Education and the Growth

The Journal of Philosophy of Education Book Series

The Journal of Philosophy of Education Book Series publishes titles that represent a wide variety of philosophical traditions. They vary from examination of fundamental philosophical issues in their connection with education, to detailed critical engagement with current educational practice or policy from a philosophical point of view. Books in this series promote rigorous thinking on educational matters and identify and criticise the ideological forces shaping education.

Titles in the series include:

Education and the Growth of Knowledge

Perspectives from Social and Virtue Epistemology

Edited by
Ben Kotzee

WILEY Blackwell

This edition first published 2014
Originally published as Volume 47, Issue 2 of *The Journal of Philosophy of Education*
Chapters © 2014 The Authors
Editorial organization © 2014 Philosophy of Education Society of Great Britain

Registered Office
John Wiley & Sons Ltd, The Atrium, Southern Gate, Chichester, West Sussex, PO19 8SQ,
United Kingdom

Editorial Offices
350 Main Street, Malden, MA 02148-5020, USA
9600 Garsington Road, Oxford, OX4 2DQ, UK
The Atrium, Southern Gate, Chichester, West Sussex, PO19 8SQ, UK

For details of our global editorial offices, for customer services, and for information about
how to apply for permission to reuse the copyright material in this book please see our
website at www.wiley.com/wiley-blackwell.

The right of Ben Kotzee to be identified as the author of the editorial material in this work
has been asserted in accordance with the Copyright, Designs and Patents Act 1988.

Wiley also publishes its books in a variety of electronic formats. Some content that appears
in print may not be available in electronic books.

Designations used by companies to distinguish their products are often claimed as trademarks.
All brand names and product names used in this book are trade names, service marks,
trademarks or registered trademarks of their respective owners. The publisher is not
associated with any product or vendor mentioned in this book. This publication is designed
to provide accurate and authoritative information in regard to the subject matter covered. It
is sold on the understanding that the publisher is not engaged in rendering professional
services. If professional advice or other expert assistance is required, the services of a
competent professional should be sought.

Library of Congress Cataloging-in-Publication Data

Education and the growth of knowledge : perspectives from social and virtue epistemology
/ edited by Ben Kotzee.
     pages cm
  Includes bibliographical references and index.
  ISBN 978-1-118-72131-5 (pbk.)
  1. Knowledge, Theory of.   2. Social epistemology.   3. Virtue.   4. Education–Philosophy.
I. Kotzee, Ben.
  BD161.E38 2013
  121–dc23
                              2013026526

Cover image: Abstract Painting by Clive Watts – Ringer #1 © Shutterstock

Cover design by Design Deluxe.

A catalogue record for this book is available from the British Library.

Set in 11.25 on 12 pt Times by Toppan Best-set Premedia Limited

Printed in Malaysia by Ho Printing (M) Sdn Bhd

01   2014

Contents

Notes on Contributors

Jason Baehr Department of Philosophy, University Hall, Suite 3600, Loyola Marymount University, One LMU Drive, Los Angeles, CA 90045, USA

David Bakhurst The Department of Philosophy, John Watson Hall, Queen's University Kingston, Ontario, Canada, K7L 3N6

Heather Battaly Department of Philosophy, 800 N State College Blvd, Cal State Fullerton, Fullerton, CA 92834-6868, USA

Jan Derry Institute of Education, 20 Bedford Way, London WC1H 0AL, UK

Sanford Goldberg Department of Philosophy, Crowe 3-179, 1880 Campus Drive, Northwestern University, Evanston, IL 60208-2214, USA

Ben Kotzee Jubilee Centre for Character and Values, School of Education, University of Birmingham, Edgbaston, Birmingham B15 2TT, UK

Duncan Pritchard Department of Philosophy, University of Edinburgh, Dugald Stewart Building, Edinburgh EH8 9AD, Scotland, UK

Emily Robertson Syracuse University School of Education, 230 Huntington Hall, Syracuse, NY 13244, USA

Jeremy Wanderer Philosophy Department, University of Massachusetts Boston, 100 Morrissey Blvd., Boston, MA 02125-3393, USA

Christopher Winch Department of Education & Professional Studies, Waterloo Bridge Wing, Franklin-Wilkins Building, Waterloo Road, London SE1 9NH, UK

Introduction: Education, Social Epistemology and Virtue Epistemology

BEN KOTZEE

Since the heyday of analytic philosophy of education, a chill has come over the relationship between the philosophy of education and analytic epistemology. Whereas, once, it would have been a commonplace to understand education mainly in terms of what it contributes to 'the growth of knowledge', the relationship has been more complicated for some time. On the one hand, many consider formal education to be occupied at least as much with shaping the young as moral and political subjects as it is with fostering knowledge about the world; on the other, scepticism about knowledge, about its communication and—to be clear—about analytic epistemology itself has led to philosophy of education shaking off, or at any rate forgetting, what it has in common with that branch of philosophy that studies knowledge and its acquisition. Readers will need little reminding, one may suppose, how hesitant educational thinkers are to suppose that there exists one clearly defined body of knowledge that all children must master, nor how little patience contemporary educational thinking has with the idea that education works by the 'transmission' of this knowledge from teacher to learner (compare, in this regard, educators' struggles, on both sides of the Atlantic with the idea of a 'core knowledge curriculum').

Epistemology itself, however, does not stand still. During the last decade or two, traditional epistemology—that focuses on the analysis of the concept of knowledge—has come under attack from two different currents in the subject. According to the fast developing field of social epistemology, the preoccupation of traditional epistemology with the individual knower is misplaced. As far as the nature of knowledge goes, social epistemology emphasises how forms of knowledge often depend on social factors for their possibility; furthermore, social epistemology holds that one may best understand how to foster the growth of knowledge by thinking about those social institutions (such as science, politics, the media or the education system)

Education and the Growth of Knowledge: Perspectives from Social and Virtue Epistemology, First Edition. Edited by Ben Kotzee. Copyright © 2014 The Authors. Editorial organisation © 2014 Philosophy of Education Society of Great Britain. Published 2014 by John Wiley & Sons Ltd.

that contribute to spreading knowledge. Next to social epistemology, virtue epistemology—the recovery of a tradition of thinking about the human intellect that goes back to Aristotle—offers its own diagnosis of the state of the subject today. According to virtue epistemology, traditional epistemology's focus on knowledge as a particular kind of cognitive content is misplaced. Rather than focusing on what the knower knows, virtue epistemology turns its attention to the knower him/herself. The question, for virtue epistemology, is not so much what knowledge is as what it is to be a good knower.

What the two fields of social and virtue epistemology share is not only a criticism of the *metaphysics* of knowledge (still occupied with the Gettier problem and how to deal with epistemic luck), but also a clear focus on the *normative* dimensions of epistemology. Not simply interested in what knowledge *is*, both social and virtue epistemology regard it as epistemology's task to understand how to *further* knowledge or how to be a good knower. The connection with the work of the philosophy of education is obvious and pooling the conceptual resources of the two subjects promises much by way of solving questions of mutual concern. New tools to understand knowledge, knowers and mechanisms to spread knowledge will be of great interest to the study of education; furthermore, an understanding of education as a system of formalised (or, at any rate, patterned or practised) interactions between those who teach something and those who learn it should be of great interest to the study of how to further knowledge.

In this collection, a number of contributors from the fields of epistemology and the philosophy of education consider the relationship between the two subjects today. The contributors focus on core questions in social and virtue epistemology such as the nature of testimony, the nature of teaching, intellectual virtue and vice, knowing how and the importance of epistemic diversity and consider what epistemology implies for education and *vice versa*. In so doing, the case is made for greater cooperation between the fields.

SOCIAL EPISTEMOLOGY AND THE AIMS OF EDUCATION

The origins of what is now called social epistemology can be traced to Steve Fuller's *Social Epistemology* (1988) and Alvin Goldman's *Knowledge in a Social World*. In *Knowledge in a Social World* (1999), Goldman starts from what he thinks is the basic goal in our cognitive lives: information seeking. What we want in our cognitive lives is not only information, but also true information; what is of epistemic *value*, according to Goldman, is truth—a position he calls 'veritism' (1999, p. 3).[1]

Having identified truth as the aim of our epistemic practices, Goldman posits that one task of epistemology is to evaluate knowledge-gathering practices in terms of how well or badly it contributes to increasing the stock of true belief that people hold collectively. The point is that true information can be sought from different sources: we can seek it ourselves by paying attention to evidence that is available to us such as observation or experiment, or we can seek it from other people—informants who, we think, know the truth. Goldman (1999, p. 4) notices that much epistemology has focused on the first of these: the individual approach of finding out the truth for oneself. 'Individualist epistemology' amounts to the study of justification—the study of how individual thinkers should gather and use evidence in order to determine what to believe. By contrast, Goldman notes that the second matter, how we gain true information from other people, is relatively under-explored (at least in standard epistemology). In addition to the concerns of individualist epistemology, Goldman thinks that epistemology should study the social practices that we engage in to share true information between people. He calls this enterprise 'social epistemology'.

Goldman examines some general mechanisms by which people gather true beliefs and share them—for instance testimony (the telling of truths) and argumentation (convincing others of truths). More interesting in the current context, Goldman also investigates a number of forms of social organisation that have the collection and dissemination of knowledge as their purpose: the social structures that are science and education, but also the legal system and parliamentary democracy have as their central aim the gaining and sharing of information.

Regarding education, specifically, Goldman writes:

> The fundamental aim of education, like that of science, is the promotion of knowledge. Whereas science seeks knowledge that is new for human kind, education seeks knowledge that is new for individual learners. Education pursues this mission in several ways: by organizing and transmitting pre-existing knowledge, by creating incentives and environments to encourage learning, and by shaping skills and techniques that facilitate autonomous learning . . . (1999, p. 349).

It would be fair to say that a transmission model such as Goldman's is out of kilter with much current educational thinking—a fact of which Goldman is very aware. Thus, he defends his veritistic view of the aim of education against a number of other views, such as the multicultural view that what is true is relative to a culture, the postmodernist view that there is no such thing as ultimate truth for education to transmit and the view that the aim of education is not so much that students end up believing specific truths (or even believe a sufficiently large stock of truths whatever they are), but that students should be able to think critically for themselves.

Especially this last objection—that the ultimate aim of education is critical thinking amongst students and not true belief as such—is important. Harvey Siegel has formulated the following criticism of Goldman's position. Siegel points out that critical thinking or rational processes of belief formation are educationally valuable independent of whether they lead to true beliefs or not. In making the argument, Siegel points out that mere true belief, held without rational justification, cannot be the aim of education. If it were, that would imply that educational methods such as brainwashing or indoctrination would be acceptable, as long as they ended up in students believing truths (Siegel, 2005, p. 350). Or take this (slightly fanciful) example: imagine that one could get students to believe a large number of truths by giving them some kind of pill (or by subjecting them to some kind of brain manipulation process); Goldman would have to applaud such a method as having a high veritistic value and, hence, as being educationally laudable. Our educational instincts, however, are tilted against the idea that this would be laudable; the very point of education, we would be inclined to say, is not just that students end up believing truths come what may, but that they begin to believe them because they understand them or can begin to see—rationally—that they are true. In geometry, for instance, we aim not just at students knowing the various geometrical theorems, but also that they be able to demonstrate them. We see this quite clearly in the educational practice of testing (Siegel, 2005, p. 351). Not only in mathematics, but in other disciplines too, we test for justification of answers alongside the correct answer; in a mathematics exam, for instance, we mark not just the answer, but also the student's workings—an incorrect answer with some good workings is worth something and a correct answer without good workings is defective. What this shows is that education does not just aim at instilling true beliefs, but aims, instead, at instilling justified beliefs.

In a later paper, Goldman (2006) reacts to Siegel's point about appropriate methods in education and acknowledges that the aim of education is knowledge read in the traditional sense as justified true belief (rather than in the veritistic sense of true belief). Yet, Goldman maintains that the justification condition is not terribly hard to meet: because of the anti-reductionist stance that Goldman takes towards testimony, he holds that students are justified in believing what their teachers say without further evidence that their teachers are good sources of knowledge (Goldman, 2006, pp. 11–2). One might say that, for Goldman, the hard problem will still be to ensure that education transmits true beliefs; that those beliefs will also be justified can be taken 'as read' on the basis of features of the social situation and as a result of the testimonial authority of the teacher.

Above, we saw that—aside from a remaining dispute over the justification of teachers' testimony—both Goldman and Siegel hold that the aim of education is to foster justified true beliefs amongst students. Yet, while Siegel (in this paper) seeks to reconcile the aims of education with what is manifest about educational practice, the account seems of limited use to general epistemology. Siegel may conclude that our aims in education must include both justification and truth, but this does not imply that justification and truth are general epistemic aims outside of the classroom. Put differently, while Siegel succeeds in reconciling education's aims with what is manifest in our educational practice, this provides no explanation for that practice. While it is clear that teachers *do* seek to promote critical thinking, the problem is that we are still without an account of what is so specifically valuable in it that our education system *should* foster it.

VIRTUE EPISTEMOLOGY AND THE ROLE OF INTELLECTUAL CHARACTER

For Virtue Epistemology, the question of what is valuable about good thinking is one of its guiding concerns. (The question is also taken up by the authors in this volume, notably Goldberg, Pritchard and Baehr.) In Plato's *Meno*, Socrates sets the hearer the following problem. Imagine that we want to travel from Athens to Larissa, but do not know the way. Should we trust a blind man to tell us the way to Larissa? Imagine that the blind man describes the road to Larissa correctly; imagine, also, that the blind man has never taken the road himself. The blind man, then, gives information that is correct—true—but not because he *knows* the road to Larissa . . . he just happens to be right about it. Socrates's point is that if the blind man describes the way correctly, then we will reach our destination whether the blind man *knew* that it is the correct description of the road to Larissa or not. What matters, the point is, is that the blind man offers the *correct* or *true* description of the way to Larissa and not whether he is justified in believing that that is the way, is rational in believing that that is the way, etc.

While we clearly do value knowledge more than mere true belief, if we accept Socrates's reasoning, knowledge—as a belief that is both true and justified at the same time—is not more valuable than mere true belief. The problem of the value of knowledge, as it is commonly interpreted, is that, even though we *do*, we have available no explanation of *why* we value knowledge more than mere true belief.

In *Knowledge and the State of Nature*, Edward Craig (1990) provides a way of working towards the answer. As Hobbes asks how the rule of law and democratic cooperation could have arisen out of a state of nature in which everyone fended for themselves, so Craig asks how intellectual cooperation could have arisen between people who, first and foremost, look after their own epistemic interests. In showing how the concept 'knowledge' contributes to intellectual cooperation, Craig attempts to show what its importance or value is to human society.

Let us turn back to Socrates's tale about the road to Larissa. The example is set up to make us see that, if the blind man tells the truth, it is as good that we believe *that* as it is to believe what is justified. In a sense this is a profoundly misleading example. In any realistic situation of asking someone the way, the problem will typically be that our guide tells us the way (as the blind man does) *but that we do not know whether to believe him or not*. The advice that, if we believe what the blind man says and it is true, it will be useful to us (as useful as knowledge) is empty advice. The real question as we encounter it in our daily cognitive lives is whether we should believe the blind man or not (not what will be valuable if we believe him and what he tells us is true or not.)

Based on this sort of observation, Craig points out that our real cognitive problem has more to do with whether we should believe other epistemic agents than it has to do with something else.

> It is not just that we are looking for an informant that will tell us the truth about P; we also have to be able to pick him out, distinguish him from others to whom we would be less well-advised to listen (Craig, 1990, p. 18).

This leads Craig to think that our main epistemic problem is telling whether we should trust people. Expanding the point somewhat, we can only solve the question of whether something is good to believe or is likely true by paying attention to the trustworthiness of people; there is no independent route to truth. Craig turns this observation into a different way of thinking about epistemology. The concept 'knowledge', he holds, is a concept that helps us pick out good informants, not good information. We have the concept 'knowledge' to pick out those who will tell us what we want to know (rather than to pick out some feature of what they think and say). Craig's account is a character-based or agent-based account of knowledge of a minimal sort. It explains knowledge in terms of what a good informant says or does or in terms of how they cooperate intellectually with others.

Why we want good informants is a matter that we can explain in terms of our practical interests. Firstly, we want good informants in order that they can inform us of things we do not know about which may help us to satisfy our desires (if I am thirsty, then someone who can tell me where the closest water source is, is of value to me). What we want, here, of course, is true information about where the nearest water source is; however, as we saw above, the realistic situation we find ourselves in is that we *cannot directly tell* whether someone is telling the truth or not—we have to find some other way of gauging the goodness of the information one's informant offers. Furthermore, knowing that informants are fallible, we take a certain amount of risk in acting on what an informant tells us. If I am thirsty and someone directs me to a water source a minute's walk away, I do not lose much by following his advice and walking to where he says the source is. However, say that he says the water source is an hour or two away. If I go there and he is wrong, I have lost very much . . . so he had better be right! This is where procedures for telling whether someone is likely to be right come in—it is the source of the demand that we make of other people that they are not only right about things or tend to be right about things, but that they are reliable—that they have some form of justification for what they believe. The demand becomes even more clear when we engage in collective action together (Craig, 1990, pp. 82–97).

While Craig's is only a minimal character-based account, the concern he raises with being a good informant goes to the heart of virtue epistemology. Pritchard (this volume) calls virtue epistemology '. . . arguably the dominant viewpoint in contemporary epistemology . . .'. One central concern of virtue epistemology is the value problem outlined above—what makes knowledge more valuable than (mere) true belief. In his famous paper 'The Raft and the Pyramid', Sosa (1980) recovers the concept of intellectual virtue from its Aristotelian origins and puts it to work to explain the difference between true belief and knowledge: a person can be said to know something if their true belief results from a disposition on their part to form true beliefs reliably. Sosa shifts our focus in defining knowledge away from features of the belief in question (principally, that it be a rationally justified belief) to the person who forms the belief. Since 'The Raft and the Pyramid', a number of competing suggestions have been made regarding what it is about the person in question that 'turns' mere true belief into knowledge. On Sosa's view, if a person forms true beliefs reasonably reliably on the basis of natural cognitive powers such as vision or memory, that person may be said to know what she believes—this is the position of virtue reliabilism. Others (for instance Zagzebski, 1996) demand more. According to virtue responsibilism, a true belief is knowledge if it results from an acquired intellectual character trait like curiosity, open-mindedness or (intellectual) thoroughness. Recently Sosa (2007) and Greco (2010) have introduced the concept of 'credit' into the debate—an agent knows what she truly believes if she deserves credit for that belief, that is, if we would say that the fact that she has that belief is admirable or to be applauded. Furthermore, figures like Roberts and Wood have considered what a turn to virtue epistemology implies for the study of epistemology as such. Much of the import of epistemology may lie not in coming to understand what knowledge *is* but in better regulating inquiry. As Roberts and Wood write, epistemology must equally study '. . . *training* that nurtures *people* in the right intellectual dispositions' (2007, p. 22).

One may say that, in being able to offer an account both of what is valuable about knowledge and what is valuable about being a good informant, the resources are available in virtue epistemology to explain why we want good informants and what it is to be one. It also appears obvious why education *should* attempt to form good intellectual character. If, by educating young people, our aim is to bring them into our society in such a way that they can (eventually) cooperate with us, we have a clear interest in forming their minds in such a way that they will be good informants. In shaping young people's intellectual capacities with social cooperation in mind, the interests of social epistemology, virtue epistemology and education come together.

THE CHAPTERS

In his chapter, Sanford Goldberg starts from two beguilingly simple claims regarding the cognitive development of children into mature thinking adults. (i) The very aim of education is (especially according to the ideal of a liberal education) the development of intellectual autonomy or the fostering of the child's ability to think for herself. (ii) However, at least the young child is massively dependent on her teachers for what they tell her about a world that she has not yet had the chance to discover. (Perhaps equally problematically, the child relies on teacher figures for guidance—by example as much as by word—regarding how to be a diligent and careful thinker and what it is to know at all.) How does one reconcile these twin claims of epistemic dependence and epistemic autonomy? Goldberg proceeds by reconceiving what intellectual autonomy means: if one sees intellectual autonomy as not being dependent on anyone else for the reasonableness of what one knows, then the young child must fall short of coming to know the things that her teachers tell her. However, if that is the case, then it is hard to see how the child ever comes to know much by way of testimony and it becomes harder still to understand how any adult could ever have succeeded in building up a stock of genuine knowledge of the outside world if it is not by building up this stock on the foundation of real testimonial knowledge acquired early on. For Goldberg, the realistic cognitive situation of the adult is not epistemic independence, but epistemic *dependence*. The task of education is not to achieve an unrealistic independence, but rather to learn to manage this dependence.

Equally interested in social epistemology's concern with *testimony*, David Bakhurst presents an account (derived largely from McDowell) regarding how to deal with the classic problem in the philosophy of testimony—whether to understand knowledge gained through testimony in terms of having evidence for the reliability of the testifier (reductionism) or whether to accept that testimony can give rise to knowledge even absent such evidence (anti-reductionism). The challenge Bakhurst sets up is that of providing an account of testimonial knowledge as non-inferential knowledge that is nevertheless an advance on traditional anti-reductionist accounts. Bakhurst points out the similarities between learning something by way of testimony and learning it by way of perception and holds that what McDowell provides is an account in terms of 'doxastic responsibility'—the individual knower must judge, for individual situations and individual people, what testimony is to be trusted. Like Goldberg, Bakhurst considers whether there is a tension between epistemic autonomy and epistemic dependence in the classroom; he finds not and sketches how McDowellian epistemic dependence is reconcilable with liberal education.

Bakhurst asks what the philosophy of testimony may contribute to the philosophy of education. In his chapter, Jeremy Wanderer reverses the question: what can consideration of the notion of teaching reveal about the nature of testimony? In his chapter, Wanderer discusses Anscombe's little known remarks regarding 'teachers' (also introduced by Bakhurst in his chapter). Quick to point out that we are dealing, here, not with real teachers of real subjects, but with the abstract notion of teaching as a form of testifying or telling, Wanderer makes clear that his contribution belongs to the philosophy of testimony, rather than to applied philosophy of education. However, the discussion of Anscombe's distinction between 'teaching' and 'teaching philosophy' is of no little interest to any philosopher interested in what teaching and learning amount to (a concern shared by epistemology and philosophy of education). By conceptualising the difference between believing a teacher personally and coming to see that what the teacher says is true, Wanderer shows that the relation between epistemology and philosophy of education need not be one-way application of 'pure' philosophy to an applied concern—the concept of teaching is and should be a central concern of epistemology.

Sharing Bakhurst's interest in the development of reason in the child, Jan Derry takes up another theme in her chapter: the role that inference or reasoning plays in making thought at all possible. Derry asks what Brandom's inferential account of reasoning suggests about the development of rationality in the child and in what sense this contributes to the project of social epistemology. Firstly a view regarding the nature of linguistic meaning, Derry shows what Brandom's inferential account of language implies regarding the nature of knowledge. She argues that Brandom contributes to both the project of the philosophy of language and that of epistemology. In so doing, she also illustrates the relevance of classic questions regarding the development of the child's ability to talk and reason to social epistemology.

Picking up a theme that is also present in Goldberg's chapter, Duncan Pritchard asks after how we should conceive of the development of cognitive agency in the child. Pritchard sketches the relevance of virtue epistemology to the philosophy of education simply: while, in educating them, we are of course interested in bringing children to believe truths about the world (rather than falsehoods), it is misleading to suggest that this is all that we are trying to do. Rather than transmit information to passive minds, what serious education sets out to do is to enhance the cognitive agency of the child. Still, Pritchard holds that a focus on developing cognitive agency is not enough—depending on how amenable the cognitive environment is that the child finds herself in, quite little cognitive agency may be required for knowledge. For Pritchard, cognitive achievement comes in degrees (from weak to strong). In a descriptive sense the process of education works by enabling the child to be capable of stronger and stronger cognitive achievement; furthermore, in a normative sense, strong cognitive achievement is also the ultimate goal of education (in that, ultimately, in their lives as adults, children will have to be able to cope in both friendly and unfriendly epistemic environments). Signalling a more active cognitive capacity, *understanding* (rather than knowledge) serves, for Pritchard, as an example of strong cognitive achievement.

Like Pritchard, Jason Baehr sees the development of intellectual virtue as a central educational aim. Baehr sketches the general structure of intellectual virtue as consisting in a motivational component and a cognitive or rational one. Being intellectually virtuous involves both loving cognitive goods (i.e. being motivated or driven to seek knowledge, truth and understanding) and being disposed to seek these cognitive goods in a way that is skilled and intelligent (making the intellectually virtuous person thereby more likely to attain knowledge, truth and understanding). Having explained how fostering both the motivational and rational components of intellectual virtue should form part of the aims of education, Baehr considers seven measures for fostering intellectual virtue in the classroom, involving elements such as direct instruction, modelling, assessment and, of course, practice. Virtues thinking—in both its classical Aristotelian form and in the shape of its Neo-Aristotelian revival—would suggest that these strategies need to be applied in concert.

Heather Battaly turns the focus away from epistemic virtue to epistemic vice. Curiosity, open-mindedness and intellectual sensitivity are all epistemic virtues—they are all characteristics of a good knower inasmuch as they are conducive to that person's knowing well. These virtues all contribute to the knower's capacity and propensity to discover not only what is ordinary, mundane or to be expected, but to come to know what is new, interesting, fresh and inventive. Battaly discusses a concern in academic life on both sides of the Atlantic today—academic research is increasingly driven not by intellectual curiosity, but by the rather more mundane priorities of the funders of that research. Battaly makes two signal contributions in her chapter. Firstly, she criticises programmatic attempts to govern research funding, such as the Research Excellence Framework (REF) in the United Kingdom and the 'Seven Breakthrough Solutions' programme in the United States, as 'epistemically insensible'—the thinking behind these programmes are unmindful of, or indifferent to, research that is not of obvious economic value. Secondly, she makes plausible that it is not only individual people that can be epistemically virtuous or vicious; groups, policies or an intellectual climate can be equally so and we can bring to bear the language of virtue in thinking through how to manage and reform them.

Long devoted to understanding propositional knowledge or 'knowing that', epistemology has recently witnessed a new wave of interest in practical knowledge or 'knowing how'. Christopher Winch considers recent work in this area and thinks through what the debate between intellectualists and anti-intellectualists about the nature of knowing how implies for the philosophy of education, firstly, but also for vocational and professional education. What does educating a person for a certain profession, trade or occupation come down to? Winch holds that intellectualist accounts of knowing how (such as those associated with Stanley and Williamson) are often guilty of construing knowing how too narrowly as skill or technique. Instead, Winch illustrates that knowing how should be construed more capaciously: knowing how involves both more complicated capacities, best described through using adverbial verbs (such as planning, controlling, co-ordinating, communicating and evaluating), and the overall executive capability that Winch calls 'project management'. Occupational capacity, as Winch sees it, involves acquiring a range of nested (and ever more complicated) capacities that are all clearly forms of knowing how, without being merely 'skills'.

Returning to a central concern in social epistemology, Emily Robertson asks after the importance of epistemic diversity to knowledge. Is it important to the body of human knowledge that socially diverse perspectives—not just the perspectives of the dominant social group, but also that of marginalised groups—are reflected in it? As Robertson makes clear, those who believe in the value of epistemic diversity typically do so for one of two reasons: (i) either they believe that diversity contributes to a larger—and richer—stock of knowledge that is valid for everyone or (ii) they hold that what counts as knowledge is relative to social identity and that epistemic diversity is a matter of the existence of diverse 'situated knowledges'. More sympathetic to the first interpretation, Robertson holds that social epistemology provides the proper way to approach the question and sketches the implications for education.

The contributors to *Education and the Growth of Knowledge: Perspectives from Social and Virtue Epistemology* have made many fruitful contributions to questions on the intersection between epistemology and philosophy of education. It is to be hoped that the volume sparks new interest amongst philosophers of education in advances in epistemology and amongst epistemologists in enduring questions in education.

NOTE

1. In making the argument for veritism, Goldman considers a number of alternatives, such as that what is really epistemically valuable is consensus, or social benefit or rational procedure (1999, pp. 69–79).

REFERENCES

Craig, E. (1990) *Knowledge and the State of Nature: An Essay in Conceptual Synthesis* (Oxford, Clarendon Press).

Fuller, S. (1988) *Social Epistemology* (Bloomington, IN, Indiana University Press).

Goldman, A. (1999) *Knowledge in a Social World* (Oxford, Oxford University Press).

Goldman, A. (2006) Social Epistemology, Theory of Evidence and Intelligent Design: Deciding What to Teach, *Southern Journal of Philosophy*, 44, pp. 1–22.

Greco, J. (2010) *Achieving Knowledge: A Virtue Theoretic Account of Epistemic Normativity* (Cambridge, Cambridge University Press).

Roberts, R. and Wood, W. (2007) *Intellectual Virtues: An Essay in Regulative Epistemology* (Oxford, Clarendon Press).

Siegel, H. (2005) Truth, Thinking, Testimony and Trust: Alvin Goldman on Epistemology and Education, *Philosophy and Phenomenological Research*, 71.2, pp. 345–66.

Sosa, E. (1980) The Raft and the Pyramid: Coherence Versus Foundations in the Theory of Knowledge, *Midwest Studies in Philosophy*, 5, pp. 3–26.

Sosa, E. (2007) *A Virtue Epistemology: Apt Belief and Reflective Knowledge* (Oxford, Oxford University Press).

Zagzebski, L. (1996) *Virtues of the Mind: An Inquiry into the Nature of Virtue and the Ethical Foundations of Knowledge* (Cambridge, Cambridge University Press).

1
Epistemic Dependence in Testimonial Belief, in the Classroom and Beyond

SANFORD GOLDBERG

1. THE CORE ISSUE

The process of education, and in particular that involving very young children, often involves students' taking their teachers' word on a good many things. At the same time, good education at every level ought to inculcate, develop, and support students' ability to think for themselves. How should we think of these two things as forming part of a coherent pedagogical package? For reasons that will emerge, I will call the challenge of responding to this question the 'Epistemic Dependence (ED) challenge'.

The ED challenge is a *challenge* because of the tension that exists between (i) the very young child's massive dependence on her teachers, and (ii) the aim of education to free students to think for themselves. The tension would seem to be this: insofar as teachers aim to develop and support the child's *intellectual autonomy*, it seems curious that the process of pedagogy relies so heavily on the child's (apparent) *lack* of intellectual autonomy in the trust she exhibits towards her teachers throughout the process. To be sure, as the child matures, she is more critical in her extension of trust. Even so, the older child's trust dispositions remain susceptible to certain kinds of exploitation to which an adult's trust is not.[1] How can we accommodate these facts into an account of good pedagogy—one that gives pride of place to the aim of inculcating students' intellectual autonomy? This is the ED challenge.

My goal in what follows is to address the ED challenge. I aim to establish two main claims. First, while there may be some tension in the combination of (i) and (ii), this tension amounts to an *insurmountable problem* for good pedagogy—as opposed to something to be managed in the pedagogical process itself—only on a too-stringent understanding of what is involved in intellectual autonomy. Second,

Education and the Growth of Knowledge: Perspectives from Social and Virtue Epistemology, First Edition.
Edited by Ben Kotzee. Copyright © 2014 The Authors. Editorial organisation © 2014 Philosophy of Education Society of Great Britain. Published 2014 by John Wiley & Sons Ltd.

once we see this, we will be in a position to endorse a natural view about how to square (i) and (ii).

I will proceed as follows. I begin by underscoring what I see as the epistemological 'ideal' that lies behind a very natural understanding of intellectual autonomy (Section 2). I call this 'Cartesian Epistemic Autonomy', or CEA. Following this, I argue against CEA as an ideal. The assumption of CEA as an ideal renders the ED challenge insoluble, since CEA itself forces us to reject the hypothesis that cognitively immature children can acquire knowledge through testimony (Section 3), and this cost is prohibitive (Section 4). I then develop an alternative conception of intellectual autonomy, on which such autonomy is compatible with a kind of epistemic dependence on others (Section 5). And while this dependence is seen most dramatically in the case of the cognitively immature child, it persists in somewhat modified forms throughout human life.

2. CARTESIAN EPISTEMIC AUTONOMY

It is easy to appreciate why many have thought that there is a tension between the sort of dependence students (especially very young ones) have on their teachers, on the one hand, and the pedagogical aim of inculcating student independent-mindedness, on the other. Some theorists may fear that this tension poses an insurmountable problem for any account of good pedagogy. However, I believe that such a fear is based on a too-demanding, if initially tempting, conception of intellectual autonomy. In this section I describe that tempting, though ultimately unacceptable, conception.

On the conception in question, cognitively healthy, mature humans are represented as *epistemically autonomous subjects*. An epistemically autonomous subject is one who judges and decides for herself, where her judgements and decisions are reached on the basis of reasons which she has in her possession, where she appreciates the significance of these reasons, and where (if queried) she could articulate the bearing of her reasons on the judgement or decision in question. I will call reasons of this sort 'fully autonomous'.

This conception of humans as epistemically autonomous subjects goes hand-in-hand with a certain picture of epistemic assessment. According to this picture, the subject's own fully autonomous reasons constitute *the only material to be assessed* in assessing the (epistemic) well-supportedness of the decision, judgement, or belief. In particular, nothing beyond the goodness of these reasons has any bearing on how (epistemically) well-supported her judgement, decision, or belief is.

As a corollary, the epistemically autonomous subject counts as having acquired *knowledge*—as opposed to having formed a merely true judgement or a merely true belief—only if the judgement or belief was formed on the basis of an appropriately strong fully autonomous reason (or set of such reasons).

I will speak of a subject as *completely* epistemically autonomous when she is no way dependent on others for the knowledge that she has. One who is completely epistemically autonomous acquires all of her knowledge at first hand. No human being is completely epistemically autonomous in this sense. But a slight complication to the conception I am describing will enable us to accommodate the fact that we depend on others for a good deal of what we know. To this end, let us distinguish between *informational* and *epistemic* dependence. Roughly speaking, a subject, H, *informationally* depends on another subject, S, when H would not have had access to the truth of a given proposition were it not for S's having told her. To illustrate: I wasn't at yesterday's ballgame, so if someone hadn't told me who won, I wouldn't have had access to that truth. Now, the mere fact of H's informational dependence on S does not yet determine anything about the *epistemic goodness* of the belief H forms through accepting S's telling. On that score the key question is whether the epistemic goodness of H's testimonial belief is to be determined exclusively in terms of the epistemic goodness *of H's own reasons*—in particular, the epistemic goodness of those reasons H has for regarding S as credible on this occasion. If so, then we can speak of H as *epistemically independent* of, even as she is informationally dependent on, her source.[2] In short, the conception of humans as epistemically autonomous subjects can allow that each of us is *informationally* dependent on others; its core commitment, rather, is to a standard of epistemic assessment on which each of us is *epistemically independent* of others.

It might be helpful to present the resulting picture in a slightly different way. According to the picture on offer, it is compatible with one's intellectual autonomy that one believes something because another said so. What intellectual autonomy (so conceived) requires, rather, is that when one does so, one must have fully autonomous reasons for regarding the attestation as reliable. In effect, the present picture demands that the intellectually autonomous subject have an attitude of *a priori* agnosticism regarding others' say-so. On this view, the fact that another person said so, by itself, has no epistemic significance whatsoever: it does not and cannot provide any support to the subject's belief in what was said. Rather, the epistemically autonomous subject regards all testimony as having the status of *acceptable only if she herself has adequate, fully autonomous reasons for regarding the attestation as reliable.* To fail to live up to this standard—to accept another's say-so under conditions in which one does not have such reasons—is, according to the conception we are describing, to fail to be intellectually autonomous.

I will use the phrase *Cartesian Epistemic Autonomy* ('CEA') to designate the foregoing conception of intellectual autonomy. CEA is a tempting conception of intellectual autonomy for at least two related reasons. First, the claim that none of us is ever epistemically dependent on another can seem to be a piece of common-sense. For how can the epistemic goodness of *your* belief ever depend on facts about *another person*—for example, the reasons or evidence *she* has? But there is a second, related reason why CEA is a tempting conception of intellectual autonomy. It is tempting to suppose that we are, each of us, masters of the epistemic goodness of our own system of belief, at least in the following sense: truth (and anti-Gettierization) aside, the epistemic goodness of a belief can seem to be a matter of how well the subject herself responded to her reasons (or evidence), *and nothing more*. In particular, when it comes to how well you are doing, epistemically speaking, it is not the case that you are ever dependent on how any *other* subjects responded to *their* reasons or evidence: such facts about other people are in principle always irrelevant to the epistemic assessment of your own beliefs. Insofar as this too appears to be a piece of common-sense, CEA can strike us as nothing more than a theoretical gloss on these aspects of common-sense.

3. THE EPISTEMOLOGY OF TESTIMONY: THE CASE OF VERY YOUNG CHILDREN

If your conception of intellectual autonomy is CEA, then the ED challenge is going to take a particularly extreme form. In particular, CEA is incompatible with a key aspect of the educational process itself—namely, the acquisition of knowledge through the acceptance of the teacher's say-so.[3] After bringing this result out in this section, I argue that for this reason we ought to question our commitment to CEA itself.

My claim here is that CEA undermines the prospects for a student's acquiring testimonial knowledge through accepting her teacher's say-so. To see why this is so, it will be helpful to assume that knowledge requires true beliefs formed on the basis of (epistemically) good reasons.[4] If we combine the 'good reasons' condition on knowledge with CEA itself, we get the following necessary condition on Testimonial Knowledge:

CEA-TK A subject S knows that p through testimony that p only if (a) S has reasons ψ for regarding the observed testimony as credible,[5] (b) S appreciates the significance of ψ, (c) S can articulate the bearing of ψ on her belief that p, and (d) ψ are (epistemically) good reasons with respect to the proposition that p.

My claim will be that if CEA-TK is true, very young (cognitively immature) children will be incapable of acquiring testimonial knowledge—whether from their parents, their guardians, or their teachers.[6]

To bring this out, I want to offer the following case:

ICE CREAM Two-year-old Sally is told by Father that there is ice cream for dessert tonight. (Father speaks from knowledge.) Sally understands the testimony, accepts Father's say-so imme-diately, and so without further ado forms the belief that there is ice cream for dessert tonight. To be sure, Sally's acceptance is not blind. For example, if Father had made an effort to convey that he was only pretending—had he used unusual gestures while speaking, smiled exaggeratedly, winked, or given some other salient indication of insincerity that Sally recognized— Sally would not have believed him.[7] In addition, if Father had said something 'silly'—for example, that Fido (their pet dog) is really a giraffe, or that trees walk and talk—Sally would not have believed him.[8] We can add as well that Sally (like young children generally) shows a strong tendency to prefer testimony from people she recognises (such as her siblings, friends, or parents), as well as testimony from those she regards as authorities (such as her preschool teachers, or her babysitters), to testimony from strangers.[9] Still, Sally's cognitive immaturity, together with her relative paucity of background knowledge,[10] limit her ability to scrutinise the testimonies she observes: she is significantly less discerning than a normal, cognitively healthy adult. (In all of these respects she is a typical, normal, healthy young child.[11])

Now Sally believes her father, and so believes the truth that there is ice cream for dessert tonight; but does this belief of hers constitute *knowl-edge*? According to CEA-TK, Sally's testimonial belief amounts to knowledge *only if* it satisfies CEA-TK's conditions (a)-(d). But I want to argue that this necessity claim—that Sally has knowledge only if she satisfies CEA-TK (a)-(d)—is false. To do so, I will argue that while Sally's testimonial belief *does* amount to knowledge, it *fails* to satisfy CEA-TK's conditions (a)-(d).

I submit that Sally knows that there is ice cream for dessert tonight. If we are forced to the conclusion that Sally doesn't acquire knowledge *here*, we are likely to be forced to the same conclusion in most or all other cases involving Sally's reliance on the word of another. Simply put, as a case of a young child's reliance on testimony, ICE CREAM is about as good as it gets, epistemically speaking: her source is a parent, and hence is someone whom she recognises as both a family member and an authority; the source's testimony was knowledgeable; the topic is one on which the source might reasonably be expected (by adults, anyway[12]) to be knowledgeable; as hearer, Sally herself is a cognitively healthy and normal child; and there were no conditions present that would have prompted any reasonable listener to question the source's credibility. If this case fails to be one in which Sally counts as having acquired knowledge, it is hard to see how there could be *any* case in which Sally counts as acquiring testimonial knowledge. Since a good deal (and arguably most) of the knowledge a young child has comes from testimony, the result of denying that Sally knows in this case would be substantial scepticism about the extent of Sally's knowledge. And what goes for Sally goes for any very young (cognitively immature) child.[13]

Even so, Sally's testimonial belief fails to satisfy CEA-TK's conditions (a)-(d). Some will question whether Sally satisfies conditions (a)-(c): can a child of Sally's cognitive immaturity really be said to 'have' reasons whose bearing on her belief she appreciates and can articulate? But in the spirit of concessiveness I want to grant that she can be ascribed reasons. My claim is rather that whatever reasons we might plausibly ascribe to Sally in ICE CREAM, in the hope of showing that she satisfies (a)-(c), these reasons will not enable her to satisfy condition (d)—at least not on any plausible reading of 'good reasons' on which such reasons are the sort that can support claims to knowledge. To see this, consider the sort of reason(s) we might credit her with having. Presumably, these reasons derive from Sally's counterfactual sensitivity to certain forms of testimonial unreliability. Simply put, had Father's testimony been obviously insincere or patently false, Sally wouldn't have accepted what he said. We might package this counterfactual sensitivity on Sally's part as a reason, or a collection of reasons, that Sally has for regarding Father's testimony as credible. These reasons are: that Father was the speaker; and that his testimony was not defective in either of these ways.[14] (Or, to put a more positive spin on it, perhaps the reason is that Father's testimony was both sincere and not obviously false.) Now I want to claim that Sally does not satisfy (d) because these reasons are not substantial enough to underwrite Sally's claim to *knowledge*.

Sally's reasons do not constitute a basis sufficient to underwrite the claim that she knows (through Father's testimony) that there will be ice cream for dessert tonight. We can bring this out as follows. Father, being like any other ordinary adult human being, is such that not all of his sincere statements are true. What is more, on (virtually) every occasion on which he would testify (sincerely but) falsely, the falsity of his statement would elude his two-year-old daughter. But for this very reason we can say that, had the present case been one in which Father's testimony was sincere but false, Sally herself would have reacted as she did in ICE CREAM: she would have believed him. But this shows that she would have had *precisely the same reasons* for accepting Father's testimony in a case in which his testimony was sincere but false, as she has for accepting his testimony in the actual case (where that testimony was both sincere and true). But if she would have had precisely the same reasons for accepting Father's testimony *whether or not Father spoke truly*, despite the fact that Father (being fallible) speaks falsely often enough to make this something to which a responsible hearer ought to be sensitive, then Sally's reasons themselves are not strong enough to underwrite Sally's claim to know.[15] And this makes clear that even if we do credit Sally with having such reasons for accepting Father's testimony, and even if we allow that Sally appreciates the bearing of these reasons on what she believes, and that she can articulate them if queried, still, Sally's having these reasons does not suffice to render her true testimonial belief *knowledge*.

At this point an obvious rejoinder will have occurred to the defender of CEA. Sally is relying on Father, and, while it is true that he sometimes speaks (sincerely but) falsely, he wouldn't have said something false *to Sally*. In particular, he is more careful with the claims he makes to his two-year-old daughter, and more careful still when those claims pertain to dessert!

Though attractive in many ways, this response is not in the spirit of CEA itself: it appeals to facts which, by the lights of CEA itself, can have no bearing on the epistemic assessment of Sally's beliefs. After all, the facts in question are facts *about Father* and his speech dispositions towards his daughter. While Sally is so positioned that she can in effect take advantage of these aspects of Father's speech dispositions towards her, she herself is unaware of any of this. And if she is not aware of any of this, then none of these facts can count among the reasons that she has (and whose bearing on her beliefs she appreciates and can articulate). In short, she is in no position to satisfy CEA-TK's conditions (a)-(d). But then, for the reasons given above, the conclusion stands: given CEA-TK, Sally does not count as acquiring knowledge through Father's testimony.

We can now generalise this result in two ways.

First, we can generalise beyond the ICE CREAM case, to speak of very young (cognitively immature) children and their sources more broadly. The point here is that if CEA undermines testimonial knowledge in a case as good as that of Sally and her Father, then it will undermine testimonial knowledge in most or all cases in which a very young child relies on another's testimony. This is because the relevant features of the case that generate this result have to do with the sorts of reasons such children can be credited with having. I argued above that, in the case of Sally and Father, reasons of the sort that are available to a young child like Sally were not sufficient to underwrite knowledge; and I submit that a corresponding argument could be given in any case in which a cognitively immature child relies on the word of a speaker whose fallibility is ordinary.

Second, while my case against CEA so far has rested on the assumption that knowledge requires good reasons, we can also generalise this result so as to dismiss any background assumptions about the nature of knowledge. For whatever one's views regarding the materials required for knowledge, and whatever one's views on the conditions on testimonial knowledge in particular,[16] the fact remains that whether Sally's belief satisfies these necessary conditions on knowledge depends not just on Sally's reasons (alternatively: the reliability of *her* cognitive processes), but also on those reasons possessed by Father (alternatively: the reliability of *his testimony*). Even if we allow that cognitively immature children are not blind consumers of testimony, the materials that they contribute to the support of their own testimonial beliefs—their reasons, the reliability of their cognitive processes, etc.—do not contribute enough, by themselves, to support the claim to knowledge. Since CEA requires precisely this sort of epistemic independence, CEA itself is problematic.

4. TESTIMONY AND TESTIMONIAL KNOWLEDGE IN EARLY EDUCATION

As an argument against CEA, the case from ICE CREAM in Section 3 might be represented as follows:

(1) Sally knows (through accepting Father's testimony) that there is ice cream for dessert tonight; but

(2) if CEA is true, Sally does not know (through accepting Father's testimony) that there is ice cream for dessert tonight; so

(3) CEA is false.

In the previous section I spent most of my efforts defending (2). But proponents of CEA might think to respond to this argument by rejecting (1). While I did provide some argument for (1) in the previous section, perhaps proponents of CEA will think to redouble their efforts to deny (1). In this section I reinforce my argument on this score, by providing two programmatic reasons in defence of claims like (1).

Before doing so, it is worth bearing in mind what the proponent of CEA must do, if she aims to defend CEA by rejecting (1). We will be in a position to offer an argument like that of (1)-(3) so long as there is a *single case* in which a very young child knows through testimony, but fails to satisfy CEA-TK's conditions (a)-(d). So it is not sufficient to reject (1); the defender of CEA must hold that there is *never* a case in which a version of (1) and (2) both hold. That is, the defender of CEA must hold that there is never a case in which a young child knows through testimony, yet where the child fails to satisfy CEA-TK's conditions (a)-(d). Now if my case for generalising from ICE CREAM were sound, it would show that, given CEA and the (undeveloped) capacities and (limited) background information of the typical cognitively immature child, no such child ever has reasons that are substantial enough by themselves to underwrite knowledge.[17] In that case, the defender of CEA who hopes to respond to my argument by rejecting (1) must reject not only (1), but also every other claim to the effect that some cognitively immature child knows through testimony. In short, the defender of CEA must reject the very idea that cognitively immature children acquire knowledge through testimony. I contend that this rejection is too costly, and in two ways.

It should be uncontroversial that teaching of any sort aims at getting students to learn—to learn the relevant facts, skills, or what-have-you. It should be uncontroversial as well that when the teaching in question aims at teaching facts, it aims at getting students to *know* those facts. Insofar as pedagogy which aims at teaching facts does not eventuate in the students' acquisition of factual knowledge, then, to just that extent the pedagogical process itself can be said to have failed to attain one of its aims. Herein lies a first cost associated with the move to defend CEA by rejecting the idea of testimonial knowledge in early childhood. To make this move is to imply that early childhood educators systematically fail to attain one of the aims of education—the inculcation of factual knowledge in its students.

But there is a second cost associated with the move to defend CEA by rejecting the idea of testimonial knowledge in early childhood. When we represent someone as knowing that such-and-such is the case, we represent her as having met all relevant epistemic standards in arriving at her belief that such-and-such is the case. Correspondingly, when we represent someone as failing to know, despite having a true belief, we represent her as *failing* to have met all relevant epistemic standards. So insofar as the proponent of CEA rejects the idea of testimonial knowledge in early childhood, our proponent implies that very young children systematically fail to meet epistemic standards whenever they form beliefs through accepting others' testimony. And this fails to do justice to the children themselves. For while it is true that their reasons, and their appreciation of and ability to articulate those reasons, fail to underwrite their claim to know, *this is no strike against their performance as believing subjects.* On the contrary, in the circumstances in which they find themselves e.g. when in school, their dispositions to trust give rise to beliefs that are true significantly more often than not. Indeed, it is precisely the young child's disposition to trust that enables her to acquire the knowledge she will subsequently employ as she grows and becomes a more critical thinker. No doubt, the fact that young children's disposition to trust (when employed in school settings) has this happy outcome is not to be traced to their capacity to discern reliable from unreliable testimony. Rather, the fact that their trust gives rise to a preponderance of true beliefs can be traced to the fact that they are employing this (underdeveloped) capacity in an environment that is, and has been structured to be, *highly friendly*. In particular, classroom interactions are highly structured, with the teacher at the centre of a good many (if not all) of the learning activities; the set of people who have access to the children, and the other informational materials available in the classroom, are both highly restricted (and vetted in advance by relevant adult authorities); the informational exchanges involving the children in the classroom are monitored by the teacher(s), who correct and redirect these interactions as they perceive the need to do so; and so forth. In such settings, the children's disposition to trust, though still immature, actually aids them: since the environment is a friendly one, their more trusting nature results in many true beliefs (and not as many false beliefs as one might fear). For just this reason, regarding the child as failing to live up to relevant epistemic standards seems wrongheaded in the extreme. Once again, CEA delivers the wrong verdict.

Might the defender of CEA reply by arguing that whether a subject's reasons are good enough to support a claim to knowledge *itself* depends on the nature of the context in which she acquires those reasons? If so, the defender of CEA might allow that the young child does acquire testimonial knowledge while in the classroom, since the reasons she has, though not good enough to underwrite her claim to know *if she were in an ordinary adult setting*, are good enough to underwrite her claim to know in the classroom.

But while such a reply might thus seem attractive, the proponent of CEA ought to reject it, for two reasons.

First, this reply amounts to a highly unattractive kind of epistemic contextualism. The proposal is that a young child's reasons for accepting a piece of testimony are good enough, e.g. when he is in school, but not good enough when he is on the playground (unsupervised by teachers). But do we really want to say that little Frank knows (when he is in class) that school buses are yellow, but fails to know this when he is on the playground, or otherwise unsupervised?[18] Or is the view rather that, because Frank acquired these reasons in the classroom, where they were good enough to support his claim to knowledge, these reasons are good enough when he is subsequently on the playground as well? Either way, this proposal runs contrary to a point on which virtually *all* epistemologists (contextualist and non-contextualists alike) agree, namely, that a subject's 'strength of epistemic position'—e.g. the epistemic goodness of her reasons—is not context-sensitive in this way.[19]

Second, not only does the present proposal amount to one or another implausible form of epistemic contextualism, it also seems highly unmotivated in connection with CEA. The proposed move is essentially a recognition of the relevance (to epistemic assessment) of factors having to do with the antics and practices of *other people*—factors which *do not constitute any part of the believing subject's own epistemic perspective* (her beliefs, her reasons, etc.). It is hard to see how this is in the spirit of CEA.

In sum, the idea that cognitively immature children can nevertheless acquire testimonial knowledge is one that plays an important role in how we think about the aims of early childhood education, and it is one that informs the epistemic standards that we bring to bear on very young children themselves. We abandon this idea only at great costs. CEA, which requires us to abandon it, is thus a costly doctrine. Before paying such a price, we ought to see whether we can avoid doing so.

5. AT WHAT SORT OF INTELLECTUAL AUTONOMY SHOULD EDUCATION AIM?

Let us take stock. One of the central aims of education is to inculcate, develop, and support students' capacity to think for themselves. A tempting picture holds that to think for oneself is to depend epistemically only on oneself. This picture derives from a view of epistemic subjects, CEA, according to which all epistemic subjects are *Cartesian Epistemic Subjects*—subjects whose beliefs are only as epistemically good as the fully autonomous reasons on which those beliefs are based. However, CEA runs into trouble when we consider the dependence of cognitively immature children on their caregivers, parents, and teachers. That this dependence is distinctly epistemic is seen in testimony cases: even on the concessive assumption that cognitively immature children have reasons of their own for regarding their sources as credible, still, these reasons fail to be the sort that can underwrite knowledge. As a result, the cost of insisting on CEA is to deny that such children acquire knowledge (as opposed to merely true belief) through testimony. This is an unhappy result.

In order to see whether we can avoid this result, we must face a new version of the Epistemic Dependence challenge. As initially formulated, the ED challenge was to square (i) the epistemic dependence of very young children on their teachers (and other caregivers), with (ii) the educational aim of getting students to think for themselves. We now see that, all else equal, it would be best to meet this challenge *without* surrendering the idea that (iii) cognitively immature children can nevertheless acquire testimonial knowledge from their teachers (and other caregivers). We can do so if we reject CEA in favour of an alternative conception of intellectual autonomy.

Before getting to this proposal, however, it is worth noting that there is another, more theoretically conservative way to meet the new version of the ED challenge. The conservative reaction would be to hold on to CEA, but to regard CEA as applying to a more restricted domain—perhaps that of cognitively mature, healthy adult human beings.[20] To see how this does the required job, suppose that CEA applies only of the restricted domain of cognitively mature, healthy adult human beings. Then the proponent of CEA could allow that cognitively immature children fail to have the sort of reasons CEA requires for testimonial knowledge, without having to conclude that therefore they fail to acquire testimonial knowledge. Stronger still, the proponent of CEA might claim that cognitively immature children *do* acquire such knowledge; the proponent of CEA could claim this so long as she endorsed the view that the acquisition of testimonial knowledge requires less *of cognitively immature children* than it requires of cognitively mature, healthy adults.

Relative to this conservative reaction, the move that I will defend—to reject CEA altogether, and replace it with a different conception of intellectual autonomy—can seem radical. Still, I believe that there are clear reasons for favouring my more radical reaction over the conservative reaction just described. Here I offer three.

The first is a methodological one. All else equal, it is preferable to have one account that covers all epistemic subjects, rather than having a separate account for cognitively immature subjects. (We might think of this as an injunction to favour simple theories over more complicated ones.) The theoretically conservative reaction runs afoul of this methodological stricture, since in effect it offers at least two different accounts of the conditions on testimonial knowledge: one for cognitively immature subjects, and another for cognitively mature subjects. Of course, the methodological principle itself is applicable only if all else *is* equal: there may be strong independent reasons to favour two distinct accounts. But in the absence of such reasons, we have a first consideration in support of rejecting CEA outright, rather than restricting its domain to cognitively mature subjects.

A second reason in support of rejecting CEA outright, rather than merely restricting its domain to cognitively mature subjects, is that CEA would appear to be false even if we restrict our attention to the domain of cognitively mature subjects. This is a point that has been argued at length elsewhere,[21] so here I will be brief. One claim that has been made on this score is that it is not the hearer's own reasons, but rather the speaker's reasons, that determine whether the hearer counts as knowing through testimony (Burge, 1993; Faulkner, 2000; Goldberg, 2006a; Schmitt, 2006).[22] To this a second, weaker claim can be made: whether or not the speaker's reasons (or the reliability of her testimony) are required to determine whether the hearer knows through accepting the speaker's testimony, still, these reasons (reliability) enhance the strength of the hearer's epistemic position, and so should be factored in to a complete epistemic assessment of the hearer's testimonial belief. Either way, factors beyond those pertaining to the hearer's own reasons are relevant to the epistemic goodness of her beliefs. CEA is thus a false claim even if we restrict our attention to cognitively mature subjects.

But there is a third reason in support of rejecting CEA altogether, rather than simply restricting its applicability to the 'cognitively mature' phase of an epistemic subject's life: CEA fails to be able to accommodate a striking feature of our (mature) reliance on the word of others. Intuitively, when one relies on another's say-so, one is depending on her to have had her own epistemic house in order. This is precisely why one is relying on her in the first place: one takes her to have the relevant reasons (or to be relevantly reliable) on the matter on which she just testified. But by the lights of CEA, nothing pertaining to another person is *ever* relevant to the epistemic standing of one's own beliefs. Thus it would seem that this striking feature of our reliance on the word of others cannot be accommodated by CEA.

Still, CEA had one thing going for it: it provided a (natural and tempting) conception of intellectual autonomy, from which we could derive a corresponding standard for assessing whether the educational process succeeded in its aim of getting students to think for themselves. If we reject CEA outright, and so reject both this conception of intellectual autonomy and the corresponding characterisation of what good pedagogy should aim at, what should replace them?

Let us agree that the pedagogical process ought to aim to elicit, support, and develop those capacities that enable the student to think for herself. (While I reject the idea that success in this endeavour is to be understood in CEA's terms, I do not reject the idea that this is part of the aim of education.) What does this aim look like, and how should we understand successful pedagogy in this respect, once we recognise that students are epistemically dependent on their teachers and other caregivers? Perhaps everyone (proponents of CEA included) can agree on this much: the student who thinks for herself is one who, in the course of forming and revising her attitudes and values, does not ascribe undue weight to the opinions of others or to the role of tradition. Nor should it be controversial to suppose that pedagogical success on this score involves instilling the capacities required to have the appropriately critical distance from the opinions of others. But what it is to ascribe 'undue' weight to the opinions of others, or to have a distance from others' opinions which is 'appropriately critical'?

Whatever the correct answers may be, they won't be the answers that CEA would give us.[23] According to CEA, the epistemic ideal at which epistemic subjects ought to be aiming is *complete epistemic independence* of others. Such independence is assumed in the very standards CEA would have us use in epistemic assessment: only a subject's own completely autonomous reasons are to be taken into account when assessing the epistemic standing of her beliefs.[24] On this picture, one ascribes undue weight to others' opinions to the extent that one depends epistemically on them. Further, it would seem that the 'appropriately critical' distance from others' opinions is precisely the sort of *a priori* agnosticism I described in section 3 above. Simply put, any other attitude towards the say-so of others appears to give undue weight to the opinions expressed, and so would not be 'appropriately critical'. To be sure, the reasonable proponent of CEA will acknowledge that human subjects cannot always attain this ideal. (That is the lesson from childhood reliance on testimony, as seen above.) But the proponent of CEA will regard this as a regrettable fact about the human condition, rather than a reason to question the ideal itself. (We will be reminded that something can be an ideal even if it isn't always, or even regularly, attainable.)

In response, I submit that CEA's picture amounts to a *false epistemic ideal*: it is not merely that young children can't attain this ideal; it is rather that *this is not the ideal at which we ought to be aiming even in the maturity of adulthood*. To see this, it will be helpful to revisit several of the central lessons of the cognitively immature child's reliance on testimony. (After doing so I will argue that similar things can be said in connection with mature adults as well.) First: while the cognitively immature child can acquire knowledge through testimony, when she does so, it is not her autonomous reasons, so much as those that are had by the testifier, that render her true belief *knowledge*. Second: even if we allow that the cognitively immature child has reasons for accepting testimony (whose bearing on her testimonial belief she appreciates), these reasons are not robust enough to protect her from the range of insincerity and incompetence found in the testimonies of the adult world. That she can nevertheless come to acquire knowledge through testimony reflects the epistemic happiness of her classroom or home environment. Third: the 'happiness' of her epistemic environment is the result of a good deal of deliberate effort and attentiveness on the part of her teachers and other adult caretakers, about which she is largely (if not wholly) ignorant. In this context, where what we might call the child's *informational environment* is the result of a good deal of prior deliberation and is highly regulated and monitored by teachers and other adults, the task the child faces in connection with managing the flow of information is made easier by the friendliness of the school environment.[25]

I submit that these points, taken together, point to an alternative ideal. The young child, as epistemic subject, is situated in an environment that has been so tailored to enable her epistemic dependence on others to result in her reliable acquisition of true beliefs. At least for her, epistemic independence, far from being an ideal, is such that were she (counterfactually) to aim at it, *doing so would dramatically hinder her education*. For suppose that epistemic independence were the ideal. In that case, given her cognitive immaturity, the young child would then face one of two unattractive options: either to believe others' say-so under conditions in which she fails to have sufficiently strong autonomous reasons for acceptance; or to refrain in a systematic way from believing any say-so at all. In the former case, she would be acquiring what by the lights of CEA's ideal are insufficiently-grounded beliefs—beliefs which fail to be knowledge even when true. In the latter case, she would be depriving herself of a good deal of true information about her world. And so we see that if

CEA's picture really is an epistemic ideal, the educational process of young children must be seen as a necessary evil.

I suspect that there will be proponents of CEA who do not flinch in acknowledging this much. They will shrug off this result by claiming that children are not ideal epistemic subjects to begin with, so of course the process of educating them will deviate far from the ideal. At the same time, they will insist that the process of education is one in which the distance between what the student is capable of and what the ideal requires is ever narrowed—ideally, to the point where there is no distance whatsoever. This will remain an attractive picture to many.

The only way to dislodge the attractiveness of this picture is to insist that versions of the very points made in connection with cognitively immature children *persist into the maturity of adulthood*—and indeed last throughout human life. This is precisely what I take to be the case. First: while the mature adult regularly acquires knowledge through testimony, when she does, it is not her own autonomous reasons, but rather those that are had by the testifier, that render her true belief *knowledge*.[26] Second: while the mature subject typically has reasons for accepting testimony (whose bearing on her testimonial belief she appreciates), and while these reasons *are* often robust enough to protect her from the range of insincerity and incompetence one finds in the testimonies of the adult world, even so, she still relies (in an ineliminable way) on others in her community for enforcement of testimonial norms. Consider the role that others play in 'policing' testimonial norms. If every time that one observes what strikes one as false testimony one reacts by raising questions or expressing doubts, then, assuming hearers are broadly knowledgeable and speakers are sensitive to even mild rebuke, this sort of practice will have a dampening effect on the prevalence of unreliable testimonies. In this way, our testimonial environments are 'cleaner' than one would predict in the absence of any such practice. And this 'cleanliness', in turn, makes the adult's task of discerning reliable from unreliable testimony easier than it would be if individual hearers had to rely on nothing beyond their own onboard resources.[27] Thus, while the adult's world is not structured like a grade school classroom, nevertheless adults benefit from the efforts of others in 'cleaning up' the testimonial environment. It is of course true that the adult world poses many more epistemic risks and dangers than are found in the typical classroom, and true as well that a good deal of the adult world is not 'epistemically engineered' at all. Still—and this is the third parallel between the adult case and the case of the cognitively immature child—there are some adult environments that *are* engineered so as to be easily exploited for reliable information. Consider the university, the institute, and the range of professional and scientific associations; the scholarly (peer-reviewed) journal, traditional newsprint media, and respectable book presses; the phenomenon of expertise, and the way expertise is 'signalled' to those in need of an expert's information. Of course, mature adults are often highly self-aware in the way they acquire information in these settings or from these sources; they do so only when they have reasons to regard these settings or sources as providing highly reliable information (under certain recognisable conditions). But in the very same way that a hearer's reasons for accepting a piece of testimony do not render her testimonial belief knowledgeable even when true, so I submit that a hearer's reasons for regarding a source as credible do not exhaust the considerations that bear on the rationality of her acceptance. Rather, the context of acceptance is one in which the task of monitoring testimony is itself distributed.[28]

I submit that these considerations point out the objectionably individualistic character of CEA's epistemic ideal even for mature adults. Rather than thinking that we ought to be aiming *to reduce as much as possible our epistemic dependence on others* (with the ultimate goal, where possible, of eliminating this dependence altogether), I submit that our epistemic ideal ought to recognise our ineliminable epistemic dependence on others. Our aim ought to be rather to manage this dependence appropriately. Relatedly, when it comes to getting students to think for themselves, successful pedagogy is success in shaping the students' local informational environment in such a way as to prepare her to face the sorts of information management challenges[29] that are regularly faced in adulthood. The ultimate aim is to gradually increase the difficulty of the information-management challenges the student must confront so that, by the time she reaches adulthood, she will be proficient at this sort of challenge even in the decidedly less friendly adult environments. The aim here is *not* one of an ever-increasing attempt to *eliminate* epistemic dependence; it is rather to equip students to manage their dependence in a world in which this dependence has a clear payoff (in the extension of knowledge each of us can acquire) but also exposes us to the threats of manipulation and misinformation.

Still, we might wonder: why should we care that our youth be educated so that they are presented with information-management tasks that are challenging and yet still manageable?[30] Among other reasons, the value of this sort of pedagogy can be seen in the role that students play (not merely as consumers of testimony, but also) as producers of testimony. We want students to emerge as reliable informants in their own right;[31] and when successful, a process of pedagogy of this sort offers the twin advantages of achieving this aim in adulthood, while all the while preserving the reliability of the information the children get throughout the process.

I have been highlighting the continuities that exist between the information management tasks that confront the cognitively immature child and those we face in the maturity of adulthood. But there are important differences as well, and perhaps it is good to conclude by acknowledging the most salient of these. Clearly, the cognitive immaturity of early childhood makes very young children less good—in fact, significantly less good—at the information management tasks that arise in the environments in which we adults regularly find ourselves. Thus, even if little Mary (a precocious but still cognitively immature child) invariably succeeds in the very limited version of the information management task she faces in the preschool environment, still, she would fare poorly in information environments that are less highly structured and less well monitored. Here one might worry that my account of intellectual autonomy cannot acknowledge this: insofar as little Mary succeeds in her preschool environment, the objection has it, my account will regard her, implausibly, as highly intellectual autonomous. But this objection assumes that we can assess a subject's intellectual autonomy without taking into account the range of informational environments in which she can reliably employ her critical capacities to good effect. I submit that we reject this assumption. Rather, insofar as we want to think of the (degree of) intellectual autonomy exhibited by a subject, we should do so against the backdrop of the range of informational environments in which she can reliably manage the information management challenge. For this reason, it would be more apt to reserve the description 'intellectually autonomous' to those who have attained the sorts of critical capacities that suffice to enable them to succeed across a wide variety of informational environments. Despite her precociousness, little Mary does not fit that bill. Even so, when an adult does do well on this score, and so is properly described as exhibiting a high degree of intellectual autonomy, this should not cause us to lose track of the fact that such a subject continues to be epistemically dependent on others throughout her adult life—Cartesian ideology to the contrary notwithstanding.

ACKNOWLEDGEMENTS

I would like to thank Ben Kotzee and an anonymous referee for their very helpful comments on an earlier draft of this chapter. I would also like to express my deepest appreciation to my wonderful colleague Kyla Ebels-Duggan, for several illuminating conversations on this topic (as well as insightful comments on an earlier draft of this chapter).

NOTES

1. See Koenig *et al.*, 2004 and Heyman and Legare, 2005.
2. Strictly speaking, this characterisation of epistemic independence needs to be qualified. It should read: a subject H's testimonial belief is epistemically independent of her source when, *bracketing the question of truth (and the anti-Gettier condition on knowledge)*, the epistemic goodness of H's testimonial beliefs is to be determined exclusively in terms of the epistemic goodness of H's own reasons. However, for ease of exposition I will ignore this qualification in what follows.
3. Although I will restrict my discussion to cognitively immature children, I think similar points hold with respect to older children and even adults as well.
4. As we will see below, similar points can be made even if one thinks that knowledge requires, not good reasons, but reliable belief-forming processes.
5. Strictly speaking, condition (a) should read: (a) S has reasons ψ for believing that p. I am here assuming that in testimony cases, these reasons are reasons to regard the observed testimony as credible.
6. One might worry that any theory that rejects CEA-TK will be overly-liberal in its implications for the extent of testimonial knowledge—i.e. that any such theory will regard as testimonial knowledge many cases that are not cases of testimonial knowledge. I will respond to this sort of worry below; but for a more detailed treatment, see Goldberg and Henderson, 2006 and Goldberg, 2008.
7. According to the developmental psychology literature, preschool children can distinguish, more or less reliably, those speakers who are engaging in obvious story-telling. See Dias and Harris, 1990; Harris, 2002; and Richards and Sanderson, 1999.
8. Children as young as sixteen months react differently to true and false testimony in cases involving the labelling of simple objects; see Koenig and Echols, 2003.
9. Although this sort of discernment of (and differential responses to) various types of testimonies and testifiers is especially striking at the age of six, children do make some distinctions of this sort even earlier. For the literature on this topic, see Baldwin and Moses, 1996; Bar-Tal *et al.*, 1990; Heyman and Legare, 2005; Lutz and Keil, 2002; and Mills and Keil, 2004.
10. Even among children who have initiated the move to a more sceptical trust, the effects of this move are limited by the fact that children typically do not have a great deal of relevant worldly knowledge on which to draw when assessing the likely truth of testimony in real-life cases. The result is that, while the young child may reject false testimony when she has observational knowledge contradicting the testimony (Harris, 2002; Mitchell *et al.*, 1997), in everyday life children often confront testimony regarding whose truth they have no relevant first-hand information (Koenig *et al.*, 2004).
11. According to the developmental literature, it is not until late elementary school that children regard discrepancies between a speaker's verbal and nonverbal communication as indicating dishonesty (Rotenberg *et al.*, 1989). What is more, children younger than six are likely to endorse self-report as a means to learn about such highly-esteemed qualities as the intelligence of the self-reporting person (Heyman and Legare, 2005), thereby rendering themselves potentially gullible in matters in which others have a strong motive to lie.

Finally, even older children (six to ten) are susceptible to suggestibility by sources they regard as powerful (Wheeless *et al.*, 1983) or whom they perceive as in a position to reward or punish them (Loftus and Ketchum, 1991; Ceci and Bruck, 1993). This brief review of the empirical literature suggests that the move to more 'sceptical trust' develops gradually, and in any case is significantly less well developed in three-year-olds than it is in four-year-olds (Koenig *et al.*, 2004).

12. This qualification is very important. It would appear that preschoolers are highly insensitive to an interlocutor's access to the truth of what she is reporting. This of course is one of the lessons of the widely-cited 'false belief test' (Wimmer and Perner, 1983). Their result was extended by Taylor and colleagues (Taylor *et al.*, 1994), who showed that this insensitivity in young children extends to include not only features of locally observed objects, but also more general information about the world. More recently, Wellman *et al.* (2001) have drawn the general lesson implicit in the foregoing studies: that, until the age of four, children do not appear to appreciate that beliefs (whether their own or others') can be false.

13. More on this below.

14. Sally wouldn't put it like this, of course. But I let this pass for the time being.

15. Here I am assuming a relatively weak modal condition on knowledge: S knows that p through method M (alternatively: on the basis of reasons R), only if M (alternatively: having R) would not easily have lead S to form a false belief. (This is a widely shared assumption among epistemologists across the spectrum of views in epistemology.) Assuming that Sally's method is that of trusting Father (when he is sincere and doesn't say something obviously false), Sally fails to satisfy this condition.

16. For example, whether one requires good reasons to regard the testimony as reliable, or one holds instead that a lack of reasons to doubt the reliability is sufficient. This is close to the issue at the heart of the so-called reductionism/anti-reductionism debate in the epistemology of testimony. I will return to this briefly below. For my reasons for thinking that this debate cross-cuts the issue presently before us, see Goldberg, 2006a.

17. At least not in any environment with the usual amount of sincere but false testimonies.

18. This level of epistemic instability is worse than anything associated with contemporary versions of epistemic contextualism. Those versions allow for instability across conversational contexts in which the attribution of knowledge is being made, whereas on the present proposal the subject's knowledge is gained or lost even when no attribution is under consideration.

19. Even those authors who are otherwise highly sympathetic to extant versions of epistemic contextualism would agree on that much. What is sensitive to context on their view is not *the epistemic goodness* of one's reasons, but *the epistemic standards* that these reasons need to satisfy if one is to count as knowing.

20. This would mirror a move made by Elizabeth Fricker in the epistemology of testimony literature. Faced with the objection that very young children do not (typically or ever) have positive non-testimonial reasons for regarding their sources as credible, Fricker (whose theory requires these) responds by restricting the demand for such reasons to the 'mature' phase of a subject's life. See Fricker, 1994, 1995.

21. Versions of this claim can be found (implicitly or explicitly) in Burge, 1993; Faulkner, 2000; Goldberg, 2005, 2010, 2011; and Schmitt, 2006. What is more, although she doesn't make this an explicit part of her view, Lackey (2007) would appear to support the claim that CEA is false of cognitively mature subjects as well: her condition on justified testimonial belief requires reliability in the testimony.

22. A similar claim has been made in terms of reliabilist epistemology; see Goldberg, 2010.

23. In the paragraphs that follow I am deeply indebted to a discussion with Kyla Ebels-Duggan.

24. Again, let us disregard the complications introduced by the truth and anti-Gettierization conditions on knowledge.

25. This was a point I was concerned to make in Goldberg, 2008, where I spoke at length about the restriction in the messages to which the child has access and the support the child receives in assessing them.
26. See note 21 for references.
27. See Goldberg, 2011 for discussion.
28. See Goldberg, 2006b, 2011 for discussion.
29. Let the *information management challenge* be the challenge of discriminating, among all of the (spoken or written) 'messages' a hearer encounters, all and only those which are reliable, and hence worthy of belief. And let us say that a subject does well with respect to this task insofar as she reliably discriminates the true from the false messages, believing only the former.
30. I thank Ben Kotzee for suggesting that I take this issue up, and also for suggesting the sort of answer I am developing.
31. This point echoes a theme made popular by Craig (1990). One need not agree with Craig's main hypothesis, to the effect that the very point of the verb 'to know' is to flag good informants, to agree with him about the central importance of good informants.

REFERENCES

Baldwin, D. and Moses, L. (1996) The Ontogeny of Social Information Gathering, *Child Development*, 67, pp. 1915–1939.

Bar-Tal, D., Raviv, A., Raviv, A. and Brosh, M. (1990) Perception of Epistemic Authority and Attribution for its Choice as a Function of Knowledge Area and Age, *European Journal of Social Psychology*, 21, pp. 477–492.

Burge, T. (1993) Content Preservation, *Philosophical Review*, 102.4, pp. 457–488.

Ceci, S. and Bruck, M. (1993) Suggestibility of the Child Witness: A Historical Review and Synthesis, *Psychological Bulletin*, 113, pp. 403–439.

Craig, E. (1990) *Knowledge in the State of Nature* (Oxford, Oxford University Press).

Dias, M. and Harris, P. (1990) The Influence of the Imagination on Reasoning by Young Children, *British Journal of Developmental Psychology*, 8, pp. 305–318.

Faulkner, P. (2000) The Social Character of Testimonial Knowledge, *Journal of Philosophy*, 97.11, pp. 581–601.

Fricker, E. (1994) Against Gullibility, in: B. K. Matilal and A. Chakrabarti (eds) *Knowing from Words* (Boston, MA, Kluwer), pp. 125–161.

Fricker, E. (1995) Critical Notice: Telling and Trusting: Reductionism and Anti-Reductionism in the Epistemology of Testimony, *Mind*, 104, pp. 393–411.

Goldberg, S. (2005) Testimonial Knowledge from Unsafe Testimony, *Analysis*, 65.4, pp. 302–311.

Goldberg, S. (2006a) Reductionism and the Distinctiveness of Testimonial Knowledge, in: J. Lackey and E. Sosa (eds) *The Epistemology of Testimony* (Oxford, Oxford University Press), pp. 127–44.

Goldberg, S. (2006b) The Social Diffusion of Warrant and Rationality, *The Southern Journal of Philosophy*, 44, pp. 118–138.

Goldberg, S. (2008) Testimonial Knowledge in Early Childhood, Revisited, *Philosophy and Phenomenological Research*, 76, pp. 1–36.

Goldberg, S. (2010) *Relying on Others: An Essay in Epistemology* (Oxford, Oxford University Press).

Goldberg, S. (2011) The Division of Epistemic Labour, *Episteme*, 8, pp. 112–125.

Goldberg, S. and Henderson, D. (2006) Monitoring and Anti-Reductionism in the Epistemology of Testimony, *Philosophy and Phenomenological Research*, 72.3, pp. 576–593.

Harris, P. (2002) Checking our Sources: The Origins of Trust in Testimony, *Studies in History and Philosophy of Science*, 33.2, pp. 315–333.

Heyman, G. and Legare, C. (2005) Children's Evaluation of Sources of Information about Traits, *Developmental Psychology*, 41.4, pp. 636–647.

Koenig, M., Clément, F. and Harris, P. (2004) Trust in Testimony: Children's Use of True and False Statements, *Psychological Science*, 15.10, pp. 694–698.

Koenig, M. and Echols, C. (2003) Infants' Understanding of False Labeling Events: The Referential Roles of Words and the Speakers Who Use Them, *Cognition*, 87, pp. 179–208.

Lackey, J. 2007: *Knowing from Words* (Oxford, Oxford University Press).

Loftus, E. and Ketchum, K. (1991) *Witness for the Defense: The Accused, the Eyewitness and the Expert Who Puts Memory on Trial* (New York, St. Martin's Press).

Lutz, D. and Keil, F. (2002) Early Understanding of the Division of Cognitive Labor, *Child Development*, 73, pp. 1073–1084.

Mills, C. and Keil, F. (2004) Knowing the Limits of One's Understanding: The Development of an Awareness of an Illusion of Explanatory Depth, *Psychological Science*, 87, pp. 1–32.

Mitchell, P., Robinson, E., Nye, R. and Isaacs, J. (1997) When Speech Conflicts with Seeing: Young Children's Understanding of Informational Priority, *Journal of Experimental Child Psychology*, 64, pp. 276–294.

Richards, C. and Sanderson, J. (1999) The Role of the Imagination in Facilitating Deductive Reasoning in 2-, 3-, and 4-year-olds, *Cognition*, 72, pp. B1-B9.

Rotenberg, K., Simourd, L. and Moore, D. (1989) Children's Use of a Verbal-nonverbal Consistency Principle to Infer Truth and Lying, *Child Development*, 60, pp. 309–322.

Schmitt, F. (2006) Testimonial Justification and Transindividual Reasons, in: J. Lackey and E. Sosa (eds) *The Epistemology of Testimony* (Oxford, Oxford University Press), pp. 193–224.

Taylor, M., Estbensen, B. and Bennett, R. (1994) Children's Understanding of Knowledge Acquisition: The Tendency for Children to Report that They Have Always Known What They Have Just Learned, *Child Development*, 65, 1581–1604.

Wheeless, L., Barraclough, R. and Stewart, R. (1983) Compliance-gaining and Power in Persuasion, in: R. Bostrom (ed.) *Communication Yearbook 7* (Beverly Hills, CA, Sage), pp. 105–145.

Wimmer, H. and Perner, J. (1983) Beliefs about Beliefs: Representation and Constraining Function of Wrong Beliefs in Young Children's Understanding Of Deception, *Cognition*, 13, pp. 103–128.

Wellman, H., Cross, D. and Watson, J. (2001) Meta-analysis of Theory-of mind Development: The Truth about False Belief, *Child Development*, 72, pp. 655–684.

2
Learning from Others

DAVID BAKHURST

PRELIMINARIES

John McDowell begins his essay 'Knowledge by Hearsay' (1993/ 1998) by describing two ways language matters to epistemology. The first is that a person can acquire knowledge by understanding and accepting someone else's utterance—not just knowledge that 'such-and-such' has been said or written, but knowledge that such-and-such is the case. I can come to know it is raining in Liverpool because someone who knows tells me it is. This is what philosophers call 'knowledge by testimony' (thereby using 'testimony' more broadly than in everyday discourse). The second is that children gain knowledge in the course of learning their first language—not just knowledge of the language, but knowledge of how things are. In acquiring language, a child inherits a conception of the world. McDowell observes that much of this conception is not something the child has been told. Here he has in mind fundamental beliefs that form the background to our thinking and reasoning, beliefs to which Wittgenstein draws attention in *On Certainty* (1969)—such beliefs as: cats do not grow on trees (§282), motor cars do not grow out of the earth (§279), the earth existed long before our births (§§187–190), or every human being has parents (§§211, 282). We do not usually learn such things by being told them. Rather, they are implicit in the 'cognitive-practical ways of proceeding' into which we are initiated as we learn to speak (McDowell, 1993/1998, p. 415).

In *The Formation of Reason* (2011), and my writings on Russian socio-historical philosophy and psychology, I address issues bearing on the second of these topics, questions about the child's development through initiation into language and other forms of social being. Here I shall focus, as McDowell does in his paper, on the first, and specifically on how discussions of testimony can illuminate issues in philosophy of education. We shall find, however, that we cannot entirely lose sight of the second topic, to which I shall return in my conclusion.

Education and the Growth of Knowledge: Perspectives from Social and Virtue Epistemology, First Edition. Edited by Ben Kotzee. Copyright © 2014 The Authors. Editorial organisation © 2014 Philosophy of Education Society of Great Britain. Published 2014 by John Wiley & Sons Ltd.

It is easy to see why philosophers of education might be interested in testimony. Consider Jamie, a grade 9 student, who today learnt the following at school: (i) from his English teacher, that Jane Austen published six novels; (ii) from his biology textbook, that the structure of the DNA molecule is a double-helix; (iii) from his friend Luke, that Ann Boleyn was beheaded with a sword; (iv) from his classmate Stephanie, that the maths test is cancelled; (v) from Sheila, that Lucy kissed Jack behind the bicycle sheds; (vi) from a representative of the Public Health Unit, that smoking increases the risk of heart disease. All these are cases of learning from testimony as philosophers usually deploy that term. In addition, Jamie acquired other knowledge by means akin to or dependent upon testimony: (vii) he overheard Jack tell Sam that Eric held a party last weekend and (viii) from glimpsing Paula's secret journal, he learnt that Paula is fond of Harry. It seems that testimony enters into much of the knowledge acquired in school, whether inside or outside the classroom.

What, then, can philosophy of education expect of the epistemology of testimony? For many years, the individualistic orientation of analytic epistemology led philosophy to disregard the ways we learn from others. Things have now changed and testimony is a hot topic, but even so there remains a sense in which testimony tends to be treated as something of an afterthought. Having arrived at a working account of knowledge focused on how it is acquired through experience, inference, and so on, the question is only then raised about how knowledge, thus understood, could be gleaned from the words of others. If knowledge is such-and-such, how can a person come by it merely by hearing what someone else says? The epistemology of testimony then emerges as the specialised sub-discipline tasked with answering that question. Two kinds of response typically follow. Philosophers who hold that an answer can be given entirely by using the resources of the prior account of knowledge are *reductionists* about testimonial knowledge. Philosophers who think that testimony is a distinctive source of knowledge intelligible only by extending the resources of the prior account are *anti-reductionists*. The two positions are usually expressed as theories about the conditions under which an audience is *justified* in accepting a speaker's testimony. Reductionists hold that to be justified in believing the testimony of a speaker, the hearer must have good positive reasons for doing so that are not themselves based on testimony (and hence the analysis of these reasons can be given by the prior account of knowledge). Anti-reductionists, in contrast, hold that the hearer is entitled to believe the speaker's testimony without any positive reason for so doing, just so long as there are no available reasons *not* to believe the speaker (testimony thus involves a distinctive sort of entitlement to believe that requires specific epistemological treatment). So the sides line up.

One might, however, favour an alternative approach—one that starts by recognising that it is in the nature of knowledge to be shareable, and hence that there is no special issue about how one speaker can acquire knowledge from another. Knowledge is public in at least this sense: when a person's judgement amounts to knowledge, she apprehends a truth that is in principle available to others. A judgement is the sort of thing that finds expression in an assertion, and when a knower expresses her knowledge, then another person, in accepting that assertion by being willing to reassert it, thereby shares in that knowledge. Christine sees the cats are in the kitchen and she tells me so; in accepting what she says I come to know where the cats are. Understanding that the concept of knowledge is internally related to the concepts of truth, judgement, and assertion already brings the possibility of testimonial knowledge into view. So we cannot find ourselves in the position of having to supplement a plausible understanding of knowledge with an epistemology of testimony. If supplementation looks necessary, something is wrong with the initial account.

A view of this kind has been nicely articulated by Sebastian Rödl (Rödl, forthcoming). Rödl's view is consistent, I believe, with McDowell's position. I think this is the correct approach. So in what follows, I shall expound McDowell's view of testimony, supplementing it with ideas from Rödl, before considering how it illuminates two issues of relevance to education: the extent of an individual's epistemic dependence upon others and the nature of teaching.

MATTERS EPISTEMOLOGICAL

McDowell develops his position by distinguishing it from a familiar variant of the standard approach. A person should obviously not believe everything she hears: credulity is an epistemic vice. If Jamie is to acquire knowledge from Stephanie's saying that the test is cancelled, he must be justified in believing what she tells him. What form must that justification take? One possible answer, favoured by reductionists, is that Jamie must have at his disposal an *argument* from the premise that Stephanie said the test is cancelled to the conclusion that the test *has* been cancelled. Such an argument is what he will need to produce should his later assertion that the test is cancelled be challenged.

The problem, as McDowell quickly points out, is that no such argument can deliver the goods. A person does not know that *p* if the grounds for her belief that *p* are consistent with *p*'s not being the case. This follows from what McDowell calls the conditional principle that: 'if . . . the title of a belief to count as knowledge is constituted by the believer's possession of an argument to its truth, it had better not be the case that the best argument he has at his disposal leaves it open that things are not as he believes them to be' (1993/1998, p. 421). Thus unless Jamie's grounds rule out the possibility that the test is still on, he does not know the test is cancelled. But no argument he can construct could guarantee this. He may know that testimony is in general a reliable source of knowledge. He may know Stephanie is a reliable witness and an honest person. But nothing will guarantee that she is not mistaken in this case, or that she is not lying to him, or that Jamie has not somehow misunderstood her. In the absence of such guarantees, for all Jamie knows he may be wrong to believe her, and if that's the case her testimony is not a source of knowledge.

This kind of problem is not unique to testimony. Anyone familiar with the history of epistemology will know the difficulties that beset attempts to cast the justification of perceptual knowledge in the form of an argument from premises about how things appear to conclusions about how things are. No such attempts have succeeded for no argument from appearance to reality can rule out the possibility of error. A different approach is called for.[1]

The alternative McDowell favours is this. Where Jamie comes to know that Lucy kissed Jack from Sheila's telling him so, his justification can be fully characterised by the words, 'Jamie learnt from Sheila that Lucy kissed Jack'. That characterisation expresses a warrant for belief that is incompatible with error, for Jamie cannot have learnt from Sheila that Lucy kissed Jack unless Lucy *did* kiss Jack. So this approach does not invite the objection that Jamie's grounds for belief fall short of guaranteeing that the state he is in really is knowledge.[2]

This move may provoke suspicion. It is important, however, that McDowell is not trying to provide the kind of argument for which his opponent is asking by exploiting the truistic inference from (i) the fact that Jamie learnt that *p* from Sheila to (ii) the conclusion that he knows that *p* (see 1993/1998, pp. 416–7). On McDowell's view, no such argument is necessary. Sheila's testimony discloses to Jamie the fact that Lucy kissed Jack. Her telling him gives him knowledge and the ground of that knowledge is simply that he got it from Sheila. It is perfectly consistent with everyday discourse that Jamie should answer the question 'How do you know that Lucy kissed Jack?' by saying, 'I heard it from Sheila' or 'Sheila told me'. That's all the justification he needs. Of course, the question might be raised about whether Jamie should believe her, and if that question deserves an answer (it may not), then he will have to provide one if he is to count as knowing. But the considerations he adduces in that answer will be designed to secure the cogency of the original warrant (i.e. that he *did* learn it from Sheila); they are not part of that warrant.

McDowell (2011) offers an analogous account for perceptual knowledge. If I come to know there is a cat in the street by looking out the window, then the ground of my knowledge is simply that I see the cat. Similarly for memory: the ground of my knowledge that there was a silver birch in my parents' garden is that I remember there was. On McDowell's view, perception, memory, and testimony all yield non-inferential knowledge. Seeing is not a matter of first apprehending something that is less than a seeing—an appearance—and then working from there by inference to a claim that, if all goes well, amounts to perceptual knowledge. No: seeing is apprehending how things are. The same goes for remembering, and for taking the word of someone who knows. Perception, memory, and understanding the testimony of others are 'capacities for knowledge' (or 'powers of knowledge' as Rödl (2007, p. 83) has it). These capacities are of course fallible. But citing their non-defective exercise provides a warrant for knowledge.

Although perception, memory, and testimony are sources of non-inferential knowledge, McDowell makes clear that our capacities for knowledge are productive only if we exercise what he calls 'doxastic responsibility'. It is not normally doxastically responsible to make judgements about the colour of an object in poor light, and hence a person who judges in such circumstances doesn't know what colour the object is even if she happens to judge correctly. Similarly, it is doxastically irresponsible to take someone's word if one is, or ought to be, aware that he is untrustworthy or incompetent. So McDowell insists that a person acquires knowledge by testimony in the non-inferential way he describes only if she is alive to considerations relevant to whether the speaker is to be believed (that he is competent, reliable, trustworthy, in a position to know what he claims, has no special reason to deceive her, and so on). McDowell's reductionist opponent would incorporate such considerations within an argument that supposedly expresses the knower's justification. But McDowell locates them elsewhere (1993/1998, p. 433). Jamie, being doxastically responsible, learns from his teacher that Austen published six novels. That Jamie is sensitive to factors that would have given him reason to doubt his teacher had they obtained is part of what makes him doxastically responsible, but the absence of such factors is not among the grounds of his knowledge.

That McDowell rejects reductionism about testimonial knowledge makes him an anti-reductionist in a trivial sense, but it does not put him in the anti-reductionist camp as that is usually understood.[3] Anti-reductionists typically argue that a speaker's testimony immediately provides her audience with a *prima facie* reason for belief. They then proceed to embrace something like the following epistemic principle: A speaker is entitled to believe testimony just in case she has no positive reason not to (see, e.g., Burge, 1993). McDowell, however, should reject this principle in favour of a particularistic view of doxastic responsibility. It is not doxastically responsible to adopt *either* the anti-reductionist's principle *or* the reductionist principle that one should not believe a speaker unless one has independent reason to think her a reliable source. Neither is cogent as a general strategy. In matters of testimony one must be neither unduly credulous nor unduly sceptical, but the appropriate attitude to take to a speaker involves sensitivity to context. The playground requires one blend of epistemic open-mindedness and vigilance, the classroom another.[4] The kind of sensitivity to context demanded by doxastic responsibility resists codification—there is no algorithm to determine the standards to which one must adhere, just as there is no recipe to discern when a speaker is truthful, reliable, trustworthy, and so on. Of course, since our powers to perceive, remember, and understand testimony are powers of knowledge, there is a presumption that their exercise will yield knowledge, for when those capacities are deployed non-defectively in congenial circumstances, knowledge is their outcome. But this thought cannot be parlayed into an epistemic principle to guide the formation of belief.

There is a sense in which McDowell puts testimony on a par with perception and memory—they are all sources of non-inferential knowledge. But it is also true that testimony is parasitic upon other forms of knowledge. Testimony yields knowledge 'at second-hand' and if a claim to such knowledge is a good one, there must be a link to someone's acquiring the knowledge in question first-hand. When Jamie makes a knowledge claim on the basis of Sheila's words, the authority with which he makes that claim is derived from Sheila and if he is later challenged, he is entitled to refer it to her (see McDowell, 1993/1998, p. 438). If Shelia is herself relying on testimony, then she can in turn refer the challenge to her source, and so on.[5] The testimonial chain stops only with someone who gained the knowledge in question first-hand. But if the chain is sound, then Jamie can gain knowledge from Sheila by believing what she says.

One attraction of McDowell's position is that it makes better sense of fallibility than many views. Harvey Siegel (2003, p. 308) writes that 'all knowledge is fallible'. Strictly speaking, this is nonsensical. In keeping with the conditional principle noted above, if a person knows it is raining, she cannot turn out to be wrong. Knowing that p is incompatible with being wrong that p. What Siegel should have said is that anything we take to be knowledge might turn out not to be so (which is meaningful, though contentious). Perhaps Siegel's remark was a merely verbal slip. But his choice of words is nonetheless revealing because it is in keeping with a familiar but misguided approach in epistemology. Advocates of this approach start from the view McDowell rejects—namely, that justification takes the form of an argument. They then realise that no such argument can provide conclusive justification. Fearing that they are now hostage to scepticism, they abandon the conditional principle and hold instead that the level of justification required for knowledge need not rule out the falsity of the belief that p. They then suppose that this captures the sense in which knowers are fallible: they may have the best possible justification for belief and yet be wrong.

But the conditional principle should not be abandoned. I agree with McDowell when he says it is 'obviously correct' (1993/1998, p. 421). In perfectly everyday contexts, a person cannot claim to know that p while admitting that she might be wrong—the admission is tantamount to withdrawing the claim. (Consider: 'I know the train leaves at 2pm, but I might be wrong'.) To know is to be in touch with the facts; therefore one's grounds for knowledge cannot stop short of putting one in touch with the facts.[6] To deny this as a defence against scepticism is self-defeating, for the outcome is a position that is no better than scepticism. If for all a person knows she may be wrong, she does not have 'fallible knowledge'; she doesn't have knowledge at all.

We need, therefore, an alternative conception of fallibility, one consistent with the conditional principle. On the McDowell-Rödl account, it is people and their capacities that are fallible, not knowledge itself. Our perceptual powers enable us to gain knowledge of the layout of our environment, but we can find ourselves in circumstances unfavourable for their exercise. These circumstances may be 'external' to us (the light or acoustics may be bad, for example) or they may be 'internal' (we may be tired, injured, medicated, and so on). Similarly, our powers of understanding and judgement enable us to gain knowledge from the testimony of others, even though those powers sometimes let us down. We can misunderstand what is said, or misjudge the reliability or trustworthiness of our informant. The cause may be a failure of doxastic responsibility, or plain bad luck: we can end up with a false belief despite our doxastic diligence.[7] But that does not show that the exercise of our capacities is never sufficient for knowledge. And when it is, then citing their successful exercise is enough to characterise our warrant for belief (I saw it; I remember it; I learnt it from . . .).

In this our powers of knowledge are like other fallible capacities. We would not deny that an expert juggler has the capacity to juggle ten balls because she occasionally drops a ball (Rödl's example, 2007, pp. 151–52). Nor would we declare this to show that her capacity is really something *less than* the capacity to juggle ten balls (that move would imply that a genuine capacity has to be infallible). Possession of the capacity is compatible with the possibility of occasional error. Indeed, that's just what it means to say the capacity is fallible. By the same token, it would be a mistake to infer from (i) the fact that, in unfavourable circumstances, the exercise of our perceptual capacities sometimes results in false belief to (ii) the conclusion that even in favourable circumstances those capacities deliver something less than awareness of how things are.

It is not uncommon in epistemology, however, to make just that inference. It will be noted, of course, that an important difference between jugglers and believers is that while a juggler knows when she has dropped a ball, a person may be unable to tell she is in circumstances unfavourable to knowledge-formation. From my point of view, I cannot discriminate between a case in which I form a true belief and a subjectively-indistinguishable case in which I am fooled. But if that is my predicament—so the argument goes—then my grounds for belief do not take me as far as knowledge in either case.

This is a version of the infamous 'argument from illusion' (which is designed for perceptual knowledge, but can be generalised). Neither McDowell nor Rödl find the argument persuasive (see Rödl, 2007, ch. 5; and McDowell, 2011, §10 and 2013, §5). McDowell insists (2011, p. 42): 'Defective exercises of a perceptual capacity can be indiscriminable from non-defective exercises. It is a mistake to infer that even on an occasion on which the capacity is working perfectly, the current exercise of it is, for all one knows, defective'. The argument would present a problem only if the subject's grounds for belief were identical in the two cases. But this is not so. To take a perceptual example: when I learn there is a cat in the street by looking out the window, my ground for knowledge is that I see the cat; but that could not be my ground if I were mistakenly taking a fox to be a cat. So the successful and unsuccessful cases are asymmetrical. The same goes for Jamie's believing that Lucy kissed Jack. Here Jamie's warrant is his learning from Shelia that Lucy kissed Jack and this cannot be his warrant unless Lucy *did* kiss Jack. In contrast, where Shelia is fooling him, the fact that Lucy kissed Jack is not part of his grounds for belief (there is no such fact). Thus we can maintain that, in a successful case, appeal to the exercise of the subject's powers of knowledge is sufficient to characterise her grounds for belief, though this is obviously not so in cases where those powers misfire.

This response might appear only to kick the problem up a level. Suppose we grant that in the successful case the subject has grounds that rule out error. Is it not also true that the subject can never discern whether she has such grounds? Rödl (2007, p. 158) replies that the objection makes the same mistake as before. It can be true that when I am mistaken, I do not know that I am. But it does not follow that when I am not mistaken, I do not know that I am not. As Rödl would put it, knowledge is a self-conscious act; so if you know, you know that you know, even though it is sometimes true that you think you know when you don't (see also McDowell, 2013, pp. 23–24).

The McDowell-Rödl view can seem counterintuitive, but much in the view suits our sound, pre-philosophical intuitions about knowledge. For example, the natural response to Descartes's famous dreaming argument is to claim that when a person is awake she knows that she is, notwithstanding the fact that when she is asleep and dreaming, she mistakenly thinks she is awake. This is exactly what the McDowell-Rödl view allows us to say. The possibility of error is one we encounter and negotiate all the time. It is no more (and no less) problematic than we know it to be in our dealings with the world, everyday and scientific. There is no route from the recognition of fallibility to the conclusion that our best epistemic standings fall short of putting us in touch with the world.

Let us now leave these epistemological reflections and turn to questions of education.

MATTERS EDUCATIONAL

A. *Epistemic Dependence*

On the McDowell-Rödl view, the members of a community of language users are able to make what they know public: by asserting what they know, they make their knowledge available to others, who can acquire it merely by understanding and believing what has been said. As McDowell puts it: 'The idea of knowledge by testimony is that if a knower gives intelligible expression to his knowledge, he puts it into the public domain, where it can be picked up by those who can understand the expression, as long as the opportunity is not closed to them because it would be doxastically irresponsible to believe the speaker' (p. 438). There need be nothing provisional or incomplete about knowledge of this kind.

This model is one in which knowledge is a public phenomenon that may be transmitted between speakers by linguistic acts. Once we have this in view, it is easy to countenance the extent of our epistemic dependence on others. Elizabeth Anscombe (1979, p. 143) writes: 'The greater part of our knowledge of reality rests upon the belief that we repose in things we have been taught or told. . . . We must acknowledge testimony as giving us our larger world in no smaller degree, or even in a greater degree, than the relation of cause and effect.' Almost everything we know about the world beyond the confines of our immediate experience is derived from others, and much of what we know about the tiny piece of reality open to our experience is informed by testimonial knowledge. Schooling is an obvious source of such knowledge: a school is a place where knowledge is deliberately and systematically put into the public domain (by teachers) in a way that invites others (their students) to pick it up.

Although McDowell (1993, p. 438) speaks of the 'transmission' of knowledge, his view need not invite the kind of transmission model of pedagogy often derided by philosophers of education. McDowell makes clear that, even where learners are passive beneficiaries of testimonial knowledge, '[a]cquiring knowledge by testimony is not a mindless reception of something that has nothing to do with rationality' (p. 434). Jamie can learn from his textbook that the structure of the DNA molecule is a double-helix only if he understands what is written, and for that he needs an active grasp on some of the concepts involved together with enough understanding of the subject-matter to contextualise his new knowledge, at least to a degree. Just how much competence this demands is an open question not to be closed by philosophical stipulation. The key point is that only a being capable of active thought can passively acquire knowledge by testimony. In any case, even if students can be fed knowledge passively, it does not follow this is pedagogically desirable. The McDowell-Rödl view should not be faulted on such grounds.

It may yet be argued that an emphasis on epistemic dependence is in tension with McDowell's commitment to what is sometimes called 'epistemic autonomy', the view that each of us is responsible for determining the cogency of his or her beliefs. McDowell (1994, p. 12) is clear that 'active empirical thinking takes place under a standing obligation to reflect about the credentials of the putatively rational linkages that govern it.' This is central to his view of doxastic responsibility and to his conception of how freedom finds expression in a human life. For McDowell, rational agents are autonomous in the sense that they have the power to determine for themselves, not just what to do, but what to think. I wholeheartedly embrace this view in

The Formation of Reason. But how can epistemic autonomy be squared with epistemic dependence?

Some respond to this problem by denying we are as epistemically dependent as we seem. Siegel, for example, follows Jonathan Adler, and argues that the beliefs we acquire from testimony are 'typically sustained and justified by being confirmed for us in ways which do not depend on the testimony of others' (2003, p. 313). However, the example Siegel gives suggests the reverse. He claims that although testimony may be the source of our belief that smoking increases the risk of heart disease, it is 'confirmed for each of us routinely as we read both scientific and popular reports, speak with physicians, biologists, and others who do have direct familiarity with the details of research, hear pronouncements on the matter from government officials, talk to our doctors, etc.' (ibid.). But much of this confirming evidence is testimonial in kind. Even the physicians and biologists said to have 'direct familiarity with the details of the research' will be relying on testimony (after all, we do not routinely encounter people who have conducted such research first-hand). The same goes for Jamie's knowledge of DNA, the number of Austen's novels, and the fate of Ann Boleyn. Moreover, Jamie's teachers and the authors of his textbooks will be scarcely less dependent upon testimony than he is. We can hope to support a piece of testimony by fitting it into a cogent picture of the world, but we cannot free that conception from reliance on testimony.

I do not believe, however, that epistemic dependence need conflict with epistemic autonomy. Two central thoughts inform the latter idea. First, each of us is responsible for our own beliefs in the sense that, if our beliefs are challenged in a reasonable way, we are beholden to respond or give up the beliefs in question. Second, each individual must settle for herself the question what to believe. In forming a belief a person adds a component to a conception of the world, allegiance to which is partly constitutive of her identity (if I may use the concept of identity somewhat loosely). Neither idea is really in tension with epistemic dependence. First, there is no reason why an individual cannot appeal to testimonial knowledge in defending her beliefs: that I am responsible for keeping my epistemic house in order does not entail that I cannot draw on the knowledge of others. Second, I do not fail to settle what *I* think about some issue by deferring to someone else who knows what to think about it. On the contrary, believing someone who knows is a perfectly good way to decide what to think. Of course, I must aim to settle what to think by arriving at the truth of the matter, so I should only look to another for the truth. (It would not be rational for me to think *whatever* she thinks, like a customer in a restaurant who orders by telling the waiter, 'I'll have whatever she has'.) But if she can tell me how things are, then believing her is a good source of knowledge.

What makes it difficult to see these issues clearly is a tendency to portray things as a choice between extremes—on the one hand a Cartesian vision of the self-sufficiency of the rational subject, where each of us must build a conception of the world from the bottom-up, and on the other, a kind of Orwellian collectivism where our beliefs are decided for us by others. The truth is that an autonomous, doxastically responsible agent can draw on knowledge that others make available to her without surrendering control of her mental life. Indeed, the very possibility of her having a mental life depends upon her inheriting a conception of the world in the first place (the second topic mentioned in my opening paragraph), and the exercise of epistemic autonomy always presupposes a background of common knowledge. McDowell is fond of the metaphor of Neurath's boat, which portrays our epistemic predicament as akin to a mariner who must repair her boat at sea. There is no epistemic dry dock; we must fix problems in our conception of the world by relying on beliefs we take to be in better shape than those under threat. We should remind ourselves that none of us built our boats from scratch. Indeed, we found ourselves afloat. And while each of us is responsible for keeping our boat from sinking, we may rely on others to furnish us materials and to show us what to do with them.

Of course, just as an individual's epistemic situation can be empowered and enhanced by her relation to a community, it can also be diminished. What we take to be common knowledge can turn out to be common folly. This is something that a doxastically responsible individual understands. But it is also a fact that calls for a reasonable view of the extent to which individuals can be held responsible for their beliefs. Clearly, I am culpable if I hold a belief when I ought to be cognisant of evidence of its falsehood, but I can hardly be blamed if, say, the scientific culture into which I have been initiated turns out to be massively in error. There are limits to the degree to which we can control our epistemic fate. Nonetheless, there is room within those limits for epistemically autonomous beings to operate, even though such beings are dependent on others for resources without which the exercise of their powers of autonomy would be greatly impoverished.

B. Testimony, Teaching, and Trust

One concept prominent in recent discussions of testimony, of which McDowell and Rödl make little, is *trust* (see, e.g., Faulkner, 2011 and

McMyler, 2011; also Moran, 2005, 2006). There is an important distinction between believing what someone has said or written and believing a *person*. When Jamie glimpses Paula's journal and learns she likes Harry, Jamie might ask himself whether he should believe what she has written. But if Paula *tells* Jamie herself, then she is asking him to believe *her*, or as Anscombe puts it (1979, p. 151), to 'trust her for the truth'. She is giving Jamie her word and thereby taking responsibility to back him up if he relies on the knowledge she is offering him. This introduces a distinctive interpersonal relation to the exchange. If Jamie believes her, he is entitled to feel wronged if she turns out to be misleading him—her deception would be a breach of trust. Similarly, if Jamie refuses to believe Paula when she is telling him the truth, she may justifiably resent his unwillingness to trust her word. Whether this notion of trust is relevant to the justification of testimonial belief, as McMyler and others maintain, it is undeniably central to the interpersonal relations that mediate communication and the ethics of conversation.

How does this illuminate the situation of teacher and student? Clearly trust is an essential element in their relation, though its character will vary depending on the students' age and the stage of their education. Is epistemic trust—trusting another for the truth—a part of this? Anscombe (1979, p. 147) seems to think so. She contrasts the teacher with the linguistic interpreter. The latter is blameless if what he says is untrue so long as his translation is accurate. The teacher, in contrast, 'even though in no way an original authority, *is* wrong if what he says is untrue, and that hangs together with the fact that his pupils believe (or disbelieve) *him*'. If Anscombe is right, then students accept the knowledge they are offered because they trust their teachers for the truth.

This might be thought a significant finding of relevance to our understanding of authentic pedagogy (and a possible premise in an argument defending traditional teaching styles against new learning technologies that threaten to displace the teacher). However, though there is undoubtedly a breach of moral trust where a teacher deliberately misleads students about some subject-matter, or presents herself as a reliable authority when she is not, I do not think that the kind of trust involved in believing someone's testimony is as central to the teacher-student relation as might appear. As Anscombe herself writes (1979, p. 145), two pages before the passage just quoted, in teaching philosophy 'we do not hope that our pupils *believe us*, but rather, that they will *come to see* that what we say is true—if it is'. Here is a vital distinction. When a teacher presents some subject-matter to her students, there is a sense in which she speaks, not in her own voice, but for the subject-matter itself. As Rödl (forthcoming) puts it, '[t]he teacher does not speak as a particular subject but as the science'. She presents to her students, not *her* knowledge as such, but common knowledge in which she invites her students to share. She thus speaks in her own voice only in asides and her role is that of facilitator or conduit. She is to initiate her students into some part of the conversation of mankind, to use Oakeshott's famous expression, and she does not typically portray her own voice as part of that conversation. A teacher must aspire to a certain intellectual transparency so that the students 'look through her' to the shared subject of their inquiries.

This interpretation fits the following facts. First, a student may not usually cite her teacher's authority to justify a knowledge claim about the subject of instruction. A student cannot normally support a claim in an essay or examination by maintaining that she learnt it from her teacher; rather, she must invoke further claims from the subject-matter in question. This is not because students are barred from relying on testimonial knowledge—there is usually no requirement that they provide first-hand justification. It is because the teacher is not treated as a source of knowledge of the kind envisioned in philosophical discussions of testimony. The teacher's role is to direct students to the subject-matter so that they hold beliefs about it in recognition of the truth and not because they have been told what to believe.[8] Second, there is something inauthentic about teachers designing assignments to test whether their students know what they have been told rather than testing their knowledge of the subject-matter in question. Third, a teacher can be successful even if she does not believe the subject that she teaches. A creationist can effectively teach evolutionary theory, so long as she does not allow her creationist beliefs to interfere. If the students know their teacher's true beliefs, they do not learn by trusting her for the truth and she does not take herself to be offering them knowledge (they may trust her for the truth in the way we trust a thermometer to give the correct temperature, but this is a different kind of trust). For all that, she may do an excellent job.

Throughout this chapter I have followed philosophical convention in treating all knowledge learnt from what one is told by others as knowledge by testimony. But the discussion above suggests that we should distinguish teaching from testifying, if I may put it like that, and work with a narrower view of testimony. On this view, a person, A, gains testimonial knowledge from another person, B, just in case (i) B, knowing that p, informs A that p in order that A, by believing B, should come to believe that p, and (ii) B thereby entitles A to invoke B's authority to justify p. In short, B gives A her word that p and A believes that *p* on B's authority. Of course, a student may form beliefs by taking her teacher's word for it, and in that case the knowledge the student acquires is testimonial in kind, but here the student is accepting what she is told rather than learning what she is taught. Teaching can begin with such acceptance, but it cannot end there.

To this we must add the further, and perhaps obvious, point that teaching is not only telling. As McMyler nicely points out (2011, pp. 144–145; see also Moran, 2006, pp. 279–280), there is a distinction between *telling* someone that p and *arguing* that *p*. While in the former case, the speaker asks her audience to believe *her* that *p*, in the latter the audience is invited to believe that *p* in light of the reasons the speaker presents to them. And arguing for *p* is not the only speech act to contrast with telling. There's also *presenting evidence* that *p*, *setting out the proof* that *p*, *challenging* not-*p*, together with less direct ways of stimulating an audience to think so as to lead them to the belief that *p* (see Moran, 2005, pp. 344–347). These modes of persuasion are central to the teacher's art, but they need not involve testimony.

Sceptics about epistemic dependence might take solace from in this discussion. Siegel, for example, might respond to my earlier criticism by claiming that his position is simply that we are not as reliant on testimonial knowledge as is commonly thought: for instance, we are not forced to believe there is a link between smoking and heart disease on anyone's say-so, for we can critically evaluate the reasons that favour so believing. However, though this is so, it remains the case that in order to evaluate such reasons, we have to take a huge amount for granted. It may be that we are not dependent upon the testimony of specific individuals, but we certainly defer to conceptions widely held within our epistemic community, and here we find dependence with a kinship to testimonial knowledge. It is also important not to obscure the fact that in educational contexts students must accept a great deal on the authority of their teachers. This is especially true in the early years of a student's education (where teaching does involve a lot of telling), but it persists into high school and college. Things could scarcely be otherwise, since students are hardly in a position independently to justify all they are taught (even if they were motivated to do so). This is entirely consistent with the ideals of a liberal education, understood as initiation into a world-view, conceived as an evolving conversation. Such initiation aims to equip students so that they are able, in the course of time, to subject any part of their world-view to critical reflection, but all we can reasonably ask is that they be ready critically to reflect on beliefs that have been thrown into reasonable doubt, not that they actually aspire to some kind of epistemic independence.

CONCLUSION

I began by defending an account of testimonial knowledge based on the work of John McDowell and Sebastian Rödl. On this account, when B tells A that *p*, A's warrant for believing that *p* can be no more (and no less) than *A learnt from B that p* (or *A heard it that p from B*, or *A has it on B's authority that p*), so long as A is not doxastically irresponsible in believing B. Testimony is treated as a source of knowledge in its own right—one of the ways in which we can bring the world into view and one source we can cite in answer to the question 'How do you know . . .?'. But at the same time, this account of testimony is part of an attractive general approach to epistemology —one that offers parallel views of perception and memory. The McDowell-Rödl approach does not recognise the epistemology of testimony as a distinctive sub-branch of epistemology, one that comes into focus only after a working account of knowledge is on the table, for the possibility of testimony is inherent in the very idea of knowledge. Knowledge is the kind of thing that can be shared and held in common. There is therefore nothing mysterious about how, by articulating her knowledge in a linguistic act, one person can make that knowledge available to another.

I suggested that the McDowell-Rödl view has important consequences for philosophy of education. It enables a more satisfying account of fallibility than often figures in philosophy of education— one that sees fallibility as a characteristic of people and their powers of knowledge, rather than of knowledge itself. It provides a plausible view of the epistemic dependence of the individual on the knowledge of other individuals and the common knowledge of the community, and it assists us in making an important distinction, sometimes obscured, between offering testimony and teaching. There is a difference between believing something on the say-so of another and believing something in virtue of one's initiation into a body of common knowledge and traditions of common inquiry. Both are important dimensions of the social character of knowledge, but while the epistemology of testimony concerns the former, the philosophy of education must concern itself principally with the latter.

With this in mind, let us revisit the distinction with which we started: McDowell's contrast between knowledge the initiate gains in the course of learning her first language and the testimonial knowledge available to mature speakers. Two refinements suggest themselves. First, notwithstanding McDowell's formulation, the distinction is not best put as one between knowledge we acquire by being told what is the case and knowledge that doesn't derive from telling. For a child learning her first language is in fact told a great many things that she subsequently comes to believe at least partly because she has been told them, even though, at the time of the telling, she lacks the conceptual resources actively to understand what she is told. Only consider the running commentary on actions and events to which parents submit babies and infants. Being so addressed is essential to acquiring the concepts necessary to understand and evaluate utterances. As the child gains the concept *cat* she comes by knowledge of cats that includes much that she *has* explicitly been told. (Of course she does not acquire this knowledge through the exercise of concepts she already possesses, as in standard cases of testimony. This is, I take it, McDowell's principal point.) Second, we should not suppose these two modes of knowledge-acquisition can be clearly held apart, essentially applying to different stages in a person's life. Mature speakers continue to acquire a good deal of knowledge implicitly in the course of learning from what they are told.

These refinements bear on the contrast between teaching and testifying. For the situation of the student is sometimes closer to that of McDowell's initiate than the mature recipient of testimonial knowledge. In harmony with the reflections that concluded the last section, students are told much by their teachers, and come to believe what they are told at least partly because they are told it, but often they neither receive this as testimony, nor affirm it in recognition of reasons. Rather, they embrace it as part of the world-view into which they are being initiated. Moreover, in addition to learning from what they are told, students gain knowledge in much less overt ways. They acquire styles of thinking and reasoning; they acquire conceptions of salience and relevance; they learn conversational and intellectual virtues—how to listen, how to ponder, how to reflect, and so on; they pick up concepts that are not overtly explained and they exercise conceptual skills that no-one tells them how to deploy. Some of this *could* not be explicitly taught, but must be shown, and in some cases the showing cannot advertise itself as such. A philosopher cannot tell her students how to reason. She needs to teach by example. She must encourage her students to reflect on and reason with the reasoning of others, though the students may better learn from example the less they try explicitly to emulate it. This is part of what it is to be initiated into an intellectual tradition and an important dimension of our epistemic dependence on others.

I hope to have shown that, although the recent enthusiasm for the epistemology of testimony may have less to offer philosophy of education than might appear, reflecting on testimony can initiate inquiries that uncover some of the depths and complexities of the ways we learn from others, a subject-matter undoubtedly worthy of sustained exploration.[9]

NOTES

1. Some may think the solution lies in dropping the conditional principle and holding instead that the level of justification required for knowledge that p is compatible with the falsity of the belief that p. I consider and reject this idea later in my argument.
2. Another alternative is an externalist account, according to which empirical knowledge depends not, or not only, on the quality of reasons for belief that are in principle within the knower's cognitive reach, but on the obtaining of further 'external' conditions about which the knower need know nothing, such as whether her belief issued from a reliable belief-causing mechanism. McDowell (1993/1998, §7), however, rejects externalism. If knowledge is 'a standing in the space of reasons' (as he puts it following Sellars), then when a person knows, her grounds must consist in considerations that are at least potentially within her grasp—the sort of thing she could cite to support her claim.
3. Faulkner (2011, pp. 102–103, note 73) contests this, wrongly in my view. See McDowell, 1994, pp. 419–420, note 11.
4. Moreover, circumstances can act to raise the standards of doxastic responsibility. For example, when a serious accusation is made it is often doxastically responsible for hearers to reserve judgement (pending investigation, as it were), whether or not the accuser is known to be generally epistemically reliable.
5. Some theories make much of the fact that a recipient of testimonial knowledge is entitled to defer a challenge to this knowledge back to her source. McMyler (2011, e.g. p. 169), for example, maintains this reveals how testimonial knowledge involves shared epistemic responsibility. Such views have to cope with the fact that testimonial knowledge can survive even if its source is no longer available to address the deferred challenge. In such cases a recipient can refer *to* her source (I heard it from Lewis), but cannot refer something *back to* her source (Lewis being, e.g., no longer alive).
6. It might be objected that in everyday discourse we employ a variety of conceptions of knowledge and some are far less demanding than the one I favour here. For example, in educational assessment, we sometimes count a student as knowing that p merely on the basis of her ticking the right box, sometimes we demand that students present reasons to support their beliefs to count as knowing, and sometimes we ask not just that they cite reasons, but that they show they understand how those reasons support their view. So on what grounds do I privilege the demanding notion of knowledge favoured by McDowell and Rödl? I do so because I believe that conception of knowledge is central to everyday empirical inquiry. We do not count someone as knowing when the train leaves, or what the weather is doing, or who won the match, or where the enemy is camped unless she has a true belief about the fact in question, together with a warrant for belief that discloses that fact to her.
7. McDowell has interesting things to say about our propensity to construe reason as a domain immune from luck at 1993/1998, pp. 440–43. I discuss his view further in Bakhurst, 2011 (see, e.g., pp. 79 and 129).

8. This point invites consideration of the literatures on indoctrination and the character of liberal education, but a fuller discussion must await another occasion.
9. A version of this paper was presented to the Department of Applied Linguistics at Penn State in October 2012. I am grateful to members of the audience on that occasion for their perceptive comments and criticisms. Thanks also to Ben Kotzee, Andrew Davis, and Sebastian Rödl who read the manuscript and made many helpful suggestions.

REFERENCES

Anscombe, G. E. M. (1979) What Is It to Believe Someone?, in: C. F. Delaney (ed.) *Rationality and Religious Belief* (Notre Dame, IN, Notre Dame University Press), pp. 141–151.

Bakhurst, D. (2011) *The Formation of Reason* (Oxford, Wiley-Blackwell, 2011).

Burge, T. (1993) Content Preservation, *Philosophical Review*, 102, pp. 457–488.

Faulkner, P. (2011) *Knowledge on Trust* (Oxford, Oxford University Press).

McDowell, J. (1993/1998) Knowledge by Hearsay, in his *Meaning, Knowledge, and Reality* (Cambridge, MA, Harvard University Press), pp. 414–443.

McDowell, J. (1994) *Mind and World*, 2nd edn., 1996 (Cambridge, MA, Harvard University Press).

McDowell, J. (2011) *Perception as a Capacity for Knowledge* (Milwaukee, WI, Marquette University Press).

McDowell, J. (2013) Acting in the Light of a Fact, in: D. Bakhurst, B. Hooker and M. Little (eds) *Thinking About Reasons: Themes From the Philosophy of Jonathan Dancy* (Oxford, Oxford University Press), pp. 13–28.

McMyler, B. (2011) *Testimony, Trust, and Authority* (Oxford, Oxford University Press).

Moran, R. (2005) Problems of Sincerity, *Proceedings of the Aristotelian Society*, 105, pp. 341–361.

Moran, R. (2006) Getting Told and Being Believed, in: J. Lackey and E. Sosa (eds) *The Epistemology of Testimony* (Oxford, Oxford University Press), pp. 272–306. Originally published in *Philosopher's Imprint*, 5 (2005), pp. 1–29.

Rödl, S. (2007) *Self-Consciousness* (Cambridge, MA, Harvard University Press).

Rödl, S. (forthcoming), Testimony and Generality, *Philosophical Topics*.

Siegel, H. (2003) Cultivating Reason, in: R. Curren (ed.) *A Companion to the Philosophy of Education* (Oxford, Blackwell), pp. 305–319.

Wittgenstein, L. (1969) *On Certainty*, G. E. M. Anscombe and G. H. von Wright, eds; D. Paul and G. E. M. Anscombe, trans. (Oxford, Blackwell).

3
Anscombe's 'Teachers'

JEREMY WANDERER

In a largely neglected paper, G. E. M. Anscombe explores what she describes as a largely neglected topic in epistemology, viz. that of believing someone, where 'belief' takes a personal object—'believing x that p' (p. 142).[1] One striking feature of the paper is the prominent role played by the paired activities of teaching and learning in Anscombe's explorations of what it is to believe someone. Whilst not all instances of learning from another involve believing that person and not all instances of teaching aim at being believed personally, Anscombe seems to suggest that there is a categorical connection between learning from teaching in key cases and believing that person, such that investigating what it is to believe someone is an investigation into the nature of learning from teaching in these cases, and vice versa.

Anscombe's remarks in the paper are terse and tentative. My aim here is to focus on her reflections on learning from teaching as a way of developing an understanding of what it is to believe someone. Whilst I will pay close attention to the text, this is *not* an exercise in Anscombe exegesis. It is an attempt to construct a framework for thinking about these issues that is inspired by Anscombe's brief but suggestive discussion.

I THE CAST

The case of learning from teaching that involves believing someone is illustrated in Anscombe's paper through a series of implied contrasts. Let us begin with a perfunctory characterisation of these contrasts, to be developed more fully in subsequent sections.

One contrast is between *the teacher and the interpreter*.

> Consider belief reposed in what an interpreter says—I mean the case of believing the sentences he comes out with. If you believe those communications, probably—i.e. in the normal case—you

Education and the Growth of Knowledge: Perspectives from Social and Virtue Epistemology, First Edition. Edited by Ben Kotzee. Copyright © 2014 The Authors. Editorial organisation © 2014 Philosophy of Education Society of Great Britain. Published 2014 by John Wiley & Sons Ltd.

are believing his principal: your reliance on the interpreter is only belief that he has reproduced what his principal said. A teacher, on the other hand, even in no way an original authority, is wrong if what he says is untrue, and that hangs together with the fact that his pupils believe (or disbelieve) him (p. 147).

Even if the teacher herself is merely transmitting information acquired second-hand from another original informant, there is a sense in which she is not a mere conduit through which the information is transmitted from informant to learner. The teacher endorses the claim, so that if we believe what the teacher has said, it may be a case of believing her. In this she differs from an interpreter, who has not endorsed the transmitted claim, so that if we believe what the interpreter has said, it is not a case of believing him.

One contrast is between *the teacher and the megalomaniac.*

For it would be a megalomaniac who complained of not being believed when he agrees that the thing that was not believed was, anyway, not true. . . . Compare the irritation of a teacher at not being believed. On the whole, such irritation is just—in matters where learners must learn by believing teachers. But if what was not believed should turn out to be false, his complaint collapses (p. 151).

The megalomaniac described here cannot be one who is unable to recognise a distinction between what he asserts to be true and what is true, for he explicitly concedes that his judgement was in error. Rather, he desires that others agree with him merely because he says so, irrespective of its truth. The teacher also wants others to believe what she says, and may likewise experience irritation when this does not come to be, but—unlike the megalomaniac—she aims for being believed precisely because she takes the claim to be true.

One contrast is between *the teacher and the teacher of philosophy.*

[W]hat someone's saying a thing may bring about, is that one forms one's *own* judgment that the thing is true. In teaching philosophy we do not hope that our pupils will believe us, but rather, that they will *come to see* that what we say is true—if it is (p. 145).

This comment is made in the course of illustrating the difference between merely believing what someone said and believing someone. Teaching philosophy is portrayed as a special kind of teaching in which the teacher does not aim at being believed personally, in the hope that the students will grasp for themselves the truth of what she says. In contrast, the kind of teaching highlighted by Anscombe in the paper is one in which the teacher aims to be believed personally, and this precludes the learners forming their own judgments on the matter.

Here, then, are Anscombe's 'teachers': the interpreter, the megalomaniac, the teacher of philosophy and the teacher. Although the first two are not 'teachers' in the sense that Anscombe aims to explicate, both may occupy the institutional role of being a teacher, and will be familiar to many from past experiences of formal educational encounters. The third deserves the title of 'teacher', albeit one for whom there is no categorical connection between teaching and being believed personally. It is the fourth, the teacher who aims at being believed personally, that is the primary focus, illustrated by contrast with the other three cases.

My use of the term 'the teacher', with the definite article and without qualification or modification, to describe the fourth case may suggest that what follows is an attempt at an analysis of the paradigmatic case of teaching, either in the descriptive sense of giving an account of 'what we mean by the concept' in everyday discourse, or in the normative sense that this should be treated as the core case of teaching from which all others may be derived.[2] Whatever Anscombe's own intentions in this regard, this is resolutely not an intended implication of the ensuing investigation. Its aim is, inter alia, to shed light on the distinctive kind of teaching that Anscombe treats as aiming at being believed personally. Whilst it is assumed that this kind of teaching is somewhat familiar to most, no stance is taken here on either the descriptive or normative centrality of this kind. My persistence here with the use of term 'the teacher' as a title for this kind echoes the language used in the target text; one should treat this as shorthand for 'the Anscombean teacher', i.e. as the kind of teacher that is Anscombe's focus.

Before characterising this kind of teacher, by exploring in further detail the contrast with the other kinds of 'teachers' just noted, let us first consider the manner in which Anscombe frames the issues.

II SETTING THE SCENE

Anscombe's discussion of what it is to believe someone begins, somewhat peculiarly, with a puzzle.

> There were three men A, B and C talking in a certain village. A said 'If that tree falls down, it'll block the road for a long time.' 'That's not so if there is a tree-clearing machine working,' said

B. C remarked 'There *will* be one if the tree does not fall down'. The famous Sophist Euthydemus, a stranger in the place, was listening. He immediately said 'I believe you all. So I infer that the tree will fall down and the road will be blocked.' Question: What's wrong with Euthydemus? (p. 141).

Euthydemus' logic is 'impeccable' (p. 145). If we take B's 'that's not so' to refer to the whole of A's statement, then the conjunction of the claims of A and B's implies that (i) *there will not be a tree clearing machine working*. So, when C adds the further contention that there will be a clearing machine if the tree does not fall down to (i), Euthydemus can infer that (ii) *the tree will fall down*. Finally, combining (ii) with A's initial statement, Euthydemus rightly concludes (iii) *that the road will be blocked*. Yet, Anscombe is correct in noting that something has gone wrong with Euthydemus; '*insane* is just what Euthydemus' remark is and sounds—it is not, for example, like the expression of a somewhat rash opinion or excessive credulity' (p. 146). So, where has he gone wrong?

A, B and C were engaged in a conversation, 'talking in a village'; Euthydemus is an outsider to the conversation, 'a stranger . . . listening' in. The mere fact Euthydemus is an eavesdropper on a conversation does not preclude him from believing A, B and C.[3] Highlighting his status as outsider, however, serves to signify his insensitivity to the dynamics of engaged conversation. Euthydemus treats each statement independently of each other, as if they were entered into a timeless register of facts, without regard for how each subsequent statement may require an alteration or retraction of the previous claim. B's utterance is best read as casting doubt on A's; it constitutes a challenge that calls for A to defend, modify or retract the statement. Euthydemus cannot, therefore, believe them all, since—given B's challenge—he cannot simply treat A's claim as still available without some further response from A.

Discussions of the epistemology of testimony usually concentrate on isolated instances of social interaction—a stranger asking for directions, the reporting of a fact gleaned from reading the Sunday papers. In contrast, by starting her discussion of what it is to believe someone with this puzzle, Anscombe firmly places the topic within the wider setting of conversational activity. As I use it, *conversational activity* denotes a very broad category that includes all discursive interpersonal encounters. *Reasoning* is a species of this genus, where interlocutors display a commitment to allowing the activities of others to affect their own participation in the activity. *Engaged reasoning* is a sub-species of reasoning, whereby the interlocutors are further committed to producing activities that call on those addressed to alter their own normative commitments in light of these performances, such that the reactions of others to these calls are treated as grounds for altering one's own normative commitments on the matter under discussion.[4] The paradigmatic activities of teaching and learning under investigation here, as well as the interrelated phenomenon of believing someone, all have their home in this activity of engaged reasoning.

A substantive part of Anscombe's paper sets out some of the necessary background conditions for such engaged reasoning.

> [T]he recipient can at any rate *fail to believe* (as opposed to disbelieving) NN out of a variety of attitudes. He may not notice the communication at all. He may notice it and take it as language and make something of it but not take it as addressed to himself. Or he may notice it and take it as language and yet, whether or not he takes it as addressed to himself, he may make the wrong thing of it. And he may take it as addressed to himself and not make the wrong thing of it but not believe it comes from NN. Only when we have excluded all the cases—or, more probably, simply *assumed* their exclusion—do we come to the situation in which the question simply is: Does X believe NN or not? (p. 150).

At minimum, then, learning from teaching requires the learner (i) to notice the communication; (ii) to take it as meaningful; (iii) to take it as addressed to him; (iv) to correctly interpret it and (v) to believe that it comes from the teacher. If all background conditions such as these are fulfilled then it becomes possible for the learner to disbelieve the teacher as opposed to fail to believe her. This is an important distinction, one that relates to what I have elsewhere described as the difference between ignoring and rejecting a claim.[5] If these background conditions are not fulfilled, then it is possible for the learner to fail to believe the teacher—he can ignore her. However, once the background conditions are fulfilled and the learner recognises that he is being addressed by the teacher in meaningful communication in the appropriate way, then the possibility of ignoring her is no longer available. Any response, even silence, is taken as an active response by the learner to the teacher's claim. In turn, once these background conditions are recognised by both parties to be fulfilled, the teacher and learner are involved in engaged reasoning, such that any response by the learner is itself a call to the teacher, providing the teacher with potential grounds for altering her own stance on the issue.

By starting with the puzzle of Euthydemus, Anscombe invites the suggestion that the appropriate framework for thinking about the activity of teaching which aims at being believed personally is that of engaged reasoning. Let us elaborate on this suggestion by considering each of Anscombe's 'teachers' in turn.

III THE INTERPRETER

The *interpreter* here is best thought of as a translator, viz. an intermediary—such as a court or sign-language interpreter—who transfers a stable meaning across a physical or conceptual divide that may exist between speaker and audience. Anscombe uses the verb 'reproduce' in describing this activity: even though the production of the interpreter may require great skill and effort on her part, it aims to merely replicate (lit. 'fold back') the original performance. Much to the chagrin of many a skilled interpreter, the successful act of interpreting in this sense is transparent, and lies outside the audience's awareness. C. N. Bialik's description of reading in translation as 'kissing a bride through a veil' is thus doubly apt: transparency is both an aspiration for the act of interpreting and rendered largely unachievable by the very interpretive performance itself.

It is intriguing to contrast this case of the interpreter with that of an official spokesperson.[6] Suppose both the president's interpreter and spokesperson state in the name of the president that 'the threat is imminent'. In both cases the statement reports to be a claim made by the president; in both the claim is produced by an actor explicitly standing as an intermediary between president and audience; both can be said to be representing the president on this matter; and we can attribute an action to the president on the basis of both their performances. Yet the grounds for this attribution differ between the cases. The spokesperson has been formally authorised by the president to speak on his behalf. As a result, she can speak for him even if there was no prior act of assertion, and the president has agreed to take responsibility for this assertion even if he would rather not. In contrast, the interpreter need not have been explicitly authorised by the president to speak on his behalf any more than any other interlocutor, but functions to enable the president's initial act reach an audience through a potential barrier that prevents it from so doing. As a result, there does need to be a prior act of asserting by the President to be interpreted, and the president can repudiate the interpretation should he so wish. Despite these differences, however, neither interpreter nor spokesperson is believed personally. This is not because they are insincere in their respective utterances, but because they are detached from their utterances in a manner that precludes them from being treated as the author of the act.[7]

It is rare for any actual teacher to see themselves functioning merely as an interpreter of the claims of others (in the narrow sense of interpreting just outlined), nor as functioning as a spokesperson for others. Nevertheless, it is common for someone occupying the social role of teacher to speak in a detached manner that—if recognised by the learner—precludes them from being believed personally. Here is a much discussed recent example, involving a devoutly Christian fourth-grade teacher who teaches her biology students that 'modern-day *Homo sapiens* evolved from *Homo erectus*' because of her recognition of her duties as a teacher to teach the syllabus despite believing in the truth of creationism.[8] Let us grant that her students can acquire knowledge on this teacher's say-so. This is, nonetheless, patently not an ordinary case of learning from teaching. It is not that the teacher is being insincere in her utterances (she may make no attempts to hide her own convictions, for example, whilst ably defending the asserted claim from students' challenges). Rather, the claim is one from which the teacher is detached. One way of thinking about this is to note the teacher here is isolating one aspect of her self-identity, without striving for integration with others, such that the testimony is not one that she herself can be said to author. (One could even imagine her inserting a disclaimer to this effect—'Look, I am just speaking here in my capacity as a school employee' or 'I'm just towing the party line here'—which serves to make explicit her own detachment from the speech act). As a result, whilst her students may come to believe that modern-day *Homo sapiens* evolved from *Homo erectus*, they do not believe *her* that this is the case.

Here we have three examples of detached speech: the interpreter, the spokesperson and the creationist teacher. It would be misleading to say that what makes any of these instances of detached speech is that the speaker is putting a claim into the public domain without endorsing the claim, since this construal fails to distinguish these activities from related kinds of unendorsed acts such as conjecturing or guessing or playing devil's advocate. The point is that in all three cases, the claim is put forward as authored, although the identity of the author differs from the identity of the speaker. In the first two cases, it is someone else (the principal) who should be held responsible for the claim. In the third case, the author is the speaker herself under another guise.[9] In all three cases of detached speech therefore, one can come to believe what is said without believing the speaker.

Can the audience of these detached acts be said to believe the act's author, as opposed to the speaker? In the case of the creationist teacher, it seems straightforward that the appropriate response is no. Belief takes a personal object when the object is indeed a person and not a person playing a role that is temporarily detached from other aspects of their self. The case of the spokesperson is more complicated, and it is arguable that here too the answer should be no. Whilst the president's authorisation of the spokesperson's acts ensures that he must take responsibility for those performances, this sense of responsibility seems to differ from that of a speaker—he stands *by* those acts rather than stands *for* them. It is thus not surprising that the relevant context to be considering the spokesperson is a formal institutional setting, where the issue of who is to be held culpable for the claim runs separate from the question of defending the claim's veracity. If this is right, it is only Anscombe's case of the interpreter where it is possible for the audience to believe the principal in the personal sense.

We suggested earlier that the appropriate framework for thinking about the idea of believing someone personally is that provided by engaged reasoning, a social context in which the normative standing of a given performance by each interlocutor in a conversation is beholden to the response of other interlocutors addressed by that performance. Our reflections on the case of the interpreter serve to emphasise that the engagement here is between persons via their authored performances, where the relevant aspect of authorship is one that precludes detachment from the act. If the performer were to make their detachment from a performance manifest, or if the addressed audience suspected such detachment, one could learn from the performance but it would not be a case of believing them personally.

IV THE MEGALOMANIAC

Unlike the interpreter, the megalomaniac is emphatically not detached from his verbal performances, yet he too is not believed personally. To understand why this is the case, we need to clarify the notion of authority implicated in the social context of engaged reasoning.

The megalomaniac is introduced in the course of a discussion of the irritation experienced in not being believed. Following an act of teaching, a teacher typically desires the esteem of her pupils.[10] The teacher does not simply crave generic positive approbation from them; she takes herself to be a certain kind of authority on the matter at hand, and craves their recognition of this status. When her students learn from this act and believe her that p, i.e. believe her personally, they recognise her as the relevant kind of authority and display the esteem in which they hold her. She thus experiences irritation and insult when she becomes aware that they fail to believe what she asserts—they have failed to accord her the esteem she takes herself to deserve. As Anscombe suggests, her irritation is a form of 'complaint' at the failure to be accorded what she deserves, even though esteem is not something that can be demanded. Should it transpire later that she was mistaken in the claim, she may want to save face or desire that her students continue to hold her in high esteem, but she can no longer genuinely treat herself as deserving the esteem that is conveyed in their recognition of her as a relevant kind of authority on the matter. She thus ought not to feel irritation or insult when they do not believe her. 'Falsehood lets one off all hooks' (p. 151).

In this context, the megalomaniac is one who continues to crave the esteem of his pupils in the form of their recognition of him as the relevant kind of authority on this matter, even in cases of acknowledged falsehood. On one understanding, his megalomania is such that he misunderstands the nature of the relevant kind of authority, thereby assuming he actually deserves recognition as an authority on this matter just because he 'asserted' something, whether or not he takes himself to be right or wrong on the matter.[11]

Insight into the nature of the relevant kind of authority can be had by comparison with the case of a general who continues to experience insult when his troops do not obey his order to advance, even though he is now aware that the order was a disastrous strategic move. Here too there is disparity between the esteem deserved and the esteem sought, though one need not appeal to the diagnosis of megalomania to understand why the sense of insult persists. Whence the difference?

The key seems to be captured in a distinction due to R. B. Friedman between two types of authority: 'being *in* authority' and 'being *an* authority'.[12] The general is the paradigmatic example of one *in* authority. In acknowledging the general's authority to command by performing the commanded act, the soldier recognises that the general has this authority in virtue of being legitimately placed in this position within the system of authority. Here, in the case of *in* authority, 'the system of authority is logically prior to the person',[13] since there is no reason to defer to the person if he is does not occupy this position within the system and so lacks authority. This kind of authority is undermined if the soldier follows this command because he judges that the general is wise or that the command is sensible. As a result, recognition of authority through compliance is still deserved, even if the command is unwise in the circumstances. The paradigmatic example of being *an* authority is the teacher. In recognising the teacher's authority, the pupil recognises that the teacher has this authority in virtue of some expertise she has, where this arose independently from the system of authority itself. Here, in the case of *an* authority, 'the person is prior to the system', since there is a reason to defer to her expertise even if she is not recognised to have this authority. It does not undermine the authority of the teacher if one concurs precisely because one judges that she is wise. As a result, recognition of authority through compliance is not deserved by the teacher should the counsel itself not turn out to be sensible in the circumstances.

In a successful instance of commanding, the soldier complies with the command because he recognises that the general is *in* authority. This may involve some 'calculation' by the soldier, i.e. rational deliberation as to whether the general's performance on this occasion has the appropriate standing. Yet part of recognising that authority is a commitment to limiting this calculation in practice to establishing the credentials of the performance as authoritative in the context of the normative system within which that he takes himself to be operating, and not let any further calculation as to whether the ordered action is the best thing to do effect his decision to perform. This is not a description of two different stages, but of two aspects of the same activity—the form that recognition of the ' 'mark of (in) authority' takes is that is that of 'surrendering private judgment'.[14] Of course, the soldier may refuse to perform as commanded, and it is possible that such refusal be taken as criticism of the command itself which may lead to an alteration of the command. Nevertheless, the act of command is not a call for a response but for compliance, and refusal is a transgression of the command.

By contrast, recognising the teacher as *an* authority cannot take the form of surrendering private judgement, for compliance by surrendering private judgement (and thereby treating the teacher as one in authority) robs the act of the very authority that the teacher attempts to exercise. An exercise of this kind of authority is a move within ongoing reasoned discourse, and acts as a call for response. Its authority comes in part from the absence of unanswered criticism, an authority that is always provisional since it is always open to potential challenge. If the absence of criticism is simply because private judgement has been surrendered, then the performance lacks this kind of provisional authority. The pupil's failure to concur need not be a transgression, provided that the rejection of the call may be accompanied by reasons for the failure, which would then call on the teacher to defend the claim in response. Of course, there may be discrepancy between teacher and pupil as to what constitutes reasonable criticism here. If the teacher desires the esteem of the pupil in a case where he deems the criticism unreasonable or that the pupil is predisposed not to recognise him as an authority on the matter ('You showed yourself very ready to disbelieve me' (p. 150)), then being disbelieved may lead to irritation and insult.

Being an authority thus involves vulnerability, by making exercises of this authority open to ongoing criticism. The disciplinary climate in some educational settings may not be able to tolerate such vulnerability, and the resultant disparity of standing between teacher and pupil in such settings is such that the former cannot be *an* authority to the latter because the only space open for the learner to respond is that of transgression and not criticism.[15] In such a climate, it is possible for the teachers to teach and for the pupils to learn from such teaching, much as one can learn from the megalomaniac. But this would not involve learning from teaching in the sense that is under investigation here as it does not involve the recognition of the teacher as an authority, and thus not a case of being believed personally.

V THE TEACHER OF PHILOSOPHY

The phrase 'teaching philosophy' as used here denotes a distinctive kind of teaching and learning, one that is in no way limited to a particular subject matter or discipline. (A teacher of history and mathematics, for example, may be a teacher of philosophy in the sense under elucidation.) Unlike the interpreter and the megalomaniac, the teacher of philosophy is engaged in the activity of teaching. Yet teaching philosophy is not a paradigmatic case of teaching under investigation, since a successful instance of learning from teaching philosophy does not involve the pupil believing the teacher that p. Anscombe provides two glosses on this difference between teaching and teaching philosophy. First, unlike a successful case of teaching, a successful case of teaching philosophy involves the pupil forming his '*own* judgment that the thing is true' (p. 145). Second, whilst the teacher hopes that her pupils will believe her, the teacher of philosophy hopes that 'they will *come to see* that what we say is true—if it is' (p. 145). To best make sense of these differences, it is helpful to focus again on the social context in which these activities take place.

Both teaching and teaching philosophy are social activities, yet the norms governing the social framework within which each take place differ. To see this, let to us return to Euthydemus. The interlocutors observed by Euthydemus address claims to others and are disposed to treat the responses of others to such addressed claims as grounds for altering their own opinions on the matter. In other words, the participants involved in that encounter are engaged in the activity earlier dubbed 'reasoning'. But the participants in question go beyond just reasoning: in making a claim, they strive for uptake of the claim by other interlocutors, such that silence of other interlocutors in response to a performance recognised as such is considered to be an act of uptake, and unanswered criticism of the claim demands retraction of the claim. In other words, the kind of conversation taking place in the case of Euthydemus takes the form of what was earlier dubbed 'engaged reasoning'. It is so called, because there is a distinct kind of engagement between interlocutors here that is not manifest in all cases of reasoning—a beholdedness of the normative standing of the person making the claim to the response of other addressed interlocutors who are taken to have recognised the call to respond, and whose own normative standing on the matter in turn is taken to be altered by the ongoing engagement.

Teaching philosophy as conceived here does not take place within the framework of engaged reasoning. I find it most helpful to think of instances of teaching philosophy which do not involve the presentation of a formalised argument but comprise an attempt to bring a particular and favoured conception of the shape of the relevant issues into view (such as Anscombe herself is doing in the paper). Here the teacher is engaged in reasoning: she clearly and sincerely puts forward a given picture with the aim of helping her pupils see this as attractive, and treats their responses as reasons for modifying her own view. But her standing on this matter is not beholden to the response of her students in the manner just outlined. Whilst she may hope that they will be moved to share her position, she will not feel irritation or insult if they do not; silence from her pupils will not be treated as acceptance of her claims; and whilst unanswered criticism of her position may cause her to change her mind, rarely is it treated as having been immediately retracted. The point here is, of course, not a descriptive claim designed to characterise typical instances of what are usually treated as teaching philosophy, but to articulate one conception of just what it is to teach philosophy, according to which the social act of teaching philosophy does not fall within norms governing the framework of engaged reasoning.

In contrast, (Anscombean) teaching, as with the performances observed by Euthydemus, does involve reasoned engagement between teacher and student. Reciprocal recognition of the act places the two in an engaged relationship, such that any further response alters both of their normative standing on this matter.[16] Thus conceived, the act of teaching is an addressed act, calling on those addressed to respond in some form, even if the response is rejection or disbelief. The form of the address is second-personal; it calls on *you* to respond. In recognising this address, one must recognise this form by judging that *I* have been addressed. Use of the first- and second-personal pronoun is deliberate, and cannot be replaced by any other way of picking out the same referent.[17] You thus call on me to respond, referring to me by representing my capacity to recognise this call with the first-personal pronoun, and I recognise the call by exercising that capacity. Once recognised, *I* respond to the act (even if it is to disbelieve), which itself is a call addressed back to *you*. In a successful instance of teaching, *I* believe *you*. In this regard, Anscombe's way of formally expressing the case of where belief takes a personal object—'*believing x that p*'—does not fully capture the sense of what it is to believe someone following an instance of learning from teaching. Better: belief takes a personal object that is expressed as '*believing you that p*'. The second-personal form of address characterises the reasoned engagement between interlocutors in the kinds of cases of teaching and learning under investigation.[18]

Anscombe explicitly acknowledges the role of address, noting the importance that 'the communication is *addressed* to someone, even if only to 'whom it may concern' or 'the passer-by' or 'whoever may happen in the future to read this' (p. 148). Nothing in my description of the form of address as second-personal requires that the addressee is personally known to the addresser. In speaking to 'whom it may concern', I am picking you out in term of your potential capacity to recognise this call, and thus I am addressing *you*. Of course, without knowledge of your recognition of the call, I am not engaged with you in the manner discussed. I nonetheless am beholden to you (and you to me) if both parties became aware of this recognition. This is why there is a genuine sense in which Euthydemus is not really an outsider to the discussion on which he was listening. Although A, B and C were speaking to each other and not him, their performances are potentially addressed to anyone and everyone, including Euthydemus. Indeed, this must be the case if they are to have the kind of authority needed to be believed personally, for this authority comes in part from the absence of unanswered criticism following the recognition of an addressed act, and this requires no artificial limitation of the potential resources for criticism, such as by excluding interlocutors by inappropriately deeming them outside the scope of the intended audience.[19]

VI TEACHING AND LEARNING

In light of the preceding discussion, it emerges that three of Anscombe's 'teachers'—the interpreter, the megalomaniac and the teacher of philosophy—are not involved in engaged reasoning with their students, either because they are detached from their performances (as with the interpreter), or because they misconstrue the structure of authority relations appropriate to the social activity (as with the mega-lomaniac) or because they do not take themselves to be directly beholden to the potential criticism of those taught (as with the teacher of philosophy). Though their students may come to learn from their performances, they are not believed personally. In contrast, the per-formances of the Anscombean teacher are moves within the activity of engaged reasoning, which may result in their being believed personally.

Whilst it is important to consider the phenomenon of believing someone personally in the context of the social activity of engaged reasoning, it is not the case that every successful instance of engaged reasoning results in being believed personally. This is because the activity of (Anscombean) teaching is a distinctive kind of perform-ance within this social activity, one for which there is a basic asym-metry between teacher (T) and learner (L): *T teaches and L is taught.*[20] In other words, the activity of teaching and learning involves a trans-action between agent and patient, a structure that ensures an asym-metric, and thus hierarchical, relation between them: *T is a teacher of L and L is the student of T.*[21] This hierarchical structure serves to distinguish teaching and learning from other kinds of performances within the activity of engaged reasoning.

Let us explore the relevant hierarchical relation by reflecting on the transactional relation between teacher and student in these kinds of cases. The predicate '. . .is the teacher of. . .' is a two-place relational predicate. Such predicates can be transposed, allowing the same rela-tion to be described from two opposing viewpoints; one can freely move between saying that 'T is the teacher of L' and that 'L is the student of T' without a change in meaning. The roles characterising occupation of one pole of these opposed viewpoints are thus internally related to the other as complementary, and neither is fully intelligible without the other. On one understanding of the roles of teacher/ student, assignment to the role characterising these opposing view-points is an institutional matter that is not fixed by the character of a given transaction.[22] Although the socially-defined roles govern the nature of subsequent transactions between them, the hierarchical rela-tion of teacher/student precedes the transaction. With regards to the kind of teaching under investigation here, this way of thinking should be resisted, and teacher and learner are best conceived as occupying positions in relation to each other as the result of engaging in the paired activities of teaching/learning. On this way of thinking, the hierarchical relation of teacher/student is established by the transac-tion and does not precede it.

To say that the transaction establishes the hierarchical relation is to say that one only becomes a teacher by teaching something to someone, and that one only becomes a student by learning something from someone.[23] A person's standing as a teacher is thus beholden to the response of a student recognising that person as a teacher by learning from them. In a sense then, the authority of the performance is 'forward-looking': the credentials of any performance as authoritative are not in place at the time of the performance itself but are dependent on the way in which the performance is responded to by others.[24] Yet part of what is recognised by the student in the successful case is the fact that teacher at the time of performing already had the relevant credentials to authorise. Prior to the activity, T has already concluded her reasoning on the matter by forming a judgement, and this is part of what is recognised by L when she comes to learn from T. As a result, the authority structure of the performance here is also 'backward-looking': the appropriate credentials for the performance to be treated as authoritative are already in place at the time of performance, and it is precisely these credentials that are recognised by the learner in the successful case of teaching.

That the teaching and learning transaction has this forward- and backward-looking structure of authority serves to distinguish it from other instances of engaged reasoning, such as the roles played by interlocutors involved in the activity of jointly deliberating for example.[25] In joint deliberation, each interlocutor takes part in activity that calls for and requires a partner, and their performances are beholden to the response of the other if they are to continue to be engaged in the activity, yet the standing of a given performance as authoritative in deliberation is solely dependent on the way in which the performance is responded to by others, and there is no comparable opposition of roles required for the activity to take place. For some, the hierarchical nature of the relation between teacher and learner is reason enough to exclude this activity from the realm of engaged reasoning.[26] But this overlooks the interplay between the forward- and backward-looking structure of authority involved in teaching and learning. Whilst learning from teaching requires recognition of another as *an* authority on the matter at hand and thus dependence on her prior judgement, the forward-looking dimension ensures that no performance is immune to criticism and thus always remains potentially revisable.

This forward-looking dimension further requires that part of what must be recognised by both teacher and student thus transacting is not just their current roles as teacher/student, but also that it must be possible for the roles to be reversible amongst the same interlocutors as part of their participation in the activity. In other words, part of the teacher recognising someone as a potential learner is the recognition of the possibility that that learner is capable of playing the role of teacher as well, and part of the learner recognising someone as a potential teacher is the recognition of the possibility of the teacher playing the role of learner as well. This must be the case so as to enable the possibility of criticism from the learner that is essential to constituting the teacher as *an* authority on this occasion.

Teaching and learning can take place outside this transactional context, where it is possible to teach even if no one comes to believe you personally (cf. the case of teaching philosophy) and to learn without being taught. These are simply not cases of learning from teaching that are under investigation here. Consider those that Anscombe calls *elementary learners*:

> I may—it is not the normal case but it certainly occurs—have to reflect on whether someone is likely to be right and truthful in a particular case when he is telling me that p. I take it that this could not be the case for learners, at least elementary learners or young children (p. 151).[27]

Elementary learners are characterised as those who believe that p having been told that p without awareness of the possible need for assessment of the author's trustworthiness on the matter. The elementary learner, one who is insensitive to the nature of acts of telling as agential performances, is incapable of teaching as this act has been described here. So, in treating someone as an elementary learner, one does not treat them as having the capacity required to teach on this occasion, such that one's teaching is not beholden to the critical response of the elementary learner. The act of teaching an elementary learner can thus only be an exercise of being *in* authority, where one's standing as teacher is fixed prior to the interaction. The elementary learner learns from the teacher, but since this activity takes place outside the context of engaged reasoning her belief does *not* take a personal object.

VII IN PLACE OF A FINALE

In the preceding sections we have engaged in an investigation into the suggestion that that there can be cases in which belief takes a personal object through a consideration of a distinctive kind of teacher, one illustrated by contrast with three others: an interpreter, a megalomaniac and a teacher of philosophy. This has not been an attempt at an analysis of the concept of teaching; the discussion leaves open a possible task in philosophy of education of locating this distinctive kind within 'a topology of the teaching concept'.[28] Nor has it been an exercise in the epistemology of testimony; the discussion leaves open the challenge of exploring how 'believing x that p' relates to more familiar epistemic concepts (if at all).[29] The investigation has, however, suggested that any further work in epistemology and/or education into the phenomenon of believing someone personally should take seriously the social framework provided by the conversational activity of engaged reasoning within which this kind of teaching and learning has its home.[30]

To end this chapter, let us further illustrate the utility of approaching the phenomenon of believing someone from within this social framework by addressing the worry with which Anscombe ends her paper. Here's the worry:

> I imagined the case where I believed what someone told me, and got the information from his telling me, but did not believe *him*. This was because I believed he would tell me what he thought was false, but also would be clean wrong in what he thought. Now I *may* . . . have to reflect on whether someone is likely to be right and truthful in a particular case when he is telling me that p. If I conclude that he is, I will then believe him that p. . . . But someone might say: 'What is the difference between the two cases, culminating in belief that p because NN has told one that p? In both cases there is calculation; in one, you believe what the man says as a result of a calculation that he is a liar but wrong, and in the other you calculate that he is truthful and right' (p. 151).

Anscombe concedes that her response to this challenge is incomplete:

> The difference between the two cases is only as stated. When you say that in the first case you do not believe *the man*, only what he tells you, and in the second you believe the man, that is just a bit of terminology: you are only willing to *call* it believing the man when you believe he is right and truthful in intent. It appears to me that there is more to be said than that about the priority of rightfulness and truthfulness in this matter, but I am not clear what it is (p. 151).

Bringing together some themes from our discussion can help us go further, for there is indeed more to be said in differentiating between these cases than concentrating on priority of rightfulness and truthfulness.

We are given two scenarios in which a learner ends up believing something based on the say-so of another, yet only one is a case in which the learner believes the teacher personally. As the challenger points out, one cannot look to the solitary activities of the learner in order explain the difference, since in both cases the learner is engaged in 'calculation'. Anscombe's own response, attempting to distinguish the activities in terms of the content of the respective calculations, does not go far enough in undermining the underlying assumption of the challenger. For the challenge arises on the erroneous assumption that one can bring the idea of believing someone into view by concentrating on the isolated activities of the learner, as opposed to conceiving this as part of a teaching-learning transaction situated in the broader social context of engaged reasoning.

In this social context, the teacher-student relation is established through the transaction of teaching and being taught. Having judged that p, a wannabe teacher puts forward her claim as to be believed by a potential student. The claim is second-personally addressed, calling on you (the potential student) to recognise me (the wannabe teacher) as *an* authority on the matter. Your recognition of this call ensures that you have responded to the call in some active way (even disbelieving), a response to which I must be responsive in return. In addressing you in this manner, I not only display my recognition of you as a potential student on this occasion, but also as a potential teacher too. In a successful case, you recognise me as *an* authority by learning from me. As a result of the transaction, we now stand in the relation of teacher and student, and your belief takes a personal object— 'believing me that p'.

In contrast, when you believe what I say as a result of a calculation that I am a liar but wrong, the transaction is missing. You may learn from me but this is not a case of learning from teaching in the sense under investigation, and we do not stand in the relation of teacher and student. As a result, the structure of subsequent interaction between us differs from those that fall within the activity of engaged reasoning, since neither of us treat ourselves as beholden to each other by our responses. You may learn from me, but your belief does not take a personal object—it is not a case of 'believing me that p'.[31]

NOTES

1. Anscombe, 1979, to which all subsequent in-text references (page number in brackets) refer.
2. See, for example, the essays collected in Macmillan and Nelson, 1968; Hirst and Peters, 1970, chapters 5 and 6; and a more recent overview in Noddings, 1998, chapter 3.

3. I return to this claim below in Section V.

4. I am drawing here on the rich framework provided by Laden (2012), although—as will emerge below—my understanding of this framework differs from his.

5. Wanderer, 2012a.

6. The following characterisation of the spokesperson is incomplete, and glosses over many important complexities including (Hobbesian) cases in which the spokesperson speaks on behalf of an institution or as a representative of the views of others. More needs to be said about these important cases than the sketch provided here.

7. Cf. Dan-Cohen, 2002, pp. 249–53.

8. Adapted from Lackey (2008, p. 48), to fit the case of my own high school biology teacher.

9. Perhaps it may be better to treat the relevant author as the institution whose requirements she is fulfilling, making the creationist teacher is closer to that of the spokesperson. Again: more needs to be said about such cases than the sketch provided here.

10. I am especially indebted here to discussions with Byron Davies.

11. An alternative interpretation is that he is not self-aware enough of the gap that has opened up between the esteem he deserves and the esteem he craves, and thus continues to feel the irritation normally reserved for cases in which one takes oneself to be accorded less esteem than one deserves.

12. Friedman, 1990.

13. Friedman, 1990, p. 81.

14. Contrast with Friedman, 1990, pp. 80–3.

15. Authority in an educational context is explored in different ways in Peters, 1966, chapter 9 and Wilson, 1992.

16. See Moore, 1982, p 32 for a brief discussion of the need for some form of mutual recognition between teacher and learner.

17. Cf. Rödl, 2008, pp. 186–196.

18. Although the discussion here may seem to imply that teaching philosophy does not involve second-personal address, this is not my intention. Both teaching and teaching philosophy involve the social activity of reasoning and both acts are second-personally addressed. Yet the form of the address differs in the case of teaching, in that its recognition ensures the kind of beholdedness to each other characteristic of engaged reasoning. I develop these ideas about second-personal address more fully in Wanderer, forthcoming.

19. This contrasts with both Faulkner (2011) and McMyler (2011, p. 67) who claim to be sensitive to Anscombe's distinction to the difference between believing someone and that which they say, whilst maintaining a difference between a hearer and an overhearer for a testimonial act.

20. The transaction that establishes the relation can be described from the viewpoint of the agent as 'T teaching L' or from the viewpoint of the patient as 'L being taught by T' or as 'L learning from T'. That there is both an active and passive description of the transaction available from the patient's viewpoint serves, amongst other things, to distinguish cases such as this that involves two potential agents, from other transactions where all we can have is the passive construal (e.g. 'the gun was fired by Brody').

21. Cf. Dewey's (1910, p. 36) comparison of teaching and selling.

22. Compare Noddings, 1998, p. 37.

23. There has been much debate as to whether 'teaching' is a success term—see Noddings, 1998, chapter 3 and Moore, 1982, pp. 31–33 for useful overviews. As noted above, my interest here is limited to the kind of teaching that Anscombe depicts and not at providing some kind of general analysis of the concept.

24. Cf. Laden, 2012, p. 68, discussed below. This forward-looking dimension is relevant to discussions of indoctrination, such as that found in Green, 1968; Snook, 1970; and Callen

and Arena, 2010. For discussion of the difficulties such dual perspectives raise for narrating the emergence of authority, see Wanderer, 2012b.

25. Cf. Laden, 2012, pp. 190–193.
26. Here I have in mind the recent work of Laden (2012). Whilst I am sympathetic to the broader social construal of reasoning he presents (as reflected in my appropriation of his terminology noted above), his apparent extrusion of the activity of teaching and learning (and judging/asserting/deciding more generally) from this activity is puzzling. One motivation he provides is a Kantian-inspired contention that no act of reasoning can be immune to criticism, which he interprets as excluding any activity, such as arriving at a judgement about what to do or believe, that attempts to bring reasoning to an end (e.g. 2012, p. 27). Yet, as Laden himself concedes, most consider the Kantian-inspired contention to be satisfied by the never-ending possibility of revision rather than absence of judgement, which is just what the characterisation of teaching and learning here allows. Privileging acts such as asserting and judging over and above other examples of reasoning may be mistaken, but extruding such activities from the space of reasoning entirely makes the space barely recognisable as reasoning at all.
27. This echoes an earlier comment about childhood—where 'we are taught to consult books like oracles, and the idea of an author is not much brought to our attention at first' (p. 146). This is best not treated as an empirical claim - see Harris, 2012.
28. Cf. Green, 1968.
29. Cf. Moran, 2005, to which the preceding discussion is indebted—not least for first bringing Anscombe's paper to my attention.
30. As noted earlier, engaged reasoning itself falls within the species of reasoning and broader genus of conversation; these are thus also the broader home of this kind of teaching and learning that should be taken seriously in further work on this topic.
31. This chapter is deeply indebted to participation in two seminars in which Anscombe's paper was discussed: the SIAS summer school on 'The Second Person', and Richard Moran's graduate seminar on 'Speech and Intersubjectivity'. In addition, I have benefitted from comments on an earlier draft by Louis Blond, Byron Davies, Catherine Elgin, Ben Kotzee and Lynne Tirrell.

REFERENCES

Anscombe, E. (1979) What Is It to Believe Someone?, in: C. F. Delaney (ed.) *Rationality and Religious Belief* (Notre Dame, IN, Notre Dame University Press).

Callan, E. and Arena, D. (2010) Indoctrination, in: H. Siegel (ed.) *The Oxford Handbook of Philosophy of Education* (Oxford, Oxford University Press).

Dan-Cohen, M. (2002) *Harmful Thoughts: Essays on Law, Self, and Morality* (Princeton, NJ, Princeton University Press).

Dewey, J. (1910) *How We Think* (Lexington, MA, D.C. Heath).

Faulkner, P. (2011) *Knowledge on Trust* (Oxford, Oxford University Press).

Friedman, R. (1990) On the Concept of Authority in Political Philosophy, in: J. Raz (ed.) *Authority* (New York, New York University Press).

Green, T. F. (1968) A Topology of the Teaching Concept, in: C. Macmillan and T. Nelson (eds) *Concepts of Teaching: Philosophical Essays* (Chicago, IL, Rand McNally).

Harris, P. L. (2012) *Trusting What You Are Told: How Children Learn From Others* (Cambridge, MA, Harvard University Press).

Hirst, P. H. and Peters, R. S. (1970) *The Logic of Education* (London, Routledge).

Lackey, J. (2008) *Learning from Words* (Oxford, Oxford University Press).

Laden, S. A. (2012) *Reasoning: A Social Picture* (Oxford, Oxford University Press).

Macmillan, C. J. B. and Nelson, T. eds (1968) *Concepts of Teaching* (Chicago, IL, Rand McNally).

McMyler, B. (2011) *Testimony, Trust, and Authority* (Oxford, Oxford University Press).

Moore, T. W. (1982) *Philosophy of Education; An Introduction* (London, Routledge).

Moran, R. (2005) Getting Told and Being Believed, *Philosophers' Imprint*, 5, pp. 1–29.

Noddings, N. (1998) *Philosophy of Education* (Boulder, CO, Westview Press).

Peters, R. S. (1966) *Ethics and Education* (London, Allen & Unwin).

Rödl, S. (2008) *Self-Consciousness* (Cambridge, MA, Harvard University Press).

Snook, I. (1970) The Concept of Indoctrination, *Studies in Philosophy and Education*, 7, pp. 65–108.

Wanderer, J. (2012a) Ignored vs. Rejected: Addressing Testimonial Injustice, *Philosophical Quarterly*, 62, pp. 148–169.

Wanderer, J. (2012b) On the Legendary Beginnings of a Style of Thinking, *Studies in History and Philosophy of Science*, 43, pp. 640–648.

Wanderer, J. (forthcoming) Alethic Holdings, in: J. Conant and S. Rödl (eds) *Philosophical Topics*.

Wilson, J. (1992) The Primacy of Authority, *Journal of Moral Education*, 21, pp. 115–124.

4

Can Inferentialism Contribute to Social Epistemology?

JAN DERRY

In his assessment of the prospects for a 'dialectical approach to justification' that would position a social activity at the centre of epistemological analysis, Alvin Goldman is gloomy. According to Goldman, 'a purely dialectical approach to justification might say that a belief of S is justified if an only if S can satisfactorily respond to critics or challengers, to their request or demands for reasons or evidence' (Goldman, 2010, p. 12). He then proceeds to list those whose approach to justification is of 'this ilk'. However, he pointedly excludes Robert Brandom from his list, suggesting that he might have been included but that as 'Brandom's targets are analyses of *semantical* concepts, not *epistemic ones*, [he] is not fundamentally, trying to illuminate epistemic justification' (ibid.). A great deal hangs on the distinction between epistemic and semantic here, for while analytic philosophers might see the semantic and the epistemic as distinct, following Brandom it would seem possible to see them as two sides of the same coin.[1] Indeed, in the case of educational theory, the reasons for treating them together would seem compelling.[2] This matter is considered below, but for the moment it may be said that it is not possible to achieve an adequate understanding of the epistemic without approaching it through the semantic i.e. it is not possible to achieve an adequate understanding of what knowledge consists in without attention to its articulation. To establish as much is an important aim of this chapter.

Goldman may be correct in saying that Brandom is not '*fundamentally* concerned with epistemic justification' but that does not diminish the possible significance of his work for social epistemology (ibid.). However, for others working in the field the connection appears stronger. Martin Kusch notes that while Goldman's version of social epistemology is central to the field it is also too limiting, since it pays

Education and the Growth of Knowledge: Perspectives from Social and Virtue Epistemology, First Edition. Edited by Ben Kotzee. Copyright © 2014 The Authors. Editorial organisation © 2014 Philosophy of Education Society of Great Britain. Published 2014 by John Wiley & Sons Ltd.

little attention to the sociology of knowledge.[3] Goldman's exclusion of Brandom implies that Brandom's approach lacks normative authority i.e. any tight connection between the 'giving and asking of reasons' and the world that judgements claim to represent. Kusch comments that while Brandom is not normally considered to be a social epistemologist there are a number of themes in his masterwork *Making it Explicit* that are relevant to the foundations of social epistemology (Kusch, 2011a, p. 884). He adds that diagnostic approaches,[4] i.e. those including work such as Brandom's, need to become more central if social epistemology is to flourish (p. 882).

Hetherington makes a related point as regards the standard analytic conception of knowledge as absolute, pointing out that 'knowledge absolutism' never admits of different grades[5] (Hetherington, 2011, p. 6) and in *Beyond Justification*, Alston notes that the 'boundaries of "epistemology" are fuzzy and controversial' and for his own part suggests that 'epistemology' 'belongs to some portion of the vast sprawling territory that we identify as philosophical reflection on the cognitive aspect of life' (Alston, 2005, p. 5). When the problem of knowledge is approached from a different direction, albeit one that was already traced by Hegel, interesting questions open. The issue at stake here is not 'justified true belief' itself: all schools of philosophy can subscribe to this in some form or other. Where an issue arises is in relation to the nature of this knowledge—whether it is individual or social—or to be precise what is meant by social. What can be questioned is a concentration by standard epistemology on the conditions for justified true belief construed in individualist terms which not only fails to do justice to the social nature of knowledge but neglects its primary character as a human phenomenon.

Kusch criticises Goldman for his deferral to traditional epistemology and failure to recognise the value of the 'diagnostic programme' in social epistemology and argues exactly for the recognition of the value of 'diagnostic approaches' to epistemology;[6] importantly, embracing the diagnostic approach does not entail relativism or constructivism. To say that knowledge is a human phenomenon does not necessarily entail either; it is perfectly possible to view knowledge as a purely human creation and at the same time to see that it cannot emerge apart from the world of which it is the knowledge. The emergence of knowledge marks the end of evolution and the beginning of history and history, it must be stressed here, is specifically human. What counts as knowledge cannot be separated from the process that gives rise to it. Social epistemology, as the term implies, recognises the process that gives rise to knowledge; however, at least in the form proposed by Goldman, it does so in a way that pays insufficient attention to the distinctive character of humans and the features which distinguish them from other life-forms. Hegel, according to Stekeler-Weithofer, sees the task of philosophy as developing human self-consciousness and turns '"meta-physics" in the sense of reflecting on the basic forms of *physis* or nature, that is, on "what there is" ... into philosophical anthropology' (Stekeler-Weithofer, 2011, p. 110). In this chapter, I will argue that, to develop an approach to social epistemology as an alternative to the competing claims of sociology and philosophy, a similar transformation needs to be made in respect to epistemology, i.e. knowledge must be considered as a moment in human practice.

PHILOSOPHICAL ANTHROPOLOGY, SEMANTICS AND EPISTEMOLOGY

The account I wish to present starts from the concern that philosophical anthropology shows in the development of human thought and language through history. Taking philosophical anthropology as the context within which to consider epistemology and its relation to semantics, it can be argued that without the essential human capacity to communicate and exhibit *shared* and *collective intentionality*, i.e. mutual understanding of conscious purpose,[7] language and knowledge would not have developed. In other words approaching the issue in terms of a philosophic anthropology leads to treating semantics (or the process in which meaning arises) and epistemology as connected from the start. The work of Michael Tomasello, who is renowned for his research into the cultural and cognitive processes that distinguish humans from other primates, is of interest here. Tomasello studies processes of social learning, social cognition and communication, especially language acquisition and shared intentionality. A key element in his account of human ontogeny is joint attention. A couple of simple examples of this involve pre-linguistic children. First take the example of a child placing blocks to build a tower as an adult holds the edifice steady. Infants from about fourteen months not only share goals but also coordinate roles so that if an adult refrains from participating in a shared activity, the infant will not only prompt the adult to re-engage but will also perform the adult's turn for her (Ross and Lollis, 1987 cited in Tomasello *et al.*, 2005). Second, take a child pointing to an object purely for interest or, as Tomasello would say, for information-giving. Shared intentionality is evidently crucial here; as Tomasello *et al.* remark: 'As the key social-cognitive skill for cultural creation and cognition, shared intentionality is of special importance in explaining the uniquely powerful cognitive skills of Homo Sapiens'

(2005, p. 687). These examples are far removed from advanced systems of production and communication in the contemporary world; nevertheless, the peculiarly human capacities they illustrate are the starting point of human development and knowledge.[8]

Tomasello's interest in language is shared by the John McDowell. McDowell does not present his work as philosophical anthropology; nevertheless, as he attaches great importance to the specifically human nature of knowing, his work can be seen as a contribution to this field. When McDowell writes that we are 'born mere animals, and . . . transformed into thinkers and intentional agents in the course of coming to maturity' (McDowell, 1996, p. 125) he implies that the specifically human nature of knowing has special significance. Thus, in response to the scepticism that has been prominent in so much philosophic work on epistemology since Descartes, McDowell, following Sellars, argues that conceptual capacities are already operative in experience and account for the content of experience. In other words they cannot be separated from becoming fully human and acquiring a second nature in which we become responsive to reasons (McDowell, 1996, p. 66).[9]

This attention to reasons has particular importance for McDowell's colleague at Pittsburgh, Robert Brandom; indeed it becomes a primary focus of his work. His concern with the 'giving and asking of reasons' indicates the influence of Hegel on his thinking. For Brandom this activity has two dimensions: the first, the Kantian dimension, entails commitments and obligations; the second, the Hegelian dimension, locates reasons, and also knowledge, immediately in the social sphere.

An aspect of the social dimension of particular concern here is education. As Aristotle in the *Physics* talks of the transformation of man who knows no music into a musical man so it might be said that education transforms students from persons without knowledge into persons with knowledge, i.e. it activates those capacities to know that all humans have in common, but it does so in ways that can allow individuals to develop unique capabilities. Of course taking this transformation in isolation invites the question of what is known as epistemic access i.e. the process by which students actually gain this transformative knowledge.

Although apparently divorced from the approach to knowledge within philosophical work on epistemology, this matter may turn out to have crucial implications in both directions: on the one hand, philosophical enquiries may prove invaluable in such matters as designing curricula and developing pedagogic approaches; on the other hand, an investigation of educational practices could possibly prove insightful for philosophic enquiries.

DEVELOPMENTAL PSYCHOLOGY

As soon as education is introduced and with it the issue of child development the works of Jean Piaget and Lev Vygotsky demand attention. Piaget was particularly concerned with the activation of capacities. Of philosophic interests is the importance he attached to Kant[10] and the connection this suggests between philosophy and education. In relation to the development of capacities, which can be traced back at least to Aristotle, Piaget is undoubtedly a decisive figure in modern thought; of particular interest here is the link he made between the development of capacities and the theory of knowledge through his concept 'genetic epistemology'.[11] It is not the connection Piaget drew between the development of the individual child and the historical development of society which matters here but the fact that his paradigm for development was the individual. Opinions differ over the extent to which, if at all, Piaget disregarded the social in the development of the individual but this does not affect criticisms of his work by Margaret Donaldson, who happens to have been one of his students. The issues these criticisms raise are relevant to those being discussed here.

In a classic experiment Margaret Donaldson and her colleague Martin Hughes replicated Piaget and Inhelder's experiment designed to test the ability of the child to de-centre and see the world from a view other than its own (Piaget and Inhelder, 1967). This is considered to be an important indication of the ability to think abstractly and thus an index of epistemic access. Piaget had designed various experiments to test the egocentrism of the child (their lack of ability to 'perspective take') and their capacity to conserve different qualities such as quantity and height, following changes. His experiments demonstrated that young children failed to conserve, and in the 'three mountains task' experiment (later reproduced in a different form by Donaldson and her colleagues), children failed to de-centre, thus supporting his characterisation that they were egocentric and unable to take a perspective other than their own. Donaldson's colleague, Martin Hughes, redesigned the 'three mountains task' and in place of asking a child to take the perspective of a doll and describe where the doll would view the objects on the mountain (e.g. the Church is on the left for the doll and on the right for me) Donaldson and Hughes constructed a 'scene' where the child had to hide a 'naughty' doll from a policeman doll (i.e. to hide the doll successfully the child had to take the perspective of the policeman doll). Children taking the 'policeman task' were able to take another perspective from that of their own and Donaldson and her colleagues explained this in terms of the fact that the task 'requires the child to act in ways which are in line with certain very basic purposes and intentions (escape and pursuit) . . .' (Donaldson, 1978, p. 24).

The important difference here is that the Hughes and Donaldson task gave children insight into the motives and intentions of the characters involved in the task unlike the doll in Piaget's mountain scene. But something more is present in the redesign that is absent in Piaget's original task and this is directly relevant to the concerns of Brandom as well as to Piaget's contemporary, Vygotsky. Vygotsky is well known for the criticism he made of Piaget's early work for failing to attend to the nature of conscious awareness and the distinctive conditions in which this becomes possible for the young child. Vygotsky explains: 'Only within a system can the concept acquire conscious awareness and a voluntary nature. Conscious awareness and the presence of a system are synonyms when we are speaking of concepts, just as spontaneity, lack of conscious awareness, and the absence of system are three different words for designating the nature of the child's concept' (Vygotsky, 1987, p. 191).

For Vygotsky systematicity relates to what is distinctive about human engagement with the world. This engagement comprises the modification of the world achieving a form of control beyond the reach of any other animal. In modifying the world humans attribute significance to everything they engage with and the resulting concepts which constitute meaning have a systematic character. It could be argued that what accounted for the success of children, in the task Donaldson and Hughes set them, was not only an appreciation of purpose but that the systematic structure of the task, in which the relationship of one element to another is clear, makes visible the 'reasons that follow from' and the 'reasons that are implied by' the task's events. In the mountain task, elements have no particular relation to one another. By contrast in the policeman task they are directly connected to each other. In the mountain task, where the child is only asked to give a description, the child's response is unconstrained and there is no need to see elements in any particular relation to each other, whereas in the policeman task the elements are interconnected from the start. This type of interconnection according to Vygotsky is absolutely crucial as 'the capacity for deduction is only possible within a definite system of relationships among concepts' (Vygotsky, 1987, p. 192).

The capacity to think abstractly is fundamental to the capacity to develop knowledge, but what Donaldson and her co-investigators bring to light is not only their attention to the semantic aspect of the experiment but also its systematic structure.[12] In the redesigned experiment the reasons or norms are visible as everything is dependent

upon everything else in a way that they are not in the original mountain task. In Brandom's terms we might say the inferential structure of
the task is available to the child. To the extent that children have access
to the norms that constitute the task, they are able to decentre or to
perspective take and thus display qualities of abstract reasoning.

KNOWLEDGE IN THE CONTEXT OF EDUCATION

As anyone familiar with contemporary debates about formal education will be aware, *knowledge*, and how it should be defined, is an
on-going area of debate. Difference of opinion arises regardless of
whether the difference concerns what knowledge is required within
the school curriculum or, beyond schooling, what form of curriculum
and with it what knowledge is required for the professions. Conceptions of knowledge no more reign independent of philosophy than do
those of cognition[13] and even a cursory glance at contemporary
approaches to knowledge reveal a common conception of *facts*
without genesis or development.[14] But is this an adequate conception
of knowledge even in the context of the school curriculum where
disciplinary knowledge is converted into a form, sometimes known
as 'schooled knowledge' in order to provide access to students?

Brandom, following Hegel, emphasises the significance of social
relations in the generation of knowledge and this directs attention to
the distinctive nature of our relation to the world and the significance
of not only the dissemination of knowledge but also of the development of reasoning processes. However what is particularly significant
here is that his work assists thinking about the systematic nature of
disciplinary knowledge. As Piaget brought to our attention, how we
understand the development of the reasoning process must itself play
some role in how we conceive knowledge. We would be in error if we
thought of reason as pure reason distinct from socially 'triangulated'
engagement with the world within which reason is both active and
passive, making the norms that then bind it. This was Hegel's refram-
ing of Kant's derivation of the conditions of our knowing. According
to Testa, Hegel answered the question of 'the conditions of possibility
of conceptual norms and therefore . . . both [of] their genesis and their
validity' that Kant himself left unanswered (Testa, 2009).[15]

It is useful to take a step back before returning to Brandom's
inferentialism and consider an example from education to illustrate
the point. The general character of knowledge is a significant area
within education research on at least three fronts: the sociology of
education, the sociology of knowledge and the practical domain of

teaching. We know that the quality of teaching and learning is affected by teachers' 'content knowledge' but how, to what extent and in what way is not precisely understood (Ball, Lubienski and Mewborn, 2001). Despite an extensive literature, the 'structure and form' of content knowledge in research has, to date, not been studied in its own right.[16] In part this is because the way that teachers approach knowledge and the assumptions they make about their field have not been objects of study.[17] The relationship between knowledge and pedagogy has long been recognised but research generally attends to one or the other but not to the relation between them.[18]

Brandom's work offers resources for thinking about precisely this relation. Central to Brandom's project is the argument that an account of meaning needs to privilege inference over representation. He contests the representationalist paradigm (of awareness understood in representational terms) inaugurated by Descartes and influential in Anglo-Saxon thought ever since. He maintains in its place that to understand ourselves as knowers we need to reverse the conventional order of explanation which privileges representation over inference. For Brandom, Hegel completed the inversion of the traditional order of semantic explanation begun by Kant, 'by beginning with a concept of experience as inferential activity and discussing the making of judgments and the development of concepts entirely in terms of the roles they play in that inferential activity' (Brandom, 1994, p. 92). Brandom's approach is at odds with thought conceived in terms of individual mental states and words understood as the names for things, events or states of affairs. A teacher may approach meaning in terms of a relation between a representation and the thing that it represents i.e. assuming words are initially understood as names for things, events or states of affairs. The learner's acquisition of appropriate meaning is then supported by additional clarification and explanation to expand what lies behind the initial thought of what is represented. However, though word meaning may be tightly connected with its referent, how this connection arises is a matter of significant pedagogical importance. For, in the light of Brandom's *inferentialism*, we can understand the forging of the connection between word and object as one that involves reversing the conceptual framework in which so much conventional pedagogical practice operates. Instead the emphasis needs to be on bringing the learner into the inferential relations that constitute a concept prior to its acquisition.[19]

What Brandom's inferentialism (Brandom, 2000) brings into stark relief is that a common conception of 'coming to know', evident in teaching practice, is founded on this mistaken prioritisation of representation over inference i.e. on the assumption that initial awareness of a concept is grasped first, primarily as a representation and then once grasped, inferences can be made. This reflects a critical misunderstanding about the nature of representations. According to an *inferentialist* approach to knowledge, students' primary focus would involve grasping the inferential connections that constitute any concept so that representations learnt are already connected through reasons to other aspects of the knowledge domain to which they belong.

Inferentialism demonstrates that the grasping of a concept is an activity that involves commitment to the inferences implicit in its use in a social practice of giving and asking for reasons. In the light of the significance of systematicity, by adopting an inferentialist orientation to knowledge—that is, one which foregrounds attention on the inferential relations between concepts that constitute representations—teachers will not only be able to use what knowledge they have more effectively in the classroom, but also to approach areas where their knowledge is weak with greater confidence and enhanced effectiveness (Bakker and Derry, 2011).

Inferentialism (Brandom, 2000) opens new ground in thinking about the nature of cognitive content by explaining how propositional contents and, in particular, how objective meanings are constituted in the social practice of what Brandom terms 'giving and asking for reasons'. It can thus assist in negotiating between constructivist ideas about learning—which emphasise the learner's construction of meaning—and traditional approaches that stress the knowledge domain as a discipline. The attention given to meaning construction on the part of the learner has inadvertently led to a neglect of the domain of knowledge within which it takes place.

Attention to philosophical anthropology is not absent from Brandom's work at the heart of which are the contrasts he makes between the responsiveness involved in human knowing and other forms of differential responsiveness to an environment. In the case of the responsiveness of a parrot or a thermostat, he asks; 'What is the knower able to *do* that . . . the thermostat cannot? After all they may respond differentially to *just* the same range of stimuli . . . The knower has the practical know-how to situate that response in a network of inferential relations—to tell what follows from something being . . . cold, what would be evidence for it, what would be incompatible with it, and so on' (Brandom, 2000, p. 162).

The knower is capable of making a judgement, whereas the thermostat is not, and this distinguishes the response of the knower from that of the thermostat. The thermostat's response is simply a moment in a series of causal stimuli whereas human responsiveness involves reasons and not just causes.

Given that education involves far more than the acquisition of information and the ability to follow procedures, Brandom's approach here is highly significant. Our aim in education is not to produce automatons such as thermostats with a reliable disposition to respond to a stimulus, but to develop our students' capacity to make judgements—that is, the capacity not merely to respond passively to events but to make decisions actively in different contexts. Neither thermostats nor parrots have concepts of temperature or redness whereas humans do. They know that saying 'That's red' is not compatible with 'That's green'. Even a very young child already have access to the inferences that constitute the concept, i.e. what it follows from and what follows from it.

If we are to understand the grasping of a concept as an activity that involves committing ourselves to the inferences implicit in its use in a social practice of giving and asking for reasons, pedagogical implications follow. Drawing on a Vygotskian approach to pedagogy, teaching involves providing opportunities for learners to use concepts in the *space of reasons* within which they fall and within which their meaning is constituted. Participation in this space does not presuppose a full understanding of a concept; rather, what is needed to start with is no more than an ability to inhabit the space in which reasons and the concept operates.

According to Brandom to grasp any one concept requires simultaneously the grasping of many concepts and here he echoes Vygotsky who says: '[t]o think of some object with the help of a concept means to include the given object in a complex system of mediating connection and relations disclosed in determinations of the concept' (Vygotsky, 1998, p. 53). For Vygotsky concepts depend for their meaning on the system of judgements (the infrastructure of commitments and entitlements) within which they are disclosed. Instead of understanding the meaning of a concept primarily in terms of its representation of an object, what has priority is the system of inferences in which the object is disclosed. Vygotsky's reference to system here is crucial, for as we saw earlier, Vygotsky argued that Piaget had failed to appreciate that conscious awareness on the part of the child was dependent upon the extent to which meaning was located within a system.

NORMATIVE AUTHORITY—THE SOURCE OF KNOWLEDGE?

Despite having introduced a developmental dimension to knowledge it may seem that we are still left with the issue of normative authority or of 'thought's bearing on the world' (Bakhurst, 2011, p.115).

As Goldman remarked when explaining the absence of Brandom from his list of those undertaking a dialectical approach to epistemology, Brandom's work is on semantics not epistemology. Brandom emphasises that through our practices we institute norms by which he means the *correct* application of concepts. Our application of concepts is the making of commitments and at the same time as norms are instituted, and as long as they are maintained, we bind ourselves to them. But since this line of argument seems to leave the norms we institute dangling in mid-air, without friction from the world in which they are exercised, it appears to deny Brandom's social pragmatism the quality of realism. This however is not the case.

For what we have with Brandom is a 'turn of the kaleidoscope' where familiar elements in an epistemological account are reconfigured and assume a new shape. It is the contention of this chapter that this reconfiguration can play a positive part in thinking about educational issues, such as the structure of knowledge.

A simple case is useful here. Imagine a child beginning to use a word; she may apply the word in roughly the right territory (inferential framework) but nevertheless without sufficient understanding to apply it correctly. Take the example of a child using the word 'dog' in a domestic context where it is applied to the four-legged friend she shares her home with. On a trip out of town she applies the same term for the four-legged creatures in the field i.e. sheep. Her conception of dog as a quadruped has not yet excluded other four-legged creatures of similar height and size. The child is beginning to develop its application of concepts but this is as yet insufficiently refined; she is not yet committed to excluding the concept sheep from the concept dog, as Brandom might put it. However, as her word use develops, the concept dog is refined and its application restricted.

How does word use develop? Through their own experiences and the 'calibration' of concept use developed in a similar way by others. Norms entailing the 'correct' use of terms such as 'dog' are not generated simply by consensus among users but by the imperatives of purposeful engagement with the world. Concept development is not restricted to the early use of language but applies throughout life and even scientific concepts such as 'innateness' or 'gene' have unsettled meanings though they may be applied correctly within specific domains.[20] If we look a little more closely at Brandom's exposition of the inferential in his account of Hegel we can begin to see just how significant Brandom and Hegel's conception of knowledge is for education. Following Hegel, Brandom has 'a "nonpsychological" conception of the conceptual because it can be detached from consideration of the processes or practices of applying concepts in judgment and intentional action' (Brandom, 2011).

Summarised most simply, at the heart of Brandom's reading of Hegel is the belief that thought can grasp the world because there is a continuous adjustment of the relationships of concepts to one another (determinate negation and mediation) to the relationships in the world. This is what Sellars calls material inference which when coupled to reasoning, makes correspondence possible, and what Brandom means when he writes of 'relations of material incompatibility and consequences . . . intelligible as already in conceptual shape'.[21]

According to Brandom we bind ourselves to norms so that they in turn bind us and in line with this Westphal argues that 'Education is a matter of acquiring norms' (Westphal, 1999, p. 148).[22] Moreover, this does not lead to the conclusion that these norms actually construct the objects they study but rather 'when the constructs work well, they do inform us about the actual features of the objects investigated' (Westphal, 1999, p. 148).

David Bakhurst reminds us that there are potential problems in applying Brandom's ideas to education; 'I fear,' he writes, 'that were the language of space of reasons to get into pedagogical discourse, the result would be ripe for parody: *Exasperated teacher to class:* Really Form 1B, I wish you would spend more time in the space of reasons!' (Bakhurst, 2011, p. 122, fn. 35) However what is absent from Bakhurst's parody is the significance of material inference for school knowledge; if teachers are to provide their students with epistemic access and to induct students into domains of knowledge, this systematicity is vital. What matters is that teachers do not simply introduce concepts that feature in particular fields of knowledge without exploring the connections between them with their students. Since, in the light of material inference the relations between concepts are determinate, attention must be paid to the *structure* of knowledge, to the fact that concepts stand in particular relations to one another depending upon the particular domain in which they function. Brandom's work is relevant here because it stresses what Hegel recognised, namely that the relations between concepts are not arbitrary and that their correspondence to the world arises in on-going activity throughout history and forms what Hegel called *Phenomenology* i.e. the science of the experience of consciousness. As Croce put it 'the demand of concrete knowledge is satisfied in the form of thought' (Croce, 1915, p. 214). It is in philosophical anthropology, with due regard to the development and actualisation of the human capacity to know, that we can fully appreciate what that 'form of thought', and with it knowledge, comprises.

NOTES

1. In his chapter on 'The Value Turn in Epistemology' Riggs points to De Rose's defence of the idea that 'a semantic theory for 'knows' holds a great deal of significance for anyone engaged in the task of determining the nature and extent of knowledge' (Riggs, 2008, p. 303).
2. Implying their connectedness, Brandom talks about the priority of *semantic* over *epistemological* issues:

   > *Making it Explicit* is a book about semantics, and the epistemology comes downstream from that. And that's not the way classical epistemology thinks about its subject. I think the soft underbelly of classical epistemology is its implicit semantics. Someone like Alvin Goldman takes it for granted that the beliefs and claims he's assessing epistemologically come with their semantics fixed. We know what they *mean*, and the question is: 'Under what circumstances would they be *justified?*' . . . apart from questions about what would and even does justify a claim, one can't treat its meaning as being settled. The elements in the *inferential* articulation of a claim with respect to what would entitle you to it and how its related to other claims that are entitled—are also elements in the *semantic* articulation of the claim (Brandom, in Prien and Schweikard, 2008, p. 165; his italics).

3. 'Alvin Goldman's version of SE is rightly regarded as central to the field as a whole; Goldman's idea of SE is too limiting; the sociology of knowledge must loom large in, or vis-à-vis every conception of SE' (Kusch, 2011b).
4. 'Diagnostic epistemology tries to analyze, explain and criticize the foundations of classical epistemology. . . . diagnostic epistemology studies the structure of the building, its central pillars and cornerstones, and the rock (or swamp) on which it rests' (Kusch, 2011a, p. 877).
5. 'One commitment whose presence within most epistemological thinking is implicit, rather than explicit, is a thesis of *knowledge-absolutism*. This is the thesis that knowledge—specifically, knowledge that *p*—is absolute. According to this thesis, no knowledge of a particular truth ever admits of varying *grades* (either within a particular context or across different contexts)' (Hetherington, 2011, p. 6).
6. Kusch writes of Goldman: 'I regard his attitude towards classical epistemology as far too deferential' (Kusch, 2011a, p. 875). He continues; 'While no one has done more for establishing SE as a vibrant field in epistemology than Goldman, in some respects his vision of the field is too limiting. He shows too little interest in social-historical and sociological studies of (scientific) knowledge' (p. 882).
7. Shared intentionality refers to collaborative interactions involving participants with a shared goal.
8. However Tomasello *et al.* do in fact point to the special significance of *collective intentionality* for developing capacities that lead to advanced systems of production and communication:

   > Human beings are also the world's experts at culture. Humans do not just interact with conspecifics socially, as do many animal species, but they also engage with them in complex collaborative activities such as making a tool together, preparing a meal together, building a shelter together, playing a cooperative game, collaborating scientifically, . . . These collective activities and practices are often structured by shared symbolic artifacts, such as linguistic symbols and social institutions, facilitating their 'transmission' across generations in ways that ratchet them up in complexity over historical time (Tomasello *et al.*, 2005, p. 675).

9. '[M]odern philosophy is pervaded by apparent problems about knowledge in particular. But I think it is helpful to see those apparent problems as more or less inept expressions of a

deeper anxiety—an inchoately felt threat that a way of thinking we find ourselves falling into leaves minds simply out of touch with the rest of reality, not just questionably capable of getting to know about it' (McDowell, 1996, p. xiii).

10. Bronckart explains that for Piaget 'the main issue . . . is nothing other than the construction of the categories of understanding in *The Critique of Pure Reason*' (Bronckart, 1996, p. 93).

11. Kitchener notes that although Mark Baldwin was responsible for the creation of a field termed 'genetic epistemology' it was Piaget who became most closely identified with it (Kitchener, 1993).

   According to Piaget, 'The fundamental hypothesis of genetic epistemology is that there is a parallelism between the progress made in the logical and rational organisation of knowledge and the corresponding formative psychological processes' (Piaget, 1970, p. 13).

12. According to Stekeler-Weithofer:

   > We can comprehend *object-level truth-conditions* only if we already refer to the *particular* constitution of the regional domain of discourse *in a larger setting of joint human practice*, as we can see, for example, if we look at the sub-disciplines of mathematics and physics, or biology and history. Therefore any concrete notion of truth and knowledge (as it is defined and developed by us) is always *limited to a regional domain*. It is limited to a *genos* in Aristotle's sense, which, as a topic of discourse, is always already situated in a larger, in a sense 'unlimited' and 'holistic' world (Stekeler-Weithofer, 2011, p.111).

13. In his chapter, 'How Analytic Philosophy has Failed Cognitive Science', Brandom argues that analytic philosophers have 'failed our colleagues in cognitive science by not sharing central lessons about the nature of concepts, concept use, and conceptual content' (Brandom, 2009, p. 196). He concludes by saying that 'the ideas in question [i.e. those that Brandom believes to be mistaken] launched the whole enterprise of analytic philosophy' (p. 224) yet while analytic philosophers have explored the ideas and become clearer about them, this progress has not been shared with cognitive science.

14. A common sense conception of knowledge may well echo a remark related to Kuhn that 'a fact is a fact. It has neither genesis or development' (Kuhn, 1979, p.viii).

15. '[F]or Brandom a Kantian perspective keeps the plane of the institution of conceptual norms distinct from the plane of their empirical application—the transcendental level from the empirical level. Hegel, by contrast, in particular in the *Phenomenology*, provides us with a model in which experience is not only the application of pure concepts but is also the development of their determinate content: in other words, empirical conceptual norms are instituted in the very process in which they are applied' (Testa, 2009).

16. However it is important to mention here Paul Hirst's major work on Forms of Knowledge and Cognitive Structures (for example, Hirst, 1965).

17. There has been a lack of attention to teachers' *orientation* to the knowledge domains with which they are concerned.

18. For example, Whitty (2010) argues 'some of the key challenges in giving disadvantaged pupils access to powerful knowledge—and giving it meaningful and critical purchase on their everyday lives—are pedagogic ones'; however, the focus of attention has either been on pedagogy or on knowledge but not their integral relation.

19. How this is done can take numerous forms none of which need to be intellectualist or overly rationalistic.

20. 'For instance, Paul Griffiths (2002) argues that the concept of innateness conflates three properties: a trait being universal within a species, a trait being an evolutionary adaptation, and a trait being insensitive to the environment in its development. Each of these properties is scientifically important, yet they are not co-extensive and empirically to be distinguished, so that the notion of innateness—as it is used by cognitive and some behavioural

scientists—often leads to illicit inferences. In a similar vein Lenny Moss (2003) argues that the term 'gene' figures in two distinct explanatory games in molecular biology. Each of these two sets of inference motivated by the gene concept is legitimate in its appropriate context, but conflation then leads to fallacious inferences and an inappropriate version of genetic determinism' (Brigandt, 2010).

21. 'The constructive suggestion Hegel offers as an alternative to this assumption is a radically new, nonpsychological conception of the conceptual. According to this conception, to be conceptually contentful is to stand in relations of material incompatibility ("determinate negation") and material consequence ("mediation") to other such contentful items. . . . Objective states of affairs and properties, too, stand to one another in relations of material incompatibility and consequence, and are accordingly intelligible as already in conceptual shape, quite apart from any relations they might stand in to the cognitive and practical activities of knowing and acting subjects. Indeed, if objective states of affairs and properties did not stand to one another in such relations, they would not be intelligible as so much as *determinate*. We could not then make sense of the idea that there is some definite way the world actually is. For that idea essentially involves the contrast with other ways the world might be (other properties objects might have). And the contrasts in virtue of which states of affairs and properties are determinate must involve modally exclusive differences ("It is impossible for a piece of pure copper to remain solid at temperatures above 1085°C.") as well as mere differences. (**Red** and **square** are different, but compatible properties)' (Brandom, 2011).

22. Referring to Peirce's remark that every 'physicist, chemist has his mind moulded', Westphal points out that:

> [t]his is not to say that the objects of human knowledge in the sciences and other disciplines are human constructs. It is to say that the concepts, techniques and procedures of disciplined intellectual inquiry are normative human constructs. When the constructs work well, they do inform us about the actual features of the objects investigated (Westphal, 1999, p. 148).

REFERENCES

Alston, W. P. (2005) *Beyond Justification: Dimensions of Epistemic Evaluation* (Ithaca, NY, Cornell University Press).

Bakhurst, D. (2011) *The Formation of Reason* (Oxford, Wiley-Blackwell).

Bakker, A. and Derry, J. (2011) Lessons from Inferentialism for Statistics Education, *Mathematical Thinking and Learning*, 13.1/2, pp. 5–26.

Ball, D. L., Lubienski, S. and Mewborn, D. (2001) Research on Teaching Mathematics: The Unsolved Problem of Teachers' Mathematical, in: V. Richardson (ed.) *Handbook of Research on Teaching*, 4th ed. (New York, Macmillan).

Brandom, R. (1994) *Making it Explicit: Reasoning, Representing, and Discursive Commitment* (Cambridge, MA: Harvard University Press).

Brandom, R. (2000) *Articulating Reasons: an Introduction to Inferentialism* (Cambridge, MA: Harvard University Press).

Brandom, R. (2009) *Reason in Philosophy* (Cambridge, MA, The Belknap Press of Harvard University Press).

Brandom, R. (2011) Knowing and Representing: Reading (Between the Lines of) Hegel's *Introduction*. Lecture Two: Representation and the Experience of Error: A Functionalist Approach to the Distinction between Appearance and Reality. The 2011 Munich Hegel Lectures, 30 May-1 June 2011, at Ludwig-Maximilians-Universität. Available at: http://afterxnature.blogspot.co.uk/2013/04/brandoms-hegel-lectures-online-handouts.html

Brigandt, I. (2010) Scientific Reasoning is Material Inference: Combining Confirmation, Discovery, and Explanation, *International Studies in the Philosophy of Science*, 24, pp. 31–43.

Bronckart, J. (1996) Units of Analysis in Psychology and their Interpretation: Social inter-actionism or Logical Interactionism?, in: A. Tryphon and J. N. Voneche (eds) *Piaget— Vygotsky The Social Genesis of Thought* (Hove, Psychology Press).

Croce, B. (1915) *What is Living and What is Dead of the Philosophy of Hegel* (London, Macmillan).

Donaldson, M. (1978) *Children's Minds* (London, Fontana Press).

Goldman, A. (2010) Why Social Epistemology is Real Epistemology, in A. Haddock, A. Millar and D. Pritchard (eds) *Social Epistemology* (Oxford, Oxford University Press).

Hetherington, S. (2011) *How to Know: A Practicalist Conception of Knowledge* (Oxford, Wiley-Blackwell).

Hirst, P. H. (1965) [1974] Liberal Education and the Nature of Knowledge, in: P. H. Hirst, *Knowledge and the Curriculum* (London, Routledge & Kegan Paul).

Kitchener, R. F. (1993) Genetic Epistemology in: J. Dancy and E. Sosa (eds) *A Companion to Epistemology* (Oxford, Blackwell).

Kuhn T. (1979) Forward, in: L. Fleck, *Genesis and Development of a Scientific Fact* (Chicago, IL, University of Chicago Press).

Kusch, M. (2011a) Social Epistemology in: S. Bernecker and D. Pritchard (eds) *The Routledge Companion to Epistemology* (London, Routledge).

Kusch, M. (2011b) Social Epistemology draft. Available at http://www.academia.edu/185820/Social_Epistemology

McDowell, J. (1996) *Mind and World* (Cambridge, MA, Harvard University Press).

Piaget, J. and Inhelder, B. (1967) *The Child's Conception of Space* (New York, Norton & Co).

Piaget, J. (1970) *Genetic Epistemology* (New York, Columbia University Press).

Prien, B. and Schweikard, D. P. (eds) (2008) *Robert Brandom Analytic Pragmatist* (Piscataway, NJ, Transaction Books).

Riggs, W. (2008) The Value Turn in Epistemology, in: V. Hendricks and D. H. Pritchard (eds) *New Waves in Epistemology* (Burlington, VT, Ashgate).

Ross, H. S. and Lollis, S. P. (1987) Communication Within Infant Social Games, *Developmental Psychology*, 23, pp. 241–248.

Stekeler-Weithofer, P. (2011) Intuition, Understanding, and the Human Form of Life, in: H. Ikäheimo and A. Laitinen (eds) *Recognition and Social Ontology* (Leiden, Brill).

Testa, I. (2009) Criticism and Normativity. Brandom and Habermas between Kant and Hegel, in: G. Tuzet and D. Canale (eds) *The Rules of Inference: Inferentialism in Law and Philosophy* (Milan, Egea).

Tomasello, M., Carpenter, M., Call, J., Behne, T. and Moll, H. (2005) Understanding and Sharing Intentions: The Origins of Cultural Cognition, *Behavioural and Brain Sciences*, 28, pp. 675–735.

Vygotsky, L. S. (1987) *The Collected Works of L.S. Vygotsky, Volume 1 Problems of General Psychology* (including the Volume *Thinking and Speech*), N. Minick, trans.; R. Reiber and A. Carton, eds (New York, Plenum Press).

Vygotsky, L. S. (1998) *The Collected Works of L.S. Vygotsky, Volume 5, Child Psychology*, R. Reiber, ed.; C. Ratner, prologue (New York, Plenum Press).

Westphal, K. R. (1999) Integrating Philosophies of Mind and of Education: Comments on Cunningham, in: *Philosophy of Education 1999* (Urbana, IL, Philosophy of Education Society), pp. 147–52.

Whitty, G. (2010) Revisiting School Knowledge: Some Sociological Perspectives on New School Curricula, *European Journal of Education*, 45.1, pp. 28–45.

5

Epistemic Virtue and the Epistemology of Education

DUNCAN PRITCHARD

INTRODUCTORY REMARKS

My goal is to explore the role of cognitive agency in the epistemology of education. In particular, what interests me is how we should think of virtue epistemology—which is arguably the dominant viewpoint in contemporary epistemology, and which puts cognitive agency centre-stage in the epistemological enterprise—as informing the epistemology of education.[1] As we will see, one is led towards a view on which education leads a pupil through a scale of cognitive attainment, from mere cognitive success to various gradations of cognitive achievement. On this picture, it is ultimately understanding—rather than, for example, cognitive success or knowledge—which is the ultimate goal of education.

I VIRTUE EPISTEMOLOGY AND THE EPISTEMOLOGY OF EDUCATION

One way of drawing out the relevance of virtue epistemology to the epistemology of education is by reflecting on what we are trying to achieve, from an epistemic point of view, when we educate children. Given that one plausible, and historically popular, account of the fundamental epistemic good—i.e. the fundamental good *from a purely epistemic point of view*—is truth, then one answer to this question, an answer which is clearly inadequate, is that we merely want our children to acquire lots of true beliefs. What is inadequate about this answer is that it leaves out so much of what we expect an education to achieve (even where we restrict our attention to the epistemic realm). For we don't just want an education to provide children with a body of true beliefs that they can call upon, but also to provide children with the cognitive skills to be able to determine truths for themselves.[2,3]

Education and the Growth of Knowledge: Perspectives from Social and Virtue Epistemology, First Edition. Edited by Ben Kotzee. Copyright © 2014 The Authors. Editorial organisation © 2014 Philosophy of Education Society of Great Britain. Published 2014 by John Wiley & Sons Ltd.

It is often said that we live in an information age, and in one sense this is entirely correct, in that information—lots and lots of information—is readily available to many people in the world as never before. But access to information is of little use if one lacks the cognitive skills to interpret this information and sift the accurate information from the inaccurate, and the epistemically useful information from the epistemically useless.[4] This has always been the case of course, though it is something perhaps more keenly felt in an 'information age'. The point is that education is to be distinguished from the mere transmission of information to passive minds and should be thought of instead as something which elicits and enhances the cognitive agency of the student.[5]

Even this is an incomplete conception of the epistemic goals of education, as we will see later on, but we are at least on the right track towards a complete conception. In particular, we have done enough to demonstrate the *prima facie* relevance of virtue epistemology to the epistemology of education. By virtue epistemology, I mean any epistemological proposal which puts the subject's intellectual virtues and cognitive faculties—her *cognitive agency*—centre-stage. There is of course a range of proposals that fall under this general heading. But rather than getting into the details of these different views, we will instead briefly dwell on what *as a minimum* is involved in virtue epistemology.

I think we can usefully express the minimal conception of virtue epistemology in terms of the idea that cognitive *abilities* are central to epistemology, in that they are directed towards epistemic goals. The ultimate epistemic goal is usually true belief, and that is what we will focus on here, though there are other plausible candidates, such as correct judgement. Like abilities more generally—which are reliable ways of achieving certain goals in appropriate conditions—by using one's cognitive abilities in suitable environments and conditions one can reliably achieve the epistemic goods in question. There is, of course, more to a cognitive ability than a mere reliable belief-forming trait. What makes a reliable belief-forming (or judgement-forming, etc.) trait a genuine cognitive ability is the way in which it is integrated within the cognitive character of the subject. A belief-forming trait, no matter how reliable, which was not integrated into the cognitive character of the subject would not count as one of the subject's cognitive abilities.

This minimal conception of cognitive ability is consistent with a wide range of very different virtue-theoretic proposals. How one fills in the details will depend very much on one's wider epistemological views. For example, while those attracted to a broadly internalist epistemology will be inclined to think of the kind of cognitive integration required for cognitive ability along fairly robust lines, such that it requires a reflective meta-perspective on the part of the subject, those attracted to a broadly externalist epistemology will be disposed to resist this demand and offer instead a less reflective, and thus less demanding, conception of cognitive integration. This contrast might also be evident in what virtue epistemologists inject into the idea of a cognitive ability too. So, for example, whereas internalist virtue epistemologists might regard cognitive abilities as essentially involving some sort of appropriate reflection (e.g. on whether the conditions and environment are suitable for the exercise of the relevant cognitive ability), externalist virtue epistemologists in contrast might well regard cognitive abilities as often being entirely unreflective.[6]

We can simplify our discussion of virtue epistemology if we focus our attention on what is common to all views of this sort: that when a subject's cognitive success (i.e. her true belief) amounts to knowledge there is a significant explanatory connection between that cognitive success and the subject's cognitive agency (i.e. her manifestation of cognitive ability in forming the target true belief). That is to say, a necessary condition for knowledge on virtue-theoretic proposals is that there be this explanatory connection between cognitive success and cognitive agency.[7]

An example will be useful at this point. Imagine a child who has come across a piece of information on the Internet—that the square root of 9 is 3, say—and who believes what she has read merely because she believes anything she finds in this way. The child has a true belief, but she does not know what she believes, and the reason why is that her cognitive agency is not playing any significant role in the explanation of her cognitive success. Indeed, what explains her cognitive success is rather the happenstance that she believes whatever she reads on the Internet, and she has happened on a truth. Compare this case with a child who has the cognitive skills to critically assess the information presented to her on the Internet. Perhaps she recognises, for example, that the site she is on is approved by her maths teachers, and hence can be relied upon to proffer mathematical truths of this kind. Perhaps she also knows enough arithmetic to appreciate that this proposition is not obviously incorrect (as 'the square root of 9 is refreshing' would be), even if she cannot check it herself. Such a child can come to have knowledge of what she truly believes in this case, but this is because she isn't merely truly believing; instead, her cognitive agency is playing a significant role in the explanation of why she is cognitively successful.

Notice that I say only that the subject's cognitive agency must play a 'significant' explanatory role in her cognitive success if she is to count as having knowledge. In particular, I am not claiming that it should play an *overarching* or *primary* role in the explanation of the subject's cognitive success. The second example just offered nicely illustrates why this is the case, in that the subject concerned, while exhibiting a relevant and significant level of cognitive ability, could not really be described as exhibiting cognitive agency to such a degree that it was the overarching element in an explanation of her cognitive success. This might be true of a child who had the arithmetical abilities to reliably check this statement for herself, but our agent falls well short of this kind of cognitive performance. Still, she exhibits enough cognitive agency to qualify as having knowledge, at least in these conditions.

I think that this is an important point to emphasise. In particular, we should notice that the kind of limited cognitive performance that can in many cases suffice for knowledge might not suffice in other cases. If our child were in an epistemically unfriendly environment, for example, then that might serve to epistemically frustrate our child's acquisition of knowledge, even if it does not prevent her from gaining a true belief. Imagine, for example, that the child has, unbeknownst to her, been redirected from a maths website approved by the teacher to one which is designed to deceive schoolchildren, and which is thus no less plausible than the 'proper' website. Our protagonist couldn't gain knowledge from such a site even if she happened to read one of the few truths that were on there. In circumstances like these it is much better to be the child who can verify the mathematical claim for herself rather than the one who merely displays a limited degree of cognitive agency of roughly knowing whom and what to trust, since only the former can have knowledge in this scenario.[8]

The immediate import of this point is that it would be unwise to simply shift the epistemological goal of education from mere cognitive success to knowledge, where the latter involves as a necessary ingredient some significant degree of cognitive agency, and hence the display of epistemic virtue. For knowledge is sometimes very easily had. In particular, in epistemically friendly scenarios—that is, scenarios where one cannot easily go wrong—not much cognitive agency is required for knowledge. Rather, what we should focus on is the development of cognitive agency in the acquisition of cognitive success, where this is a matter of degree, and where a greater display of cognitive agency can enable one to epistemically navigate even epistemically unfriendly scenarios.[9]

In particular, although I noted earlier that even a limited degree of cognitive agency can be enough for knowledge, such that we should not make it a necessary requirement of knowledge that the overarching explanation of the agent's cognitive success should be her cognitive agency, one can make this point while nonetheless emphasising the epistemic importance of cognitive successes that meet the stronger explanatory condition. Indeed, as we will see in a moment, we should not stop there, in that we should also recognise the epistemic importance of cognitive successes that meet even stronger explanatory conditions with regard to cognitive agency.

II A CONTINUUM OF COGNITIVE ATTAINMENT

It will helpful at this juncture to distinguish between mere cognitive success and different grades of *cognitive achievement*. A mere cognitive success is not a cognitive achievement, since achievements by their nature imply a significant contribution from one's agency, and this is *ex hypothesi* lacking in *mere* cognitive successes. But we could reasonably call those cognitive successes where a significant part of their explanation is the subject's cognitive agency a kind of achievement, albeit of a very weak variety. Call these *weak cognitive achievements*.[10] As noted above, weak cognitive achievements, unlike mere cognitive successes, can in certain cases—i.e. in epistemically friendly environments—be enough for knowledge.

We can contrast weak cognitive achievements with cognitive achievements proper. This is a cognitive success where the overarching explanation for the cognitive success is the subject's cognitive agency. To use terminology that is now fairly common in contemporary epistemology, a cognitive achievement is a cognitive success that is *because of* the subject's exercise of cognitive agency in just this sense (i.e. where the 'because of' relation is construed as an explanatory relation, such that subject's cognitive agency is the overarching or primary element in the causal explanation of the subject's cognitive success).[11] Call these simply *cognitive achievements* (i.e. without any rider). The foregoing might be thought to suggest that while weak cognitive achievements are not sufficient for knowledge, cognitive achievements proper are. Actually, even this is false, in that in certain kinds of epistemically unfriendly environments even this level of manifestation of cognitive agency will not suffice for knowledge, though we do not need to get into this issue here.[12]

We noted above that weak cognitive achievements are sometimes very easily had, at least in epistemically friendly environments. The same is also true, although to a lesser extent, of cognitive achieve-ments proper. In particular, in cases where it is very easy for one to attain the relevant cognitive success, then one will meet the rubric for cognitive achievements pretty easily. Indeed, take ordinary cases of perception, where one for the most passively encounters a world external to one, in an environment which is epistemically friendly with regard to judgements of this sort. Here one's cognitive success will be for the most part explained by the exercise of one's cognitive agency, even though one actually did very little.[13]

With this point in mind, it is useful to distinguish between cognitive achievements and *strong cognitive achievements*. The latter category concerns a cognitive achievement which involves either the overcom-ing of a significant obstacle to cognitive success or the manifestation of high levels of cognitive skill (i.e. higher than normal). Merely opening one's eyes in the morning might generate perceptual knowl-edge, and in the process afford one various cognitive achievements also, but it won't thereby generate strong cognitive achievements. Passive perception of one's environment is thus contrasted with active observation of one's environment. Watson may see the dirt on the subject's shoe, and so come to know that her shoes are unpolished (mere cognitive achievement), whereas Sherlock will immediately observe much more than this, seeing straight away, perhaps, that the subject before him lacks an alibi for the murder (strong cognitive achievement).[14]

In sketching this continuum from mere cognitive success, via weak cognitive achievement, cognitive achievement proper, through to strong cognitive achievement, we are clearly describing an important axis on which epistemic goodness can be measured that is relevant to the epistemology of education. Education may begin with the impart-ing of truths, but if it is done well it will quickly move onto the development of cognitive abilities on the part of the pupil. One would expect this to involve creating epistemically friendly environ-ments in which a limited display of cognitive ability can suffice for knowledge.[15] In this way, the weak cognitive achievements of the pupils are no less knowledge.[16] But a proper education would not be content to leave matters there. Instead, the educational process should continue enhancing the cognitive skills of the pupil, to encourage the level of display of cognitive agency at issue in strong cognitive achievements.

As noted above, one advantage of this cognitive enhancement is that it enables pupils to gain knowledge even in epistemically unfriendly environments. In particular, the greater the degree of epistemic unfriendliness in an environment, then the greater the degree of cognitive ability that is required in order to gain knowledge. There is thus a clear epistemic efficacy in having highly developed cognitive abilities. But the benefits of enhanced cognitive abilities do not end there.

To begin with, there is the fact that enhanced cognitive abilities entails an enhanced *epistemic autonomy*. The pupil who has highly developed cognitive abilities and who can deal with epistemic unfriendly conditions has a self-reliance that pupils who depend on the right kind of helpful conditions being in play before they can have knowledge lack. Epistemic autonomy is arguably a good thing in its own right, regardless of what further epistemic benefits it might bring.[17]

Second, the kind of enhanced cognitive abilities on display in strong cognitive achievements are not just resistant to epistemically hostile conditions, but also *flexible* in their application. Enhanced cognitive abilities will typically put pupils in the position to gain knowledge in a wide range of environments and conditions, whether epistemically friendly or hostile. In this sense, cognitive enhancement is epistemically *fecund*, in that it does not just generate cognitive success in the particular conditions in which the agent finds herself in, but also puts the agent in a position to gain further cognitive successes across a wide range of environments and conditions.

Third, strong cognitive achievements, even if one sets aside the point just made about epistemic autonomy, are plausibly of *final value* (i.e. non-instrumental value). For consider the more general category to which strong cognitive achievements belong—*viz.*, strong achievements *simpliciter*, where this means a success that is because of (i.e. primarily explained by) the subject's agency, and which either involves the overcoming of a significant obstacle or the exercise of a significant level of skill. That strong achievements are of special value, over and above whatever instrumental value they might have, is a point that goes right back to Aristotle (see, in particular, the *Nicomachean Ethics*, §I.7; Aristotle, 1984), who regards such displays of agency as being constitutive elements of a life of flourishing. Whatever is true of strong achievements will also be true of strong cognitive achievements, and thus the latter should inherit the final value of the former.[18] Indeed, insofar as one grants the previous point that knowledge does not essentially involve cognitive achievements, and hence *a fortiori* doesn't essentially involve strong cognitive achievements, then it follows that there is a kind of value in play when a pupil exhibits a strong cognitive achievement which would be absent if they merely acquired knowledge.

Fourth, the kind of development towards strong cognitive achievements goes hand-in-hand with a focus on the advancement not just of knowledge but, more importantly, *understanding*. As I have argued elsewhere, understanding and knowledge come apart. In particular, in epistemically friendly conditions one can exhibit a limited degree of cognitive agency which can suffice to enable one to gain knowledge, and yet the degree of one's dependence on factors outwith one's cognitive agency in gaining this cognitive success can nonetheless ensure that one does not count as having understanding.[19]

We can illustrate this point by returning to our example from earlier of the two children coming to know that the square root of 9 is 3, but where the one child can work this sum out for herself whereas her counterpart is trusting her informant, albeit in an epistemically responsible way (i.e. because she recognises that the information is from a good information source and she can independently tell that the information is not obviously false). While both children had knowledge, only the former student's knowledge would survive an epistemically hostile environment where there are lots of falsehoods on display, and the reason for this is that she has the ability to work out the answer for herself. In being able to perform this arithmetical sum she is thereby manifesting that she does not merely know that the square root of 9 is 3, but that she also *understands* why the square root of nine is 3. Knowledge can be merely passive, and it can depend in large part on a contribution from non-agential factors, such as being in an epistemically friendly social environment, but understanding is by its nature active, in that it requires one to be able to be able to put the component parts together (where in this case this means being able to do the required arithmetic).[20]

Unlike knowledge, understanding thus essentially involves cognitive achievement, where this means that the overarching factor in a subject's cognitive success is her cognitive agency. Indeed, often understanding will involve strong cognitive achievements, where this demands in addition that there is either an elevated level of skill on display or the overcoming of a significant obstacle to success. Acquiring an understanding of anything remotely complex will often be difficult and make a number of cognitive demands on the subject. In gaining that understanding one is thus either displaying great cognitive skill (if one gains the understanding effortlessly), or overcoming significant obstacles to cognitive success (if a great deal of effort is required to gain the understanding).[21] So, insofar as strong cognitive achievements are finally valuable in the way advertised above, it follows that understanding will also tend to be finally valuable too, and finally valuable in a way that mere cognitive success, or mere knowledge, is not.[22]

III CONCLUDING REMARKS

The upshot of the foregoing is that while the epistemic goal of education might initially be the promotion of cognitive success on the part of the pupil, this goal should ultimately be replaced with a focus on the development of the pupil's cognitive agency, where this means her epistemic virtue. In developing cognitive agency in this way one is enabling pupils to exhibit cognitive achievements, and thereby enhance their epistemic autonomy. Moreover, as we have seen, this focus on cognitive achievements as the epistemic goal of education is to be contrasted with a view on which education should be aimed at the promotion of knowledge rather than mere cognitive success. For as we have seen, it is actually understanding which is at issue here, an epistemic standing which is to be prized over knowledge.[23]

NOTES

1. For some of the key works in contemporary virtue epistemology, see Sosa, 1988, 1991, 2007, 2009a; Kvanvig, 1992; Montmarquet, 1993; Zagzebski, 1996, 1999; and Greco, 1999, 2000, 2003, 2007, 2008, 2009a, 2009b). For two useful surveys of recent work on contemporary virtue epistemology, see Axtell, 1997 and Kvanvig, 2010.

   Of course, I am not the first person to reflect on the ramifications of contemporary work on virtue epistemology for the epistemology of education, though it must be said that a lot of the discussion in this regard has often failed to 'mesh' the two debates in an even way, such that the focus tends to either be on the contemporary epistemology angle or the philosophy of education angle. (For a notable exception in this regard, see MacAllister, 2012; see also the recent debate about whether 'education' is a 'thick' concept, especially Siegel, 2008 and Kotzee, 2011.) I fear that my contribution continues this tradition by being too focused on contemporary epistemology. Still, if we are to make progress in this debate, then we need to start somewhere, so it is my hope that interventions such as this will be helpful, even despite this shortcoming.

2. Note that this is not yet to say that the fundamental epistemic good is not truth, though one might well conclude from the fact that the epistemic goal of education is not mere true belief that there are grounds for doubting whether truth is the fundamental epistemic good. I survey some of the literature on the epistemic good in Pritchard, forthcoming b, and in the process defend the idea that truth is the fundamental epistemic good from some recent challenges.

3. Of course, it might be contended that the promotion of truth has *no* role to play in education (i.e. not even a minimal role as part of a set of broader epistemic ends). I have not the space to consider this possibility here. For a useful overview of some sources of scepticism about the role of truth in education, see Robertson, 2009, §1.1.

4. One might think that the distinction between accurate and inaccurate information would map onto the distinction between epistemically useful and useless information, but I think this would be a mistake. Accurate information, after all, could be about something entirely trivial, from which no further insight could be gained. In contrast, it is possible that less accurate information about something important might enable one to further one's knowledge in a certain domain (for example, by making one realise that an important question which one thought was settled was in fact not settled at all).

5. This is, of course, a familiar point in the philosophy of education. In a recent survey piece on the epistemic ends of education, for example, Robertson (2009, §1) writes, citing Elgin, 1996 and Siegel, 1988, that 'the goal [of education] is not information *per se*, but, rather, knowledge that is significant and organized in patterns that contribute to perspective and understanding in orienting thought and action.'

6. For an example of a virtue epistemology which is cast along broadly epistemic internalist lines, see Zagzebski, 1996. For an example of a virtue epistemology which is cast along epistemic externalist lines, see Greco (e.g. 1999). For a helpful discussion of the contrast between 'responsibilist' and 'reliabilist' virtue epistemology, see Axtell, 1997. I have argued elsewhere—see Pritchard, 2005—that an externalist conception of virtue episte- mology copes better at dealing with empirical work on the acquisition of knowledge, even with regard to expert knowledge, though we do not need to take sides on this debate for our current purposes. (For further discussion of my proposal in this regard, see MacAllister, 2012.)

7. Note that even those virtue-theoretic proposals which disavow the project of offering an analysis of knowledge can accept this claim, since it merely commits one to a necessity claim about knowledge, and not to the full-blooded project of offering an analysis. For further discussion of the idea that virtue epistemology might be best thought of as reori- enting the concerns of traditional epistemology (such as offering an analysis of knowl- edge), rather than simply responding to those concerns, see Code, 1987; Kvanvig, 1992; Montmarquet, 1993; Hookway, 2003; and Roberts and Wood, 2007;

8. I think that this point about how, in suitable conditions, knowledge can be gained even though there is very limited cognitive agency on display undermines the so-called 'situ- ationist' challenge that has been posed for virtue epistemology (and which might be thought to undermine the relevance of virtue epistemology to the epistemology of education). Very roughly, this challenge has appealed to empirical work regarding the role of minor environ- mental factors in determining behaviour to argue that virtues, including intellectual virtues, do not play the kind of explanatory role in our behaviour that philosophers often claim that they play. In the epistemic sphere, this objection assumes that virtue epistemology is committed to the thesis that when an agent gains knowledge the overarching element in an explanation of her cognitive success is her cognitive agency, her intellectual virtue. But as I have indicated here, in many cases this is simply not the case, and hence virtue episte- mology should ally itself with a much weaker conception of the relationship between knowledge and cognitive agency, one that can allow other factors outwith the subject's cognitive agency to play an explanatory role in the subject's cognitive success. I develop this response to the situationist challenge to virtue epistemology in more detail in Pritchard, forthcoming a. For more on the situationist challenge as it applies in virtue ethics, see Doris, 2002 and Prinz, 2009. For a helpful development of the situationist challenge as it applies specifically to virtue epistemology, see Alfano, 2012. For a response to the situationist challenge to virtue epistemology which is very different to the line I take, see Sosa, 2009b.

9. Within reason, anyway. No incremental improvement in human cognitive virtue would suffice to deal with the sort of epistemically unfriendly scenario at issue in radical sceptical hypotheses, for example. For our purposes, however, we can reasonably bracket the problem of radical scepticism.

10. Note that elsewhere, such as in Pritchard, Millar and Haddock, 2010, chapter 2, I've tended to follow convention and reserve the notion of an achievement (and thus cognitive achieve- ment) for those (cognitive) successes which are *primarily* creditable to the subject's (cognitive) agency. If the reader prefers, she can substitute 'weak cognitive achievement' with '*quasi*-cognitive achievements'.

11. Greco is the chief exponent of a view of this sort, though his proposal has become more nuanced in recent years (in ways that do not concern us here). See Greco, 2003, 2007, 2008,

2009a. For a different account of the 'because of' relation in play here, one that is cast along dispositional lines, see Sosa, 2007, 2009a. For a comparative, and critical, discussion of these two accounts of the 'because of' relation as used in virtue epistemology, see Kallestrup and Pritchard, 2013a, forthcoming.

12. See Pritchard, Millar and Haddock, 2010, chapter 3, and Pritchard, 2012 for an explanation of why even cognitive achievements proper do not suffice for knowledge. See Kallestrup and Pritchard, forthcoming for a development of this idea.

13. The same point applies to achievements more generally, if achievements are to be understood as successes that are because of (i.e. primarily explained by) a subject's manifestation of relevant ability. Raising one's arm in normal circumstances constitutes a success that is because of one's ability in this sense (assuming we have any free will at all of course), but as achievements go it is rather limited. See also endnote 14.

14. The notion of a strong cognitive achievement is arguably much closer to the ordinary language notion of an 'achievement' than a (mere) cognitive achievement. So, picking up on the point made in the last endnote, while raising one's arm in normal circumstances isn't a strong achievement, raising one's arm when, say, one's arm is a cast (and thus there is an obstacle to arm-raising that needs to be overcome) is a strong achievement. Since we wouldn't normally describe merely raising one's arm as an achievement, but we might well describe raising one's arm when it is in a cast as an achievement, this is grounds for thinking that the ordinary language notion of an achievement roughly corresponds to what we are here calling strong achievements.

15. Ben Kotzee has pointed out to me that the idea of an educator creating epistemically friendly environments as part of the educational process is also central to Lev Vygotsky's (e.g. 1978) educational theory. See in particular his notion of the *zone of proximal development*, which effectively involves educators creating favourable learning conditions for their pupils (a process which in the contemporary educational literature is often called 'scaffolding'—see, e.g., Wood and Middleton, 1975—though Vygotsky never used this term himself). For a useful recent overview of Vygotsky's educational theory, see Davydov and Kerr, 1995.

16. The educational context thus highlights how the acquisition of knowledge can be epistemic dependent upon factors in one's social environment. See Goldberg, 2010, 2011, for an important discussion of this notion. See also Kallestrup and Pritchard, 2012, 2013b. For a useful discussion of epistemic dependence in the context of the philosophy of education, see Robertson, 2009.

17. Indeed, it has been argued—most recently by Roberts and Wood (2007, Part 2)—that epistemic autonomy is a necessary ingredient in a life of flourishing. For a defence of epistemic autonomy in the context of the philosophy of education, see Siegel, 2003. For a related, though much more qualified, endorsement of epistemic autonomy in this context, see Robertson, 2009.

18. For two very different defences of a claim of this sort, see Greco, 2009a, chapter 6 and Pritchard, Millar and Haddock, 2010, chapter 2; cf. Pritchard, 2009b. For a survey of the recent literature on epistemic value, see Pritchard, 2007 and Turri and Pritchard, 2011.

19. Although not particularly relevant for our purposes, knowledge and understanding also come apart in the other direction, in that one can have understanding while lacking the corresponding knowledge. For more on this point, see Pritchard, 2009a and Pritchard, Millar and Haddock, 2010, chapter 4. For further discussion of the epistemology of understanding more generally, see Grimm, 2010. See also Grimm, 2006 and the exchange between Grimm (forthcoming) and Pritchard (forthcoming c).

20. Note that I'm taking it as given here that in 'doing' the required arithmetic one is not merely blindly undertaking an automatic process which one learnt by rote. That would be akin still to a weak cognitive achievement, in that one is epistemically dependent to a significant

degree on factors outwith one's cognitive agency (e.g. that one was taught this process by an authoritative source, and so on). But what we are dealing with here is a strong cognitive achievement, and this is a much more epistemically demanding notion.

21. Note that this is not to insist that understanding should always involve reflection. Whether it does will depend in part on whether one casts one's virtue epistemology along epistemically internalist or externalist lines, and what one's conception of understanding is. In particular, it is compatible with the view just described that understanding might involve a great deal of tacit knowledge. For a discussion of the role of tacit knowledge even in the context of expert judgements, see Pritchard, 2005. For an independent defence of the thesis that the promotion of understanding, as opposed to the mere inculcation of truths, should be the goal of education, see Elgin, 1996, 1999a, 1999b, though note that Elgin conceives of understanding in a different way to the present author (e.g. to the extent that understanding doesn't in general require truth).

22. For more on the idea that understanding is finally valuable, see Pritchard, 2009a and Pritchard, Millar and Haddock, 2010, chapter 4.

23. Thanks to Allan Hazlett, John Ravenscroft, and Lani Watson. Special thanks to Ben Kotzee and an anonymous referee who read and commented on an earlier version of this paper.

REFERENCES

Alfano, M. (2012) Extending the Situationist Challenge to Responsibilist Virtue Epistemology, *Philosophical Quarterly*, 62, pp. 223–249.

Aristotle (1984) *The Complete Works of Aristotle*, J. Barnes, ed. (Princeton, NJ, Princeton University Press).

Axtell, G. (1997) Recent Work in Virtue Epistemology, *American Philosophical Quarterly*, 34, pp. 410–430.

Code, L. (1987) *Epistemic Responsibility* (Hanover, NH, University Press of New England).

Davydov, V. V. and Kerr, S. T. (1995) The Influence of L. S. Vygotsky on Education Theory, Research, and Practice, *Educational Researcher*, 24, pp. 12–21.

Doris, J. (2002) *Lack of Character: Personality and Moral Behaviour* (Cambridge, Cambridge University Press).

Elgin, C. (1996) *Considered Judgment* (Princeton, NJ, Princeton University Press).

Elgin, C. (1999a) Education and the Advancement of Understanding, *Proceedings of the Twentieth World Congress of Philosophy*, 3, pp. 131–140.

Elgin, C. (1999b) Epistemology's Ends, Pedagogy's Prospects, *Facta Philosophica*, 1, pp. 39–54.

Goldberg, S. (2010) *Relying on Others: An Essay in Epistemology* (Oxford, Oxford University Press).

Goldberg, S. (2011) The Division of Epistemic Labour, *Episteme*, 8, pp. 112–125.

Greco, J. (1999) Agent Reliabilism, *Philosophical Perspectives*, 13, pp. 273–296.

Greco, J. (2000) *Putting Skeptics in Their Place: The Nature of Skeptical Arguments and Their Role in Philosophical Inquiry* (Cambridge: Cambridge University Press).

Greco, J. (2003) Knowledge as Credit for True Belief, in: M. DePaul and L. Zagzebski (eds) *Intellectual Virtue: Perspectives from Ethics and Epistemology* (Oxford, Oxford University Press), pp. 111–34.

Greco, J. (2007) The Nature of Ability and the Purpose of Knowledge, *Philosophical Issues*, 17, pp. 57–69.

Greco, J. (2008) What's Wrong With Contextualism?, *Philosophical Quarterly*, 58, pp. 416–436.

Greco, J. (2009a) *Achieving Knowledge* (Cambridge, Cambridge University Press).

Greco, J. (2009b) Knowledge and Success From Ability, *Philosophical Studies*, 142, pp. 17–26.

Grimm, S. (2006) Is Understanding a Species of Knowledge?, *British Journal for the Philosophy of Science*, 57, pp. 515–535.

Grimm, S. (2010) 'Understanding', *The Routledge Companion to Epistemology*, (eds.) S. Bernecker *and* D. H. Pritchard, 84–94, London: Routledge.

Grimm, S. (Forthcoming) Understanding as Knowledge of Causes, in: A. Fairweather (ed.) *Virtue Scientia* (Dordrecht, Springer).

Hookway, C. (2003) How to Be a Virtue Epistemologist, in: M. DePaul and L. Zagzebski (eds) *Intellectual Virtue: Perspectives from Ethics and Epistemology* (Oxford, Oxford University Press), pp. 183–202.

Kallestrup, J. and Pritchard, D. H. (2012) Robust Virtue Epistemology and Epistemic Anti-Individualism, *Pacific Philosophical Quarterly*, 93, pp. 84–103.

Kallestrup, J. and Pritchard, D. H. (2013a) Robust Virtue Epistemology and Epistemic Dependence, in: T. Henning and D. Schweikard (eds) *Knowledge, Virtue and Action: Putting Epistemic Virtues to Work* (London, Routledge) chapter 11.

Kallestrup, J. and Pritchard, D. H. (2013b) The Power, and Limitations, of Virtue Epistemology, in: J. Greco and R. Groff (eds) *Powers and Capacities in Philosophy: The New Aristotelianism* (London, Routledge), 248–269.

Kallestrup, J. and Pritchard, D. H. (Forthcoming) Virtue Epistemology and Epistemic Twin Earth, *European Journal of Philosophy*.

Kotzee, B. (2011) Education and 'Thick' Epistemology, *Educational Theory*, 61, pp. 549–64.

Kvanvig, J. (1992) *The Intellectual Virtues and the Life of the Mind* (Lanham, MD, Rowman and Littlefield).

Kvanvig, J. (2010) Virtue Epistemology, in: S. Bernecker and D. H. Pritchard (eds) *Routledge Companion to Epistemology* (London, Routledge), pp. 199–207.

MacAllister, J. (2012) Virtue Epistemology and the Philosophy of Education, *Journal of Philosophy of Education*, 46, pp. 251–270.

Montmarquet, J. (1993) *Epistemic Virtue and Doxastic Responsibility* (Lanham, MD, Rowman *and* Littlefield).

Prinz, J. (2009) 'The Normativity Challenge: Cultural Psychology Provides the Real Threat to Virtue Ethics', *Journal of Ethics*, 13, 117–144.

Pritchard, D. H. (2005) 'Virtue Epistemology and the Acquisition of Knowledge', *Philosophical Explorations*, 8, 229–243.

Pritchard, D. H. (2007) Recent Work on Epistemic Value, *American Philosophical Quarterly*, 44, pp. 85–110.

Pritchard, D. H. (2009a) Knowledge, Understanding and Epistemic Value, in: A. O'Hear (ed.) *Epistemology (Royal Institute of Philosophy Lectures* (Cambridge, Cambridge University Press), pp. 19–43.

Pritchard, D. H. (2009b) The Value of Knowledge, *Harvard Review of Philosophy*, 16, pp. 2–19.

Pritchard, D. H. (2012) Anti-Luck Virtue Epistemology, *Journal of Philosophy*, 109, pp. 247–79.

Pritchard, D. H. (Forthcoming a) Re-Evaluating the Situationist Challenge to Virtue Epistemology, in: A. Fairweather and O. Flanagan (eds) *Naturalizing Epistemic Values* (Oxford, Oxford University Press).

Pritchard, D. H. (Forthcoming b) Truth as the Fundamental Epistemic Good, in: J. Matheson and R. Vitz (eds) *The Ethics of Belief: Individual and Social* (Oxford, Oxford University Press).

Pritchard, D. H. (Forthcoming c) Understanding as Knowledge of Causes, in: A. Fairweather (ed.) *Virtue Scientia* (Dordrecht, Springer).

Pritchard, D. H., Millar, A. and Haddock, A. (2010) *The Nature and Value of Knowledge: Three Investigations* (Oxford, Oxford University Press).

Roberts, R. and Wood, W. J. (2007) *Intellectual Virtues: An Essay in Regulative Epistemology* (Oxford, Oxford University Press).

Robertson, E. (2009) The Epistemic Aims of Education, in: H. Siegel (ed.) *Oxford Handbook of Philosophy of Education* (Oxford, Oxford University Press), pp. 11–34.

Siegel, H. (1988) *Educating Reason: Rationality, Critical Thinking, and Education* (London, Routledge).

Siegel, H. (2003) Cultivating Reason, in: R. Curren (ed.) *Companion to the Philosophy of Education* (Oxford, Blackwell), pp. 305–319.

Siegel, H. (2008) Is Education a Thick Epistemic Concept?, *Philosophical Papers*, 37, pp. 455–469.

Sosa, E. (1988) Beyond Skepticism, to the Best of Our Knowledge, *Mind*, 97, pp. 153–189.

Sosa, E. (1991) *Knowledge in Perspective: Selected Essays in Epistemology*, (Cambridge: Cambridge University Press).

Sosa, E. (2007) *A Virtue Epistemology: Apt Belief and Reflective Knowledge* (Oxford, Clarendon Press).

Sosa, E. (2009a) *Reflective Knowledge: Apt Belief and Reflective Knowledge* (Oxford, Clarendon Press).

Sosa, E. (2009b) Situations Against Virtues: The Situationist Attack on Virtue Theory, in: C. Mantzavinos (ed.) *Philosophy of the Social Sciences: Philosophical Theory and Scientific Practice* (Cambridge, Cambridge University Press), pp. 274–90.

Turri, J. and Pritchard, D. H. (2011) The Value of Knowledge, in: E. Zalta (ed.) *Stanford Encyclopedia of Philosophy*. Online at: http://plato.stanford.edu/entries/knowledge-value/.

Vygotsky, L. S. (1978) *Mind in Society: The Development of Higher Psychological Processes* (Cambridge, MA, Harvard University Press).

Wood, D. and Middleton, D. (1975) A Study of Assisted Problem-Solving, *British Journal of Psychology*, 66, pp. 181–91

Zagzebski, L. (1996) *Virtues of the Mind: An Inquiry into the Nature of Virtue and the Ethical Foundations of Knowledge* (Cambridge, Cambridge University Press).

Zagzebski, L. (1999) What is Knowledge?, in: J. Greco and E. Sosa (eds) *The Blackwell Guide to Epistemology* (Oxford, Blackwell), pp. 92–116.

6
Educating for Intellectual Virtues: From Theory to Practice

JASON BAEHR

My concern in this chapter is with two perennial questions in the philosophy of education and educational theory: What are the proper aims or goals of education? What are the most fitting ways of achieving these goals? The answers I defend draw heavily from recent research within virtue epistemology on intellectual character virtues like curiosity, open-mindedness, attentiveness, intellectual carefulness, intellectual courage, intellectual rigour, and intellectual honesty.[1] I argue that education should aim at fostering growth in these traits and provide some indication of what it might look to educate in this way.

I begin with a brief account of the basic structure of intellectual virtues. Next, I sketch three arguments for thinking that fostering growth in intellectual virtues should be a central educational aim. Finally, I entertain two objections to this claim. In response to the second objection, I also identify several educational practices and strategies aimed at fostering intellectual virtues. As this brief overview suggests, the chapter is broad in scope and largely programmatic. The unfortunate but necessary result is that several details will have to be left unspecified and a number of questions raised but then set aside for future consideration.

I THE BASIC STRUCTURE OF AN INTELLECTUAL VIRTUE

There is broad agreement among virtue epistemologists (e.g. Montmarquet, 1993; Zagzebski, 1996; Roberts and Wood, 2007; and Baehr, 2011) that intellectual virtues exhibit a general two-tier structure. At a basic motivational level, all intellectual virtues involve something like a 'love' of epistemic goods. An intellectually virtuous person is one who desires and is committed to the pursuit of goods like

Education and the Growth of Knowledge: Perspectives from Social and Virtue Epistemology, First Edition.
Edited by Ben Kotzee. Copyright © 2014 The Authors. Editorial organisation © 2014 Philosophy of Education Society of Great Britain. Published 2014 by John Wiley & Sons Ltd.

knowledge, truth, and understanding. It is this inherent epistemic orientation that permits a distinction between intellectual virtues and what are typically thought of as moral virtues.[2]

While intellectual virtues share a common motivational basis, each individual virtue also has its own characteristic activity or psychology—an activity or psychology that is rooted in an underlying 'love' of epistemic goods. Put formally, the idea is that for any intellectual virtue V, a subject S possesses V only if S is (a) disposed to manifest a certain activity or psychology characteristic of V (b) out of a love of epistemic goods.[3] A curious person, for instance, is quick to wonder and ask why-questions out of a desire to understand the world around her. An open-minded person is willing to consider alternative standpoints because he sees that doing so is helpful for arriving at an accurate grasp of those standpoints and of the matter at hand. And an intellectually courageous person is disposed to persist in beliefs or inquiries that she has reason to think will lead her to the truth despite the fact that doing so may put her in harm's way.

II INTELLECTUAL VIRTUES AS AN EDUCATIONAL AIM

With this general structural model before us, I turn to a defence of the claim that fostering growth in intellectual virtues should be a central educational aim.

IIA *Thickening Familiar Educational Goals*

It is a near platitude that education should aim at fostering 'lifelong learning'. But as often and pervasively as this goal is espoused in educational institutions at every level, exactly what it amounts to is far from clear. This is unfortunate, for it is plausible to think that ordinary usage of 'lifelong learning' and related terms, while typically less than very thoughtful and careful, nevertheless is an attempt to get at a reasonably substantive, determinate, and compelling educational ideal.[4] Thus it is worth trying to understand what this ideal might amount to; that is, to identify some of the specific psychological qualities, abiding convictions, ingrained habits, or essential skills that distinguish the lifelong learner from the rest of us.

The notions of intellectual character and intellectual virtue are extremely useful in this regard, for we can think of intellectual virtues as the *personal* qualities or characteristics of a lifelong learner. To be a lifelong learner, one must possess a reasonably broad base of practical and theoretical knowledge. But possessing even a great deal of knowledge is not sufficient. Being a lifelong learner also requires being *curious* and *inquisitive*. It requires a firm and powerful commitment to learning. It demands *attentiveness* and *reflectiveness*. And given the various ways in which a commitment to lifelong learning might get derailed, it also requires intellectual *determination, perseverance*, and *courage*. In other words, being a lifelong learner is largely constituted by the possession of various intellectual virtues.

This claim is confirmed and illuminated by the two-tier structural model sketched in the previous section. According to the model, intellectual virtues flow from and are grounded in a firm and intelligent love of epistemic goods. Again, this orientation forms the psychological basis of intellectual virtues. This way of thinking about intellectual virtues makes good sense of the familiar idea, also noted above, that 'lifelong learners' possess a firm and powerful commitment to the life of the mind. By providing a plausible way of understanding this aspect of the putative psychology of a lifelong learner, the structural model lends further plausibility to the idea that intellectual virtues are the personal qualities or character traits of a lifelong learner.

The possession of intellectual virtues is not merely a matter of good epistemic motivation. According to the structural model, each intellectual virtue also involves a disposition to engage in a certain sort of cognitive *activity*—an activity that distinguishes that virtue from other intellectual virtues. Moreover, as I have argued elsewhere, the possession of an intellectual virtue also requires having good *reason* to think that the activity characteristic of the virtue in question will be useful for achieving one's epistemic aims.[5] If these claims are correct, that is, if possessing an intellectual virtue involves being disposed to engage in a certain sort of cognitive activity that one has good reason think will be useful for achieving one's epistemic ends, it follows that, in addition to the motivational component just identified, intellectual virtues also have a *competence* and a *rationality* component. This also fits well with the idea that intellectual virtues comprise the personal or character-related aspect of being a 'lifelong learner', for lifelong learners presumably are not merely those who love learning and knowledge; they are also *skilled* and *intelligent* in their pursuit of these ends.

We have seen that the language and concepts of intellectual virtue provide a plausible way of fleshing out the familiar but nebulous ideal of lifelong learning.[6] But what exactly follows about the proper aims or goals of education? Unlike the concept of lifelong learning, virtue concepts are 'thick concepts'.[7] They have both a normative and a richly descriptive dimension. To say that Bob is open-minded, for instance, is to pick out something good or commendable or admirable about Bob; but it is also to convey something about what Bob is *like*—about what he is disposed to do, feel, think, say, and so on. Given this rich descriptive dimension, one benefit of 'educating for intellectual virtues' or of treating intellectual character growth as a central educational aim is that doing so provides a more *concrete* and *action-guiding* framework for making education about the formation of lifelong learners. Put another way, by thinking of lifelong learning in the relevant character-related terms, we set ourselves a clearer target and thus a target that we stand a better chance of hitting.

IIB Rigorous and Personal

In *The Child and the Curriculum*, John Dewey introduces a dichotomy between two familiar accounts of how and what students should be taught. According to one way of thinking, the content and structure of an academic curriculum should be derived strictly from the content and structure of the corresponding spheres of reality. It is the job of teachers and students to expand and conform their minds to these spheres, for this alone makes possible the kind of knowledge and understanding that are proper to education. On the other end of the spectrum is the view that curriculum should be determined entirely on the basis of the interests, inclinations, and abilities of students. Their psychology alone should dictate what is taught and how it is taught. This is essential, the argument goes, to inspiring genuine interest and motivation, which in turn are essential to genuine learning (Dewey, 1902, pp. 7–15).

Unsurprisingly, Dewey treats this as a false dichotomy. He argues that while students generally are not equipped to dictate what and how they learn, curriculum should be formulated and presented in ways that are sensitive to their actual experience or psychology. Disciplinary knowledge must, as Dewey puts it, be 'psychologized' (p. 32).

My interest here is not with Dewey's positive view about how to balance 'the curriculum and the child' but rather with the dichotomy itself. On one plausible understanding, this is a dichotomy between two fundamental educational values.[8] On the one hand, a good education ought to be *rigorous*: it ought to be demanding, stretch student thinking, and provide more than a short-term or superficial grasp of the material. On the other hand, a good education should also be *personal*: it should be attentive to and demonstrate care for who students are (e.g. their fundamental beliefs and values) and for the persons they are becoming.

A second compelling feature of an intellectual virtues approach is that it provides a plausible way of integrating or harmonising these potentially conflicting values. We can begin to see how by being a bit more precise about the proper aim of intellectual virtues. As I have argued elsewhere, intellectual virtues aim at *deep explanatory understanding of epistemically significant subject matters*.[9] An intellectually virtuous person is relatively unmoved by trivial or frivolous subject matters. After all, intellectual virtues are personally admirable traits. And a love of 'junk knowledge', for example, of the names listed in the Wichita phonebook under the letter 'R' or the number of grains in a random cubic centimetre of the Sahara, is hardly admirable.[10] Nor is an intellectually virtuous person content with a *fleeting* or *superficial* grasp of epistemically worthy subject matters. Rather, her aim is deep and penetrating understanding: she is concerned with a firm personal grasp of basic principles, underlying causes, and how the various facts within a given domain hang together.[11]

The latter point in particular underscores an important connection between intellectual virtues and intellectual rigour. Deep understanding, which again is the proper aim of intellectual virtues, is a significant and demanding cognitive achievement. For a subject matter or body of knowledge to admit of deep understanding, it must have a certain structural complexity a grasp of which requires sustained effort, reflection, concentration, persistence, and the like. For this reason, educating for deep understanding is necessarily a rigorous process.[12] And, since intellectual virtues aim at deep understanding, educating for intellectual virtues is necessarily rigorous as well. One cannot aim to promote significant growth in intellectual virtues in the absence of a serious commitment to rigour.

Rigorous educational approaches can, of course, prove intellectually stifling and oppressive. They can be excessively demanding or otherwise misaligned with the psychology or developmental stages of students. As a result they can extinguish a student's natural desire to learn. An intellectual virtues approach, by contrast, is particularly well positioned to avoid this kind of excess. For, if a teacher is attempting to nurture intellectual character growth in his students, he will pay very close attention to what his students are capable of and to their fundamental beliefs, attitudes, and feelings toward learning. His expectations of his students will be high, but this orientation will be constrained by an ongoing concern with the development of their intellectual character. In this way, an intellectual virtues educational model is poised to strike a sensible and attractive balance between promoting academic rigour, on the one hand, while also being sufficiently caring and personal, on the other.

Not every educational model can claim this advantage. The educational framework embodied in the well-known Summerhill School founded by A. S. Neill, for instance, evidently runs the risk of sacrificing intellectual rigour in an effort to be sufficiently personal. On the other end of the spectrum, certain approaches to 'classical education' favour a top-down, highly rigorous approach that threatens to neglect (if not extinguish) students' natural affinity for learning.[13]

To further illustrate the relative uniqueness of this advantage, let us compare an intellectual virtues approach with one that is more like-minded, namely, an approach aimed at fostering 'critical thinking'. Critical thinking educational models are a diverse lot. Some combine a focus on critical thinking skills with a focus on the 'critical spirit' or good intellectual 'dispositions' which are very much like (if not identical to) intellectual character virtues.[14] For our purposes, it will be helpful to consider an approach that focuses strictly on the development of critical thinking *skills* or *abilities*.[15] Let us stipulate that the approach in question is rigorous, demanding competence in complex forms of reasoning across a wide range of different content areas. While satisfying the desideratum of intellectual rigour, there is no guarantee that this approach will be sufficiently personal. The primary concern of a teacher on this model will be whether her students are developing the ability to reason in the relevant ways. She might be unconcerned with whether they are developing a motivation or inclination to think in these ways outside of class. And, even if she does have this concern, it will not (as such) be situated within a broader commitment to nurturing the intellectual character of her students, that is, to their becoming more curious, open-minded, fair-minded, intellectually courageous, persevering, and so on. In trying to impart the relevant skills, she might even be oblivious to such considerations.

A second good reason, then, for treating growth in intellectual virtues as a worthy educational aim is that doing so provides a very natural and compelling way of making education suitably rigorous *and* personal.

IIC Educational Meaning and Purpose

Many teachers enter the profession because they regard teaching as meaningful work. They expect it to bring significant purpose to their lives. They consider it their vocation. Similarly, most students can recount moments in which they experienced learning as meaningful, inspiring, and intrinsically rewarding. A worthy educational aim or framework ought to make sense of the putative meaning and purpose of teaching and learning. Specifically, it should give teachers and students a lively sense and a better understanding of the *value* of education.

Not all educational aims or approaches have this effect. Indeed, much that goes on in education today makes it difficult to see or feel the importance of teaching or learning. This is clearly the case where educational success is defined—even if just implicitly—in terms of high scores on standardised tests and where teaching is geared toward the achievement of such scores.[16] Conditions like these can make honest teachers wonder why they got into the teaching profession in the first place. They can make their initial pedagogical aspirations and expectations seem hopelessly naïve. They can also leave students doubting the value of their schooling. Similarly, at the post-secondary level, to the extent that the (implicit or explicit) aim of teaching is to disseminate information or knowledge proper to a range of academic disciplines (much of which can be accessed online at little or no cost) and academic excellence is closely associated with an ability to memorise and 'regurgitate' this information, the value of a university education might reasonably be questioned, particularly when it comes with a price tag in the hundreds of thousands of dollars.

Conceiving of education as properly aimed at nurturing growth in intellectual character virtues provides a much better way of capturing the putative meaning and purpose of teaching and learning. Again, if a teacher is educating for intellectual virtues, his aim will be to mould and shape his students as *persons*—to impact their fundamental ori-entation toward epistemic goods and the practices that facilitate these goods. He will be concerned with helping them understand *why* knowledge and learning are valuable.[17] He will also take measures aimed at getting them to *care* about these things. The value of such an impact is difficult to quibble with. Most of us desire—at least in our better moments—to be and to surround ourselves with persons con-cerned with knowledge and understanding and who are inquisitive, attentive, open-minded, intellectually honest, intellectually coura-geous, and the like. These are attractive and desirable qualities.

Intellectual virtues also have several important *practical* payoffs. To see what some of these are, note that the traits in question manifest themselves most obviously and centrally in good *thinking*. Accord-ingly, by educating for intellectual virtues, teachers are equipping their students with the skills and supporting beliefs, attitudes, and feelings that dispose them toward good thinking. As such, they are preparing them for at least two important kinds of success outside of the classroom.

First, they are helping prepare their students for successful careers. There are few jobs or professions in which the disposition to think in open, careful, critical, or innovative ways is not prized. Indeed, many have observed that given the centrality of technology to present-day economies, a good portion of the technical skills and knowledge currently taught to students will be obsolete or nearly obsolete by the time these students enter the workforce. For this reason, employers today are placing a premium on so-called 'soft skills', which are 'personality traits, goals, motivations, and preferences that are valued in the labour market, in school, and in many other domains' (Heckman and Kautz, 2012). While soft skills are not the same thing as intellectual virtues, they include such virtues as curiosity, attentiveness, perseverance, open-mindedness, and creativity. Thus by educating for intellectual virtues, teachers are helping prepare their students for success in the workplace.

Second, good thinking is often a precondition for morally responsible action, which in turn is critical to living well or flourishing as a human being.[18] In many instances, acting responsibly requires effective *deliberation*: it requires thinking carefully and thoroughly, evaluating options in an open and honest way, and maintaining the courage of one's convictions. In other words, it requires thinking in a manner characteristic of many intellectual virtues. While the ability to deliberate well is not sufficient for acting well, it is one essential ingredient. Therefore, educating for intellectual virtues involves nurturing qualities that are central to human flourishing.

We have seen that by conceiving of intellectual character growth as an important educational aim, teachers can have a positive impact on the personal formation of their students and equip them with abilities and other qualities that will benefit them substantially in the workplace and other areas of life. In this way, the aim in question is capable of illuminating for *teachers* the putative value of education.

It is also capable of having a similar impact on the experience and understanding of *students*. We can approach this point by identifying a few additional features of an intellectual virtues educational model. First, as we have already seen, educating for intellectual virtues is an inherently *personal* process: it involves thinking of students, not merely as potential 'high achievers' on standardised exams or the post-secondary equivalent thereof, but as 'whole persons' or as persons whose basic beliefs, attitudes, and feelings about knowledge and learning also matter critically to the quality of their education. This is very unlikely to escape the notice of students. Indeed, it is likely to make them feel respected and cared for as persons. Second, an intellectual virtues approach to education is necessarily *social* or *relational*. Personal change and growth occur most readily in the context of trusting and caring relationships.[19] Therefore, teachers educating for intellectual virtues will place a premium on developing such relationships with their students.[20] This is also likely to be evident to students and to enhance the felt quality of their educational experience. Third, an intellectual virtues approach to teaching is also *reflective*. It involves reflecting on and discussing with students the value of thinking and learning—both in general and with respect to the particular concepts, topics, and material at hand. In other words, it involves regularly pausing to identify or reflect on the *significance* of what is being taught. This is also likely to give students a deeper understanding of and appreciation for the education they are receiving.

In this section, we have seen, first, that a good educational aim, when appropriately pursued, will give teachers and students a lively sense and better understanding of the value of education, and second, that the aim of growth in intellectual character virtues scores very well relative to this standard.

III OBJECTIONS AND REPLIES

We have considered three arguments in support of the thesis that growth in intellectual virtues is an important educational aim. I turn now to consider two objections that might be raised in connection with this discussion.

IIIA *Intellectual Virtues or Academic Standards?*

The first objection is practical. To some, the idea of placing a premium on nurturing intellectual character growth in students might seem like a nice idea in principle, while nevertheless seeming untenable in reality. Teachers at every level are responsible for delivering content to their students. These demands are especially pressing where educational funding is tied closely to performance on standardised exams that measure competence in various academic standards. It might, then, be thought that teachers today must choose between teaching for intellectual virtues and teaching for required academic content and skills. And given the grave consequences of failing to do the latter, it might be thought that any serious concern with educating for intellectual virtues must be sidelined.

It is important at this juncture to draw a distinction between '*intellectual* character education' and character education *simpliciter* or character education in its more familiar manifestations. Traditionally, efforts at character education have tended to focus on fostering moral or civic virtues like compassion, respect, tolerance, and integrity.[21] While I think it is possible to wed academic instruction with character education understood in these ways, the present point is that this challenge is considerably less pressing when it comes to educating for intellectual virtues like curiosity, wonder, attentiveness, intellectual thoroughness, reflectiveness, or intellectual perseverance.[22] As indicated above, intellectual virtues express themselves in *intellectual actions* like thinking, reasoning, interpreting, analysing, reflecting, questioning, and so on. Thus engagement with academic content or standards provides a very natural opportunity for *practising* a wide range of intellectual virtues, which in turn is critical to the formation of these traits. In short, one important way of fostering intellectual virtues is through active and reflective engagement with academic content. Indeed, by contrast with attempts to foster most moral or civic virtues, it is difficult to imagine a systematic program aimed at fostering intellectual virtues that did not involve something like this form of intellectual engagement.[23]

IIIB Intellectual Virtues: An Explicit Goal?

A second objection acknowledges intellectual character growth as a worthy educational goal but questions the extent to which this goal should be made explicit, immediate, or deliberate. It might be said that good education will have—indeed always has had—the effect of making students more curious, open-minded, intellectually rigorous, intellectually courageous, and the like. However, it doesn't follow that a concern with such growth should be an immediate or explicit focus of teachers or students. Indeed, it might be argued that by making this goal explicit, or by allowing virtue concepts or language to pervade the learning process, educators are likely to trivialise or otherwise undermine the willingness or ability of students to pursue the very goal at issue.[24]

My response to this objection is mixed. On the one hand, I acknowledge that some who attempt to educate for intellectual virtues in a more explicit or deliberate way may be drawn to methods or resources that threaten to trivialise or subvert their objective, for example, to the sorts of posters, pencils, slogans, t-shirts, bracelets, and other trinkets that have found their way into some character education curricula.[25] Moreover, I reject the idea that the way to nurture intellectual character growth is through repeated exhortations to 'try to be curious' or 'to show open-mindedness'. As noted in the previous section, intellectual virtues come about through active engagement with ideas, claims, problems, narratives, arguments, and the like. These things— not the broader goal of becoming intellectually virtuous—are more likely to occupy the immediate focus of teachers and students operating within an intellectual virtues framework.

On the other hand, there is something *prima facie* odd and questionable about the suggestion that while growth in intellectual virtues is a worthy educational goal, educators need not concern themselves with this goal in any very explicit, deliberate, or systematic way— that, for instance, they need not offer any direct instruction in intellectual virtues, incorporate the language and concepts of intellectual virtue into their teaching and assessment practices, or think systematically about how the various elements of their courses might be related to the intellectual formation of their students.

The question, it seems to me, is whether there exists an approach to intellectual character education that incorporates an explicit and systematic focus on intellectual virtues while avoiding the kind of trivialisation and clumsiness noted above. In the remainder of the chapter, I briefly describe seven plausible and interrelated measures for fostering intellectual character growth in an educational setting.[26] Taken together, they suggest an affirmative answer to our question. They also provide a more concrete idea of what an intellectual virtues approach might look like in practice.

The first measure is predicated on the idea that intellectual character growth in students is not merely a function of interactions that occur between them and their teachers in a classroom. A *supportive institutional culture* also plays an important role.[27] A school culture that promotes intellectual character growth will be one in which the commitment to educating for intellectual virtues is a critical part of the school's identity. This commitment will figure prominently in how the school conceives of itself and how it presents itself to the world. Thus, it will bear upon the school's official mission, hiring and support of faculty, development and review of curricula, public relations and fund-raising campaigns, the stump speeches of top administrators, admissions standards, recruitment efforts, the speakers and other outside voices that are invited to campus, and so on. Institutional support may not always be overt or explicit. It might be reflected, for instance, in a school's deliberate focus on teaching for understanding (versus the short-term memorisation of isolated bits of knowledge), critical thinking, or intrinsic motivation.[28]

A second measure is *direct instruction* in intellectual virtue concepts and terminology. Research on character education also underscores the importance of this strategy.[29] The suggestion is that a rich and informed understanding of the nature and value of intellectual virtues can assist teachers and students alike in their attempts to embody or impart the traits in question. Thus, a teacher attempting to educate for intellectual virtues might begin the year or semester with a brief series of instructional lessons on what intellectual virtues are, their basic structure, what they look like in practice, their value within education and beyond, and how they differ both from other cognitive strengths like hard-wired cognitive abilities and intellectual skills as well as other character strengths like moral and civic virtues. If supported by brief explanations and illustrations over the course of the semester, this initial introduction need not consume a great deal of class time.

Self-reflection and self-assessment are also important strategies for fostering intellectual virtues. They can be used to challenge students to apply their knowledge of intellectual virtues to how they understand their own intellectual character. This might involve the use of an intellectual character self-assessment tool or other exercises that invite students to reflect in honest and concrete ways about their own intellectual character strengths and weaknesses. Such methods could be employed in class, as homework, or as part of a broader advisory or mentoring program. The overarching goal would be a kind of robust self-knowledge that encourages students to begin thinking of themselves in light of intellectual virtue concepts and categories.

A fourth strategy involves *making explicit connections between the course material and intellectual virtues and vices*. These connections can be divided into two broad categories. The first includes connections that arise from the content of the material itself. Suppose, for instance, that a history or science teacher has committed to emphasising and helping her students grow in three particular intellectual virtues. When it comes to studying certain events or figures in science or other areas, she might draw attention to and invite reflection on ways in which one or more of these virtues are manifested (or lacking) in these contexts. Similarly, a literature professor might use the concept of intellectual character as a 'through line' for an entire course. He and his students might approach each narrative with an eye to the presence and significance of intellectual character traits or through the lens of a pre-established subset of intellectual virtues or vices. The second category includes connections that arise, not from the content being studied, but from demands associated with the mastery of this content. In the midst of an especially challenging unit, for instance, a teacher might pause to remind her students of the overarching personal or character-related goal of the course and of how the present challenge is related to that goal. Similarly, she might pause to specify which virtues—whether perseverance, open-mindedness, intellectual carefulness, or otherwise—are especially relevant to acquiring a deep understanding of the material. It is important, of course, that the connections themselves be 'organic' and that they be made by teachers in a way that is authentic and natural. Where this is accomplished, students will be in a better position to see and understand, not just themselves, but also the world around them in rich and informative virtue-relevant terms.[30]

The foregoing strategies are mainly ways of facilitating a certain kind of knowledge: they involve helping students understand what intellectual virtues are and why they matter, what their own intellectual character strengths and weaknesses are, and ways in which intellectual virtues are relevant to what they are learning and encountering in the world. This orientation by itself is a significant pedagogical and educational achievement. But it is no guarantee that students will actually begin to manifest the relevant traits in their intellectual activity. The final three measures are aimed at making some headway along this dimension.

At least as far back as Aristotle, philosophers and other writers concerned with character development have maintained that character virtues (and vices) are formed through the practice or repetition of virtuous (or vicious) actions. As already noted, intellectual virtues express themselves in actions like reasoning, interpreting, analysing, judging, evaluating, and so on. Accordingly, a fifth way of facilitating growth in intellectual virtues involves providing students with frequent *opportunities to practise the actions characteristic of intellectual virtues*.[31] This might happen in class through activities or modes of interaction that require students to adopt standpoints other than their own, use their imagination to extend or apply their knowledge, give reasons in support of their claims, or ask thoughtful and well-formed questions. Such activities offer practice in virtues like open-mindedness, creativity, reflectiveness, intellectual rigour, and curiosity. Similar requirements can be built into exams, papers, and other written assignments. For instance, a teacher might encourage his students to strive for the end or goal proper to intellectual virtues by requiring them to demonstrate a firm personal *understanding* (as opposed to a mere restatement) of the material. Or he might stipulate that any time a student defends a position, the student must attempt to identify the best possible arguments against this position and then respond to these arguments in ways that are intellectually charitable and fair.[32]

A closely related strategy involves *integrating virtue concepts and standards into formal and informal assessments*. At an informal level, one important practice involves calling attention to and praising intellectually virtuous actions as they occur. Particularly where students have an understanding of what intellectual virtues are, and have come to appreciate their value, such feedback can have a powerful motivational effect. At a more formal level, if an exam, paper, or other assignment has been designed to encourage students to practise certain intellectual virtues, this ought to be reflected in the criteria or rubrics used to evaluate these assignments. Incorporating virtue concepts and standards into assessment in these ways is a further way of facilitating the practice of intellectual virtues.

A final measure is also related to epistemic motivation. It consists of the natural and authentic *modelling of intellectual virtues* by teachers and other school leaders. The experience of being taught by an exemplar of intellectual virtue can be an extremely powerful invitation to the life of the mind.[33] Witnessing how such a person reflects on, communicates, and feels about her subject matter can have a profound impact on a student's fundamental beliefs and attitudes toward thinking and learning. Indeed, it is plausible to think that a teacher's other efforts at fostering intellectual character growth will be strongly amplified or diminished to the extent that he models or fails to model intellectual virtues in his own intellectual activity. Accordingly, an indispensable part of trying to educate for intellectual virtues involves exemplifying these virtues in one's teaching and other interactions with students.[34]

We have considered seven strategies for fostering growth in intellectual virtues. Our purpose has been to determine whether there might be a way of educating for intellectual virtues that is deliberate, explicit, and systematic, but that avoids the worries about trivialisation and browbeating noted above. I take it that, when considered as a whole, the strategies just sketched warrant some optimism on this score. While far from exhaustive, they represent a multi-faceted but well-integrated approach to educating for intellectual virtues—one that includes many explicit appeals to intellectual virtue concepts but that is also thoughtful and sophisticated enough to avoid trivialising the goal intellectual character growth or otherwise undermining the willingness or ability of students to pursue this goal.

Is such an approach likely to be *successful*? This depends in part on how exactly one thinks about 'success'. If the question is whether, after several semesters or years of being educated in the aforementioned ways, most students will graduate as paragons of intellectual virtue, then success may not be very likely. Suppose, however, that success is understood in terms of 'meaningful progress' relative to the goal in question, that is, in terms of whether the strategies in question are capable of making an impact on the intellectual character of students significant enough to justify their use. While this remains largely an empirical matter, I take it that the discussion in the present section also justifies some optimism on this point.[35]

NOTES

1. This conception of intellectual virtues differs significantly from that of other historical authors like Aristotle, for whom intellectual virtues are closer to cognitive powers or abilities than they are intellectual character traits. For some recent treatments, see Battaly, 2008; Roberts and Wood, 2007; Zagzebski, 1996; and Baehr, 2011. For a recent treatment on the relevance of virtue epistemology to issues in the philosophy of education, see Macallister, 2012.
2. 'Typically thought of' is significant, since there may be a sufficiently broad notion of the moral or morality according to which intellectual virtues are a subset of moral virtues. For more on the relationship between intellectual virtues and moral virtues see the appendix of Baehr, 2011.
3. For a development of this point, see Chapter 6 and of Baehr, 2011. There I note that the present formulation holds only for 'active' virtues, which, unlike 'passive' or 'negative' virtues, have an active dimension.
4. Henceforth I use the term 'lifelong learner' to refer to the putative character of this state or ideal. Thus my aim in this section is to offer a more specific account of (at least one central part of) what teachers, administrators, and others have in mind when they uphold the value of 'lifelong learning' or trying to make their students into 'lifelong learners'.
5. See Baehr, forthcoming a. As I explain in that work, 'passive' virtues present exceptions to each of the two requirements just noted. Passive virtues are manifested in the *absence* of certain concerns or actions. Such exceptions present no problem, however, for the broader point being made here.
6. Similar arguments could be made about related notions like 'critical thinking' or the 'education of the whole person'.
7. See Williams, 1985. For a recent application of this notion to epistemology and education, see Kotzee, 2011.
8. It is, in fact, quite difficult to pin down exactly which two desiderata Dewey had in mind, if indeed there really are only two (the details seem to vary from description to another). Thus my interest here is perhaps best understood as two desiderata that are at least in the immediate vicinity of what Dewey had in mind.
9. See Baehr, forthcoming b.
10. See Roberts and Wood, 2007, pp. 156–59 or Alston, 2005, p. 32.
11. As this suggests, the kind of understanding sought by an intellectually virtuous agent is indeed *factual* or *true*. The point is that truth or true belief is not the only aim proper to intellectual virtues. For more on what it looks like to teach for deep understanding, see Perkins, 1993 and Wiske, 1997.
12. Thus, I think of rigour in this context as partly a function of the content being taught and partly a function of the sorts of demands it places on learners.
13. Each of these approaches clearly has its strengths. My point at present is that the value instantiated by each one needs to be constrained or complemented by a value instantiated by the other, and that educating for intellectual virtues provides a natural way of integrating both values.
14. See e.g. Siegel, 1985; Ennis, 1985; and Dewey, 1916.
15. If all critical thinking programs were to incorporate an additional focus on intellectual character, then an intellectual virtues approach would not have the advantage I am

suggesting. But neither would this tell in favour of a critical thinking approach vis-à-vis an intellectual virtues approach. Indeed, if the attention to intellectual character development were sufficiently strong and central, the approach in question might not differ in any important way from an intellectual virtues approach, for as indicated earlier in the chapter, intellectual virtues have a skill or ability component that requires competence in at least many of the skills proper to 'critical thinking'.

16. See Siegel, 2004.

17. Ben Kotzee has suggested to me that belief in the value of one's education is partly *constitutive* of a good education. Assuming this is right, it follows that an intellectual virtues approach—focusing as it does on, among other things, students' perception and understanding of the value of thinking and learning—easily satisfies one important requirement on any plausible educational model.

18. For an account of the relationship between intellectual virtue and morally responsible action, see Montmarquet, 1993.

19. See Siegel, 2001. As Ben Kotzee has suggested to me, intellectual (and other character) virtues may be social or relational in an even deeper sense, for it may be that such traits can be fostered only in the context of a community. For present purposes, I shall leave this an open question.

20. This is not, of course, an advantage entirely unique to an intellectual virtues approach. The point is rather that an educator operating within this framework will have an additional strong reason to form trusting and caring relationships with her students, the reason being, again, that doing so is critical to the formative goal of an intellectual virtues approach.

21. See Lickona, 1992.

22. For ways in which educating for moral character can be combined with academic instruction, see Lickona, 1992 and Elgin, 2011.

23. For a related point, see Hare, 1995.

24. See e.g. Oakeshott, 1967, p. 176.

25. For a critique of these approaches to character education, see Kohn, 1993; and for an alternative approach, see Berkowitz and Bier, 2005.

26. These are not at all exhaustive. I propose them as a kind of basic framework that could easily be added to. See Ritchhart, 2001 for several additional strategies. And see Berkowitz and Bier's treatment (2007) of traditional or moral character education for several strategies and principles that have also application to *intellectual* character education. Seider, 2012 is also instructive in this regard.

27. This is one of the findings in Berkowitz and Bier, 2007.

28. For a discussion of the latter see Stipek, 2001.

29. See Berkowitz and Bier, 2007 and 2005.

30. For additional examples along these lines, see Battaly, 2006.

31. Here as well see Battaly, 2006. Ron Ritchhart's discussion of 'thinking routines' (2001) also sheds valuable light on what might look like to give students frequent opportunities to practise various intellectual virtues. See especially pp. 85–114.

32. Of course, this is something that many good teachers already do. This underscores the way in which an intellectual virtues framework can provide educators with the concepts and language to better understand, articulate, and practise much of what they already value and are trying to accomplish with students.

33. See e.g. Oakeshott, 1967 and Walker, 2002.

34. This points to what I take to be the greatest challenge involved with educating for intellectual virtues, namely, the adequate training and formation of teachers and other school leaders. Much of the work of William Hare (e.g. 1993) sheds valuable light on how this challenge might be addressed. While Hare's focus tends to be the focus of open-mindedness in particular, much of what he says applies to the full range of intellectual virtues.

35. I am grateful to Ben Kotzee, Dan Speak, William Hare, Michael Pace, an anonymous referee, and an audience at Chapman University in the fall of 2012 for helpful feedback on earlier drafts of this paper or related material. This work was supported by a grant from the John Templeton Foundation.

REFERENCES

Alston, W. (2005) *Beyond 'Justification': Dimensions of Epistemic Evaluation* (Ithaca, NY, Cornell University Press).

Baehr, J. (2011) *The Inquiring Mind* (Oxford, Oxford University Press).

Baehr, J. (Forthcoming a) The Cognitive Demands of Intellectual Virtue, in: T. Henning and D. Schweikard (eds) *Knowledge, Virtue, and Action* (London, Routledge).

Baehr, J. (Forthcoming b) Sophia, in: K. Timpe and C. Boyd (eds) *Virtues and Their Vices* (Oxford, Oxford University Press).

Battaly, H. (2006) Teaching Intellectual Virtues: Applying Virtue Epistemology in the Classroom, *Teaching Philosophy*, 29.3, pp. 191–222.

Battaly, H. (2008) Virtue Epistemology, *Philosophy Compass*, 3.4, pp. 639–663.

Berkowitz, M. and Bier, M. (2005) The Interpersonal Roots of Character Education, in: D. K. Lapsley and F. C. Power (eds) *Character Psychology and Character Education* (Notre Dame, IN, University of Notre Dame Press).

Berkowitz, M. and Bier, M. (2007) What Works in Character Education, *Journal of Research in Character Education*, 5.1, pp. 29–48.

Dewey, J. (1902) *The Child and the Curriculum* (Chicago, IL, University of Chicago Press).

Dewey, J. (1916) *Democracy and Education* (New York, Macmillan).

Elgin, C. (2011) Science, Ethics and Education, *Theory and Research in Education*, 9.3: 251–263.

Ennis, R. (1985) A Logical Basis for Measuring Critical Thinking Skills, *Educational Leadership*, 43.2, pp. 44–48.

Hare, W. (1993) *What Makes a Good Teacher* (London, ON, Althouse Press).

Hare, W. (1995) Content and Criticism: the Aims of Schooling, *Journal of the Philosophy of Education*, 29.1, pp. 47–60.

Heckman, J. and Kautz, T. (2012) Hard Evidence on Softs Skills, *Labour Economics*, 19.4, pp. 451–464.

Kotzee, B. (2011) Education and 'Thick' Epistemology, *Educational Theory*, 61.5, pp. 549–554.

Kohn, A. (1993) *Punished by Rewards* (Boston, MA, Houghton-Mifflin).

Lickona, T. (1992) *Educating for Character* (New York, Bantam).

Macallister, J. (2012) Virtue Epistemology and the Philosophy of Education, *Journal of the Philosophy of Education*, 46.2, pp. 251–270.

Montmarquet, J. (1993) *Epistemic Virtue and Doxastic Responsibility* (Lanham, MD, Rowman and Littlefield).

Oakeshott, M. (1967) Learning and Teaching, in: R. S. Peters (ed.) *The Concept of Education* (London, Routledge and Kegan Paul).

Perkins, D. (1993) Teaching for Understanding, *American Educator*, 17.3, pp. 28–35.

Ritchhart, R. (2001) *Intellectual Character* (San Francisco, CA, Jossey-Bass).

Roberts, R. and Wood, J. (2007) *Intellectual Virtues* (Oxford, Oxford University Press).

Seider, S. (2012) *Character Compass* (Cambridge, MA, Harvard University Press).

Siegel, D. (2001) *The Developing Mind* (New York, Guilford Press).

Siegel, H. (1985) *Educating Reason* (New York, Routledge).

Siegel, H. (2004) High Stakes Testing, Educational Aims and Ideals, and Responsible Assessment, *Theory and Research in Education*, 2.3, pp. 219–233.

Stipek, D. (2001) *Motivation to Learn* (New York, Pearson).

Walker, L. (2002) Moral Exemplarity, in: *Bringing in a New Era of Character Education* (Palo Alto, CA, Hoover Institute Press).

Williams, B. (1985) *Ethics and the Limits of Philosophy* (Cambridge, MA, Harvard University Press).

Wiske, M. S. (1997) *Teaching for Understanding* (San Francisco, CA, Jossey-Bass).

Zagzebski, L. (1996) *Virtues of the Mind* (Cambridge, Cambridge University Press).

7

Detecting Epistemic Vice in Higher Education Policy: Epistemic Insensibility in the Seven Solutions and the REF

HEATHER BATTALY

Stephen Colbert:	'What do we get from knowing about the Higgs-boson? Do I get my jet-pack now, or teleportation, or light sabres?'
Sean Carroll:	'We get the happy feeling that we understand how the universe works.'
Stephen Colbert:	'So . . . how much did this cost?'

(*The Colbert Report*, airdate 29 November 2012).

The current recession, beginning in 2008, has generated a plethora of arguments for restricting government funding of public universities and of the research they conduct. The Humanities and Social Sciences have been disproportionately targeted by these arguments, but theoretical mathematics and theoretical physics have also come under fire. This is because fields like Philosophy, English, Number Theory, and Cosmology are increasingly perceived by policy-makers as failing to contribute to the economy. In the UK, such arguments have influenced the content of the Research Excellence Framework (REF)—the most recent version of the Research Assessment Exercise (RAE)—which goes into effect in 2014. The REF will be used to allocate research funding to academic departments at UK universities. It evaluates the quality of research based in part on the non-academic impact of such research. Non-academic impact includes impact on, e.g., the economy, public policy, culture, and the environment; and explicitly excludes impact on one's discipline or students. In the US, especially in Texas and Florida, such arguments have generated gubernatorial support for the so-called 'Seven Breakthrough Solutions' (Solutions), proposed by the Texas Public Policy

Education and the Growth of Knowledge: Perspectives from Social and Virtue Epistemology, First Edition.
Edited by Ben Kotzee. Copyright © 2014 The Authors. Editorial organisation © 2014 Philosophy of Education Society of Great Britain. Published 2014 by John Wiley & Sons Ltd.

Foundation, and partly implemented at Texas A&M in 2010. They call for separate tracks and budgets for teaching and research at public universities, and evaluate the quality of research based entirely on the external funding it attracts. It is no surprise that faculty at public universities, especially faculty who work in theoretical fields, are frustrated with these policies. This chapter helps to explain and justify that frustration.

It argues that the Solutions, and to a lesser extent, the REF manifest two key features of the vice of epistemic insensibility. An epistemically insensible policy (i) promotes a failure to desire, consume, and enjoy some knowledge that it is appropriate to desire, consume, and enjoy. And (ii), it does so because it employs a false conception of the epistemic good—it wrongly assumes that such knowledge is not (or is not sufficiently, in the case of the REF) epistemically good. The Solutions wrongly assume that any research that lacks 'impact', in the form of funding, thereby lacks epistemic value. The REF wrongly assumes of otherwise comparable bodies of research, that the research that lacks 'impact' has less epistemic value. Section I provides an overview of Aristotle's analysis of moral vice in people, focusing on the vice of moral insensibility. Section II applies Aristotle's analysis to epistemic vice, developing an account of epistemic insensibility. In so doing, it contributes a new epistemic vice to the field of virtue epistemology. Section III shifts our focus from the vices of people to the vices of policies.

I ARISTOTLE'S ANALYSIS OF MORAL VICE

In NE.VII, Aristotle famously argues that the vicious person consistently performs acts that are in fact bad. She also acts 'in accordance with choice' (Aristotle, 1984, NE.1151a6-7). What is choice? For Aristotle, choice requires rational desire (*boulesis*). One rationally desires x when one wants x because one believes x is good; i.e. one desires x because one values it.[1] Accordingly, choice requires having a conception of the good; having beliefs about the good. In Aristotle's terminology, people who act in accordance with their conceptions of the good 'choose' their actions. Both vicious and virtuous people choose their actions; but the vicious person's conception of the good is false, whereas the virtuous person's is true. In brief, for Aristotle, vice requires one to consistently perform actions that are in fact bad; and to do so because one has a false conception of the good.

Aristotle requires the vicious person to pursue what she believes to be *good*. It is important to note that this is *not* a necessary condition of vice. One can be vicious by knowingly pursuing the bad. One can also be vicious while lacking any conception of the good or bad. Roger Sterling, a character on the television series *Mad Men*, never bothers to develop a conception of the good or bad. But, since he is blame-worthy for failing to do so, and since he consistently does what a self-indulgent person would do, he is still vicious. Aristotle's condi-tions on vice are sufficient. His analysis of vice, unlike those just sketched, enables us to account for the vices of people who falsely and negligently believe that they are doing good. Presumably, Hitler falls in this category—he falsely believed that his actions were good (Battaly, forthcoming).

In NE.III, Aristotle provides analyses of the vices of moral self-indulgence and insensibility. In so doing, he famously argues that: (A) the virtue of temperance hits the mean, whereas the vices of self-indulgence and insensibility do not. (B) The self-indulgent person exceeds with respect to objects, occasions, and frequency because she over-values pleasure; whereas the insensible person is deficient with respect to objects, occasions, and frequency because she under-values pleasure. Finally, (C) he helps us identify which objects the temperate person does, and does not, consume and enjoy. He helps us determine which objects are 'appropriate', and which 'inappropriate' (Battaly, 2010).

Briefly, (A) Aristotle argues that each virtue is a mean in two different ways. Each virtue lies in a mean between a vice of excess and a vice of deficiency (NE.1107a3): temperance lies in a mean between self-indulgence and insensibility. Second, each virtue is a mean with respect to passions and actions. The passions associated with temper-ance and its corresponding vices are pleasure and desire for food, drink, and sex (NE.1118a32). The actions that pertain to temperance and its vices are acts of consumption—drinking scotch, eating cake, having sex—and corresponding acts of omission. The temperate person hits the mean with respect to these passions and actions. He desires, consumes, and enjoys all and only appropriate objects, at appropriate times, in appropriate amounts and frequencies. He acts in accordance with his conception of the good, which is correct. He (e.g.) drinks an appropriate amount of champagne at a wedding because he rationally desires drinking the champagne—he wants to drink it because he (correctly) believes that it will be pleasurable and that (in this case) pleasure is good.

In contrast with the temperate person, (B) the self-indulgent person exceeds with respect to the above passions and actions, whereas the insensible person is deficient with respect to them. Accordingly, the self-indulgent person either desires, consumes, and enjoys appropriate and inappropriate objects; or desires (etc.) appropriate objects on appropriate and inappropriate occasions; or desires (etc.) appropriate objects too frequently. She over-values pleasure—she falsely believes that it is good to pursue any and all opportunities for pleasure. Consequently, she fails to discriminate objects, occasions, and amounts that she should desire, consume, and enjoy from those that she should not.

In contrast, the morally insensible person **(MI1)** consistently fails to desire, consume, or enjoy objects that it is appropriate for him to desire, consume and enjoy.[2] Or, he **(MI2)** consistently fails to desire, consume, or enjoy (appropriate) objects on appropriate occasions. Or, he **(MI3)** consistently fails to desire, consume, or enjoy appropriate objects frequently enough. The morally insensible person places too little value on physical pleasure—he falsely believes that pleasure is bad. Consequently, he chooses to forego opportunities to consume objects that are, in fact, appropriate (e.g. champagne at a wedding). Traditional examples include people who have taken vows of chastity. Contemporary examples include fitness fanatics who deny themselves the pleasure of food and drink (e.g. who *never* eat chocolate cake, or drink scotch) in the name of health (Battaly, 2010, p. 219).

(C) Which kinds of food, drink, and sex are appropriate? Aristotle argues that the temperate person desires, consumes, and enjoys both objects that 'being pleasant, make for health or good condition' and 'other pleasant things if they are not hindrances to these ends . . .' (NE.1119a15-18). In other words, the temperate person desires, consumes, and enjoys objects that actively contribute to health, and some objects that are 'merely consistent' with health (Young, 1988, p. 534). Cauliflower actively contributes to health. McDonald's french fries do not, but nor do they undermine health, provided that they are consumed in limited quantities. In short, both cauliflower and french fries (in limited quantities) are appropriate objects. This means that fitness fanatics who *never* desire, consume, and enjoy foods that are merely consistent with health are insensible. Accordingly, **(MI1)** should read: the insensible person consistently fails to desire, consume, or enjoy objects that either contribute to health or are merely consistent with health.

II THE VICE OF EPISTEMIC INSENSIBILITY

In the moral realm, insensibility is less common than self-indulgence. But, *epistemically*, the reverse seems to be true—we tend to err on the side of deficiency. We are far more likely to fail to consume and enjoy appropriate truths or to consume and enjoy them too seldom, than we are to consume and enjoy truths indiscriminately or too frequently. For instance, perpetually undecided voters fail to consume truths about current events, despite the fact that it is easy for them to do so.[3] Epistemically insensible people may also fail to engage in appropriate epistemic practices—we may avoid testing our own beliefs. And, even if we do manage to consume appropriate truths and engage in appropriate practices, we might still fail to enjoy them.[4] Some students and professors consistently consume appropriate truths and engage in appropriate epistemic practices, but do not enjoy them. Students may do the required reading for a course without enjoying it; likewise, professors may slog through the research required for tenure and promotion without pleasure.

Virtue epistemologists like Linda Zagzebski (1996) and James Montmarquet (1993) have argued that epistemic virtues are character traits that are analogous in structure to Aristotelian moral virtues. Analyses of individual epistemic virtues—e.g. open-mindedness, intellectual courage, intellectual humility—are already well underway in the growing literature in the field. But, with the exception of Fricker (2007), Baehr (2010), and Battaly (2010), there have been few explicit analyses of epistemic vices. This section develops an Aristotelian analysis of the vice of epistemic insensibility. Accordingly, it argues that: (A′) the virtue of epistemic temperance hits the mean, whereas the vices of epistemic self-indulgence and epistemic insensibility do not. (B′) The epistemically self-indulgent person exceeds with respect to epistemic objects, occasions, or frequency because she over-values pleasure as an epistemic good; whereas the epistemically insensible person is deficient with respect to epistemic objects, occasions, or frequency because she under-values pleasure as an epistemic good. (C′) It helps us identify which objects the epistemically temperate person does, and does not, consume and enjoy. That is, it makes some progress in determining which objects are appropriate and which inappropriate.

(A′) Like its moral counterpart, the virtue of epistemic temperance lies in a mean between two vices: epistemic self-indulgence, and epistemic insensibility. Epistemic temperance is also a mean with respect to passions and actions; here, desiring, consuming, and enjoying *epistemic* objects. Which objects are epistemic? There are two basic sorts of epistemic objects: end-states, e.g. beliefs, knowledge, and understanding; and activities, e.g. belief-forming processes and practices, and the epistemic virtues and vices themselves. End-states like beliefs can be true or false, theoretical or practical, and can be about anything from Kate Middleton's hair-colour (or other trivialities) to the Riemann hypothesis (an unsolved problem in number theory). Epistemic activities, like belief-forming processes and practices, can be reliable or unreliable.

The actions associated with epistemic temperance and its vices paradigmatically include acts of 'consuming' propositions (e.g. when reading, listening, or conducting research) and acts of engaging in epistemic practices. They also include corresponding acts of omission. To illustrate, one might consume, or fail to consume, appropriate or inappropriate epistemic objects (e.g. truths or falsehoods about current events); consume or fail to consume them on appropriate or inappropriate occasions (e.g. while listening to a lecture, or while recovering from general anaesthesia); or consume them too frequently or too seldom. The corresponding passions include desiring and enjoying appropriate or inappropriate epistemic objects.

The epistemically temperate person hits the mean with respect to the above passions and actions. He desires, consumes, engages in, and enjoys all and only appropriate epistemic objects, on appropriate occasions, in appropriate amounts and frequencies. Like the morally temperate person, he acts in accordance with a true conception of the good—here, the epistemic good.[5] He (e.g.) consumes facts about current events because he rationally desires doing so—he wants to consume them because he (correctly) believes that doing so will be pleasurable, and that (in this case) pleasure is *epistemically* good. He values pleasure appropriately, as an epistemic good. He recognises that enjoying inquiry has a role to play in the flourishing of epistemic agents. The value that he places on enjoying epistemic objects does not blind him to other epistemic goods (like, truth). He knows which epistemic objects it is appropriate to desire, consume, engage in, and enjoy and which it is inappropriate to desire, consume, engage in, and enjoy.

In contrast, (B′) the epistemically self-indulgent person exceeds with respect to the above passions and actions. She either desires, consumes, engages in, and enjoys appropriate and inappropriate epistemic objects (e.g. truths and falsehoods about current events); or desires (etc.) appropriate epistemic objects on appropriate and inappropriate occasions; or desires (etc.) appropriate epistemic objects too frequently. Arguably, the character Edward Casaubon (*Middlemarch*) and contemporary sceptics in epistemology are epistemically self-indulgent. The epistemically self-indulgent person performs the actions she does because she over-values pleasure as an epistemic good. The value that she places on enjoying epistemic objects blinds her to other epistemic goods, like truth. As a result, she fails to discriminate epistemic objects, occasions, or frequencies that she should desire, consume, and enjoy from those that she should not—she falsely believes that it is good to pursue any and all epistemic objects, occasions, or frequencies that produce pleasure.

The epistemically insensible person is deficient with respect to the above passions and actions. Accordingly, she **(EI1)** consistently fails to desire, consume, engage in, or enjoy appropriate epistemic objects.[6] Or, she **(EI2)** consistently fails to desire, consume, engage in, or enjoy appropriate epistemic objects on appropriate occasions. Or, she **(EI3)** consistently fails to desire, consume, engage in, or enjoy appropriate epistemic objects frequently enough. To illustrate, she may fail to consume truths about current events; or fail to consume them when she has ample time; or she may only consume them a few times per year.

Vices are defects. In what way is epistemic insensibility defective?[7] Arguably, it is defective in two different ways. It is defective because it involves a blameworthy psychology; specifically a false conception of the epistemic good (see below). But, it is also defective because it produces bad epistemic effects (Battaly, forthcoming). Compare two worlds. In the first, epistemic insensibility is prevalent. Many agents fail to consume and enjoy truths about important aspects of their world. As a result, they are uninformed about (e.g.) current events, history, or science. In the second world, epistemic temperance is prevalent. Many agents consume an array of important truths about their world, and enjoy doing so. The first world is epistemically worse-off. For starters, it is likely that fewer propositions are known in the first world; the epistemically insensible are less likely to make discoveries than the epistemically temperate. But, even if the same propositions are known in each world, fewer are shared and transmitted in the first world. There may be individual members of the epistemic community who have knowledge, but the prevalence of epistemic insensibility will ensure that the epistemic community is largely uninformed. This is problematic when its members influence policy, locally or globally. If, like the students and professors above, insensible people in the first world manage to consume appropriate truths but do so without enjoyment, then they will acquire and transmit knowledge. In that case, the harm is a lack of enjoyment, which diminishes their flourishing as epistemic agents.

Like other vicious people, the epistemically insensible person acts in accordance with her false conception of the (epistemic) good. On the standard description, she wants to avoid consuming truths about (e.g.) romantic poetry[8] because she believes that it is epistemically bad to consume such truths. And, she believes that because she believes consuming them will be enjoyable, and that it is epistemically bad to enjoy epistemic objects. Like many of us, she may have been (incorrectly) told that pleasure can only undermine reason, and that there is no place for pleasure in the life of the mind. She took those teachings to heart: she falsely believes that pleasure plays no role in the epistemic good. This false belief about the epistemic good causes her to falsely believe, of some pleasure-producing epistemic objects (e.g. truths about romantic poetry), that they are inappropriate (epistemically bad). On this description of epistemic insensibility, under-valuing pleasure in epistemic objects—falsely believing that pleasure plays no role in the epistemic good—causes the epistemically insensible person to have false beliefs about which epistemic objects are inappropriate.

Would an agent still be epistemically insensible if some *other* false belief about the epistemic good generated her false beliefs about the inappropriateness of particular epistemic objects? Or, would she thereby have a different epistemic vice?[9] Suppose an agent, who satisfies (EI1), falsely believes that truths about (e.g.) romantic poetry are inappropriate, *not* because she under-values pleasure, but because she falsely believes that the epistemic good must be (say) immediately maximally practical.[10] Is such an agent still epistemically insensible? She still satisfies (EI1), and does so because of false beliefs about the epistemic good. But, her failure to consume and enjoy appropriate objects is no longer grounded in false beliefs about *pleasure*. And, one might think this a requirement of epistemic *insensibility*. What if we also suppose that our agent fails to enjoy appropriate objects because she falsely believes that they do not merit enjoyment; e.g. she falsely believes that truths about romantic poetry are unworthy of enjoyment?[11] Perhaps, the notion of epistemic insensibility can be stretched to include this agent. After all, her failure to enjoy appropriate objects would be grounded in her false beliefs about pleasure. And, false beliefs about pleasure would still play a role in her psychology, though not as fundamental a role as they play in the standard description of insensibility. The objection is that this broadened description sounds less like a vice of epistemic insensibility, and more like a vice of epistemic banality or boorishness. It should be noted that work on epistemic vice has just begun. Vices like epistemic insensibility, banality, and boorishness may turn out to be in the same family, and enjoy considerable overlap. One, or more, of these vices may be subsets of the others; or they may often be simultaneously instantiated. In short, this objection, and the boundaries of epistemic insensibility warrant further exploration.

(C′) Which epistemic objects are appropriate? For simplicity's sake, let's focus on beliefs. Aristotle argues that the morally temperate person desires (etc.) objects that actively contribute to health, and objects that are consistent with health. For Aristotle, health is a constituent of the moral good. Analogously, I submit that the epistemically temperate person desires (etc.) beliefs that actively contribute to the epistemic good, and beliefs (etc.) that are consistent with the epistemic good.

Which beliefs are these? What *is* epistemically good? This issue is hotly debated; but it is safe to say that if there are any epistemic goods, avoiding falsehoods and attaining truths are among them. Consequently, false beliefs do not actively contribute to the epistemic good. Nor are they consistent with the epistemic good. True beliefs do appear to contribute to the epistemic good. But, true beliefs can be about anything, from quantum physics to romantic poetry to Kate Middleton's hair-colour to the number of threads in my left sock. Are all true beliefs epistemically good? Are some true beliefs more epistemically valuable than others?

This is tricky terrain, indeed. The epistemological literature contains three well-defended, but competing, views about which true beliefs are epistemically good and what makes them so. Roughly, these views are:

Unrestricted Intrinsic Value (UIV): all true beliefs have intrinsic epistemic value.

Restricted Intrinsic Value (RIV): only some true beliefs have intrinsic epistemic value.

Pragmatic Value (PV): no true beliefs have intrinsic epistemic value; rather their epistemic value is pragmatic.[12]

(UIV) and (PV) agree that all true beliefs are epistemically good; that being true is enough to make a belief epistemically good. They disagree over why true belief is epistemically good: (UIV) contends it is intrinsically good; (PV) contends it is pragmatically good. In contrast with (UIV) and (PV), (RIV) is compatible with the view that some true beliefs (trivial ones) are not epistemically good. It is reasonable to think that one of these views will turn out to be correct, though I won't here attempt to decide which one. The final section argues that if one of these views is correct, then the conceptions of the epistemic good that are employed by the Solutions and the REF are incorrect.

Let's begin with (UIV).[13] Michael Lynch (2004) has argued that all true beliefs are intrinsically *epistemically* good, in virtue of being true. On his view, true beliefs in theoretical physics and theoretical mathematics have intrinsic epistemic value, even if they lack pragmatic, or instrumental, value. For Lynch, even trivially true beliefs—about Kate Middleton's hair-colour, and the number of threads in my left sock—are intrinsically *epistemically* valuable. But, they are not valuable all-things-considered. There are other things of value besides truth (e.g. our time); and sometimes those other things of value outweigh the value of truth. In short, for Lynch, all true beliefs are intrinsically *epistemically* good, but only some true beliefs are good all-things-considered.

Contra Lynch, Stephen Grimm argues for (RIV): only some true beliefs are intrinsically epistemically good.[14] Grimm and Lynch agree that true beliefs about abstract and theoretical matters have intrinsic epistemic value, even if they lack pragmatic, or instrumental, value. But, they disagree about trivially true beliefs. On Grimm's view, trivially true beliefs—about the number of motes of dust on one's desk—lack intrinsic epistemic value. In his words: 'Suppose we take away my finitude . . . in the sense of making me immortal. If . . . counting the motes of dust on my desk seemed worth doing from a purely intellectual point of view, then I can only conclude with Bernard Williams . . . that immortality would be a tedious and dreary prospect indeed, and *itself* not worth having. When the only data we have to go by tells us that there is nothing intrinsically worthwhile at all about counting motes of dusts . . . then we should take these data at face value' (2008, p. 732, his emphasis). So, contra Lynch, truth by itself isn't enough to make a belief intrinsically epistemically valuable. Rather, what makes a belief intrinsically epistemically valuable is its being true *and* its being interesting (2008, p. 735). Which beliefs are interesting? Grimm suggests that beliefs that answer the question 'Why are things this way rather than that?' are interesting (2008, p. 736). In sum, Grimm argues that only some true beliefs are intrinsically epistemically good—the interesting ones.[15] Grimm's view is compatible with claiming that trivially true beliefs are not epistemically good.

In contrast with Lynch and Grimm, pragmatists argue that (PV) no true beliefs are *intrinsically* epistemically good. The value of true beliefs is solely pragmatic, or instrumental.[16] True beliefs are valuable only because they produce something else that is valuable. In the words of William James: 'our obligation to seek truth is part of our general obligation to do what pays. The payments true ideas bring are the sole why of our duty to follow them' (1922, p. 230). Of course, pragmatists like James *define* true belief to be useful belief. For James, to say that a belief is true is just to say that it helps us 'deal, whether practically or intellectually, with . . . reality' (1922, p. 213). True beliefs *just are* beliefs that lead us into valuable relations with reality;

false beliefs do not produce such relations. So, for James, all true beliefs are pragmatically, or instrumentally, valuable; though some will be more valuable than others.

Which beliefs are true—which beliefs lead us into valuable relations with reality? And, which relations are valuable? In James's words: ' "The true" . . . is only the expedient in the way of our thinking. . . . Expedient in almost any fashion; and expedient in the long run and on the whole, of course' (1988, p. 824). Accordingly, true beliefs lead us into a *wide* range of valuable relations with reality: they enable us to survive; to make accurate predictions; and to verify our sense experiences. True beliefs get us all sorts of valuable things: some of which are morally valuable; some of which are practically valuable for our individual lives. This means that, unlike Lynch and Grimm, James treats the epistemic good as a *derivative* of the all-things-considered good. On his view, for a belief to be epistemically good (true) it must be good all-things-considered—it must be expedient in the long run.

What does (PV) say about beliefs in theoretical mathematics? James explicitly argues that beliefs in theoretical fields can be useful. True beliefs in theoretical mathematics may not aid our survival or be practically valuable in our individual lives. They may not even be directly connected to sense experience. But, they do produce valuable 'relations among purely mental ideas' (1922, p. 209). They lead us into 'useful verbal and conceptual quarters' and to 'consistency, stability and flowing human intercourse' (1922, p. 215). In short, James argues that even theoretical truths pay—they enable us to make sense of, understand, and systematise, our beliefs and experiences. What about trivial truths? Pragmatists must claim that even trivial truths have some pragmatic value, though presumably less than other truths. In short, on James's view, no true beliefs are intrinsically epistemically good, but all true beliefs are pragmatically or instrumentally good; and this pragmatic value is at once all-things-considered and epistemic.

To sum up our progress on (C'), at least some true beliefs are appropriate epistemic objects. Which ones? That depends on which of (UIV), (RIV), or (PV) turns out to be correct. Interestingly, all three views claim that true beliefs about theoretical matters are epistemically good—they *actively contribute* to the epistemic good. Recall that the epistemically temperate person desires (etc.) beliefs that actively contribute to the epistemic good and beliefs that are merely consistent with the epistemic good. Accordingly, failing to desire, consume, and enjoy true beliefs about theoretical matters appears to be a mark of epistemic insensibility. Trivially true beliefs are arguably consistent with the epistemic good. If so, people who never desire, consume, or enjoy them are also epistemically insensible.

III EPISTEMIC INSENSIBILITY IN THE SOLUTIONS AND THE REF

An epistemically insensible *person* who satisfies (EI1) fails to desire, consume, or enjoy some true beliefs that it is appropriate to desire, consume, and enjoy. And, she does so because she has a false conception of the epistemic good—she wrongly thinks that such true beliefs are not epistemically good. Analogously, an epistemically insensible *policy* promotes a failure to desire, consume, and enjoy some true beliefs that it is appropriate to desire, consume, and enjoy; and does so because it employs a false conception of the epistemic good—it wrongly assumes that such true beliefs are not, or are not sufficiently, epistemically good. This section argues that the Solutions and, to a lesser extent, the REF manifest these two conditions of epistemic insensibility.

It is important to note that policies are not people. First, policies do not perform or fail to perform actions; people do. When a person is epistemically insensible, she consistently fails to desire (etc.) true beliefs that it is appropriate to desire (etc.). When a policy is epistemically insensible it *promotes* a failure to desire (etc.) such true beliefs in the people to whom it applies. Second, there is a sense in which policies have, and employ, conceptions of the good. The motivations and beliefs which generate policies are often catalogued in their mission statements. But, a policy's employing a particular conception of the good does not entail that the majority of the committee members who created it have the same conception of the epistemic good. If Miranda Fricker's (2010) account of collectives is correct, then a collective of people can have properties that none of its individual members has. So, it may be possible for a policy produced by a collective to employ a particular conception of the epistemic good that none of its members employs. A policy can be epistemically vicious even when the committee members who created it are not (2010, p. 240).

One might worry that this is a category mistake—policies are not the kind of thing that can be virtuous or vicious. In reply, I do not argue that policies share all of the properties of a vicious person. Rather, they manifest two of the same properties that we find in epistemically insensible people: they satisfy a version of (EI1), and do so because they employ false conceptions of the epistemic good.

Further, we use terms like 'unjust' and 'cruel' to describe, e.g. policies that legalise slavery. And, when we do, we sometimes mean that such policies promote actions that harm and disrespect others. If policies can manifest some of the properties that we find in morally vicious people, then they should also be able to manifest some of the properties that we find in epistemically vicious people. Finally, if Fricker is correct, then a policy can have properties that none of its architects has. Consequently, the only place to locate the vice that we detect in a bad policy may be in the policy itself.[17]

Let's begin with the REF. The REF evaluates and ranks the quality of research at academic departments in UK universities according to three criteria: the academic quality and number of research outputs (which accounts for 65% of the overall ranking); the 'impact of research beyond academia' (20%); and the research environment (15%).[18] One of the explicitly stated purposes of the REF is to: 'reward research departments in universities that engage with business, the public sector and civil society organisations, and carry new ideas through to beneficial outcomes.'[19] Accordingly, it defines valuable research partly in terms of its 'impact'. Other things being equal, research that has greater 'impact' gets a higher overall ranking—it is deemed to be better research than that which has lesser 'impact'. The REF defines impact to be: 'any effect on, change or benefit to the economy, society, culture, public policy or services, health, the environment or quality of life, beyond academia.'[20] For instance, 'impacts' include: e.g. improving a business by introducing new products or services; influencing the ethical policies of a business or professional organisation; 'contributing to economic prosperity via the creative sector, including publishing, music, theater, museums . . .'; and enhancing the public's understanding of 'the major issues . . . faced by individuals and society' via appearances in the media.[21] Evidence of impact includes, among other things, revenue from sales and 'funding from public or other charitable agencies.'[22] But, impacts explicitly exclude: the 'advancement of academic knowledge within the higher education sector' and 'impacts on students, teaching or other activities' at one's own institution.[23] It should be noted that 'impacts' must be relatively immediate: they must occur within twenty years of the published research, and for the 2014 review, between 2008 and 2013.[24]

For the REF, is research on the Higgs-boson, or Byron's poetry, or metaphysical four-dimensionalism valuable enough to be promoted? That will depend partly on 'impact', and partly on the other submissions against which such research is measured. Compare the submissions of two Physics departments: P1 and P2 in Table 7.1. The academic quality of the outputs (articles, books, etc.) of each department will be evaluated by a panel of academic experts. This evaluation comprises 65% of the department's overall quality profile (its final ranking of research quality). Imagine that both departments focus on theoretical physics. Now suppose that 100% of each department's outputs are awarded 4* rankings (the highest). But, P1 includes Sean Carroll and other like-minded faculty, whose trade-book sales and whose appearances on television programs like *The Colbert Report* raise the impact ranking of their department to 3* (100% of their submitted case studies are awarded 3* rankings). In contrast, P2 earns an Unclassified impact ranking (100% of their submitted case studies are awarded U rankings—the lowest). Something similar occurs with respect to rankings of environment. The result is that the overall quality profiles of P1 and P2 will be (in percentages of submitted research):

P1	4*	3*	2*	1*	U
Outputs (65%)	100	0	0	0	0
Impact (20%)	0	100	0	0	0
Environment (15%)	0	100	0	0	0
Overall Quality Profile	65	35	0	0	0
P2	**4***	**3***	**2***	**1***	**U**
Outputs (65%)	100	0	0	0	0
Impact (20%)	0	0	0	0	100
Environment (15%)	0	0	0	0	100
Overall Quality Profile	65	0	0	0	35

Table 7.1: Submissions of Two Physics Departments: P1 and P2.

The REF deems the overall quality of research at P1 to be better than the overall quality of research at P2, even though the academic quality of the two bodies of research is identical. So, if forced to choose, the REF would not promote research at P2—it would forego funding some of the best research on theoretical physics in the world. Matters may get more complicated when 100% of P1's outputs drop to a ranking of 3*, and the rest of the data above remain the same.

Granted, in the scenario above, the REF will still promote theoretical research in physics (at P1).[25] But, if Physics departments that focus on theoretical research are judged against Physics departments that focus on applied research, that might not be so. Presumably, it is easier for Physics departments that focus on applied research to generate 'impact.' Accordingly, they may earn higher impact rankings than departments that focus on theoretical research; and, thus, higher overall rankings, even when the academic quality of the two bodies of research is comparable. The same holds for fields like Mathematics, English, and Philosophy.[26] Accordingly, there are some conditions in which the REF might fail to promote theoretical research: when ranking departments that focus on theoretical research against departments (in the same discipline) that focus on applied research. The latter may have an advantage in generating impact, or in being judged as having done so.[27]

To the REF's credit, it allots 65% of its overall ranking of research to academic quality, and expects different disciplines to have different kinds of impact. The Solutions do neither. The most pertinent 'Solution' is number three—'Split Research and Teaching Budgets to Encourage Excellence'—which would establish separate budgets and reward-systems for teaching and research at state universities in the US Solution Three dictates that state funding would still support 'valuable research'. What counts as 'valuable research'? The answer is: 'researchers [would] be paid based on the sponsored research dollars they attract from government, business and private donors.'[28] In short, the Solutions define 'valuable research' solely in terms of research that attracts external funding. In contrast with the REF, they define the quality of research solely in terms of impact; and then, solely in terms of one kind of impact—external funding. For the Solutions, is research on the Higgs-boson, or Byron's poetry, or four-dimensionalism valuable? Not unless it attracts investment from outside the academy.

Both the REF and the Solutions employ conceptions of the epistemic good. After all, both have views about which bodies of research are valuable. Bodies of research are epistemic objects. So, both are engaged in evaluating the quality of objects that are epistemic. Both policies evaluate the quality of research instrumentally, or pragmatically, in terms of 'impact': the Solutions evaluate research solely in terms of 'impact'; the REF, partly in terms of 'impact'. Thus, they treat the epistemic good as wholly, or partly, derivative of other goods. According to the Solutions, for a research project to be epistemically good, it must be instrumentally good, where that is defined as attracting funding. According to the REF, for a body of research to be epistemically good overall, it must have a sufficiently high overall quality profile, where that is defined partly in terms of its instrumental value— its 'impact.' In this vein, Stefan Collini observes that: 'Instead of proposing that "impact" . . . is a social good over and above the quality of the research, the [REF] makes the extent of such impact part of the measurement of the quality of research . . . research plus marketing is not just better than research without marketing; it is better *research*' (2012, p. 175, his emphasis).

Moreover, the Solutions and the REF employ *false* conceptions of the epistemic good, given that one of (UIV), (RIV), or (PV) is correct. We have seen that (UIV), (RIV), and (PV) all maintain that true beliefs about theoretical matters are epistemically good. If either (UIV) or (RIV) is correct, then true beliefs about the Higgs-boson (etc.) will be intrinsically epistemically valuable, even if they produce nothing of pragmatic value. This contradicts the Solutions, which claim that such truths will *only* be epistemically valuable if they are instrumentally valuable—if they attract funding. The REF does a bit better—it allows for the possibility that 65% of the overall epistemic value of research may be due to its intrinsic value. But, as Collini points out, the REF still judges the overall *epistemic* value of research partly in terms of 'impact'. To put the point differently, if (UIV) or (RIV) is correct, then the intrinsic epistemic value of truths about the Higgs-boson makes those truths *epistemically* valuable overall. But, this is not so for the REF. As we saw above, the REF will judge research at P1 to have greater overall epistemic value than research at P2. So, if (UIV) or (RIV) is correct, the REF under-values some of the best theoretical research in the world. It wrongly assumes of otherwise comparable bodies of research, that the research that lacks 'impact' has less overall *epistemic* value.

We get similar results if (PV) is correct. According to (PV), true beliefs about theoretical matters are epistemically valuable because they are pragmatically valuable: they help us understand, and sys-tematise, our beliefs and experiences in the long run. In contrast, the Solutions and the REF take a narrower view of the kinds of impact that influence epistemic value. First, both policies favour immediate over long-term impact. Submissions for the impact section of the 2014 REF allow for research published since 1993, provided that the impact of the research occurs between 2008 and 2013. In the academic world, impact that occurs within twenty years of publication is immediate, rather than long-term. Nor does the 2014 REF acknowledge all imme-diate impacts—it excludes impacts between 1993 and 2007. The Solu-tions does not specify a time-period during which research must be externally funded, but it implies that research that is not currently externally funded is not valuable. Second, both policies favour impact that engages with organisations outside of the academy. For the REF, helping one's students understand Byron's poetry does not count as an 'impact', but helping people outside of the academy understand it does. The Solutions, which restricts 'impact' to investment from outside the academy, endorses an even less plausible view. One's analysis of Byron might have helped multiple students, and even multiple television audiences, think differently about their lives. But, if it hasn't attracted funding, then it is not 'valuable research.' In short, if (PV) is correct, both the Solutions and the REF are employing false conceptions of impact. If we are going to evaluate research based in part, or in whole, on its pragmatic value, then we cannot arbitrarily exclude the pragmatic value of the impact one has on one's own students. We need a pragmatism that is principled—one that does not arbitrarily dismiss some things that are valuable, and one that takes long- term value into account.

As a result of their false conceptions of the epistemic good, the Solutions and, to a lesser extent, the REF satisfy a version of (EI1): they promote a failure to desire, consume, and enjoy some true beliefs that it is appropriate to desire, consume, and enjoy. Given that one of (UIV), (RIV), or (PV) is correct, it is appropriate to desire, consume, and enjoy true beliefs about theoretical matters, including true beliefs about (e.g.) romantic poetry, four-dimensionalism, and the Higgs-boson. The Solutions encourage us to ignore any and all projects that are not externally funded. But, many appropriate projects are unfunded. For instance, projects on (e.g.) four-dimensionalism, and romantic poetry, are typically unfunded: they do not attract funding from business; and funding from foundations and the National Endowment for the Humanities is hard to come by. Accordingly, the Solutions encourage us to ignore truths about *these* theoretical matters; thereby promoting a measure of epistemic insensibility in us. Granted, there is some overlap between theoretical projects that are already externally funded and theoretical projects that are appropriate. This means that, in effect, the Solutions will promote our consumption of a small subset of theoretical projects that happen to be appropriate (those already favoured by business), while simultaneously discouraging our consumption of much theoretical research (e.g. on four-dimensionalism) that is appropriate. The REF, as demonstrated above, does better on this score: provided that (e.g.) physics departments that focus on theoretical research are measured against one another, it will encourage us to consume (e.g.) truths about the Higgs-boson. But, if physics departments that focus on cosmology are measured against physics departments that focus on applied research, the REF might discourage our consumption of truths about cosmology. Whether it does will depend on how it is applied. I hope to have shown that the Solutions and, to a lesser extent, the REF manifest two key features of the vice of epistemic insensibility: they satisfy a version of (EI1); and do so because they employ false conceptions of the epistemic good.

One might object that the Solutions and the REF are not employing conceptions of the *epistemic* good at all. Rather, they are employing conceptions of the good for the state, or the good for the economy, or the good all-things-considered. I submit, with Collini, that they are employing conceptions of the epistemic good; they are just using their conceptions of what is good for the state to define what is epistemically good.[29] Moreover, failing to employ conceptions of the epistemic good would be blameworthy. Hence, objecting that the Solutions and the REF fail to employ conceptions of the epistemic good does not prevent them from being epistemically insensible (see Section I).

One might also object that (UIV), (RIV), and (PV) are not exhaustive. One could argue for a fourth view, a version of which would fit the Solutions:

Restricted Pragmatic Value (RPV): only some true beliefs are epistemically valuable because only some true beliefs are pragmatically, or instrumentally, valuable.

There is logical space for (RPV). But, the version of (RPV) that fits the Solutions bears a double burden. It must argue that no true beliefs are intrinsically epistemically good, not even the interesting ones. And, it must argue that understanding, systematising, and making sense of our experiences and beliefs is not valuable. The ongoing debate over whether pragmatism is correct demonstrates that it is not easy to argue against the intrinsic value of true beliefs. But, it is the argument against (PV) that seals the coffin. It is false that it is not valuable to understand our experiences and beliefs. One could even argue for a fifth view, which defines epistemic value in terms of intrinsic *and* pragmatic value. But, any version that fits the REF will have the burden of justifying its exclusion of long-term impact and impact on one's students.

Finally, one might object that the Solutions and the REF manifest the vice of epistemic 'philistinism' but not the vice of epistemic insensibility (Collini, 2012, p. 90). To be epistemically insensible, a policy must under-value specific truths because it under-values pleasure. But, the REF and the Solutions under-value truths because they over-value 'impact'. In reply, section II suggests that one can be epistemically insensible even if one under-values truths for independent reasons. I have also argued that the Solutions and, to a lesser extent, the REF satisfy two conditions of epistemic insensibility. If those conditions turn out to be common to a family of epistemic vices that includes philistinism and insensibility, then the argument is still on the right track.[30]

NOTES

1. Alternatively, one can want to avoid x because one believes x is bad.
2. In other words, the morally insensible person does not desire appropriate objects, nor does he consume appropriate objects, nor does he enjoy appropriate objects.
3. Epistemic insensibility is a vice, and is thus blameworthy. If one fails to consume appropriate truths due to no fault of one's own, then one is not epistemically insensible.
4. At least these agents are consuming appropriate epistemic objects. Arguably, they are less insensible than agents who do not.
5. Explaining the difference between the moral good and the epistemic good is a daunting task. It seems to require giving definitions of the moral realm and the epistemic realm. Ultimately, the moral good and the epistemic good may enjoy considerable overlap. Explaining the difference between moral insensibility and epistemic insensibility is similarly daunting. They may also enjoy considerable overlap.
6. In other words, the epistemically insensible person fails to desire appropriate objects, *and* fails to consume/engage in appropriate objects, *and* fails to enjoy appropriate objects.
7. I am grateful to an anonymous referee for raising this concern.
8. I assume that truths about romantic poetry are appropriate.
9. One can ask analogous questions of moral insensibility, and of moral and epistemic self-indulgence.
10. She correctly believes that truths about romantic poetry are not immediately maximally practical.
11. She falsely believes that such objects are unworthy of enjoyment because she falsely believes that they are inappropriate.
12. Grimm employs the categories of unrestricted intrinsic value and restricted intrinsic value in Grimm, 2009, p. 248.
13. Advocates of (UIV) include Lynch (2004), and Kvanvig (2003).
14. Advocates of (RIV) include Grimm (2008), Brady (2009), and Goldman (2002).
15. Presumably, Grimm also thinks that the intrinsic epistemic value of interesting true beliefs can be outweighed by other values, and hence that there are some beliefs that are intrinsically *epistemically* good but not good all-things-considered.
16. Advocates of (PV) include James (1922, 1988); Peirce (1992); and Hookway (2003).
17. Thanks to Ben Kotzee for this point.
18. A Brief Guide for Research Users. Online at: http://www.ref.ac.uk/users/ (Higher Education Funding Council for England, 2012a).
19. A Brief Guide for Research Users http://www.ref.ac.uk/users/
20. A Brief Guide for Research Users http://www.ref.ac.uk/users/
21. Assessment Framework and Guidance on Submissions: Main Panel D Criteria. Online at: http://www.ref.ac.uk/pubs/2012-01/ (Higher Education Funding Council for England, 2012b, p. 144).
22. Assessment Framework and Guidance on Submissions: Main Panel D Criteria. Online at: http://www.ref.ac.uk/pubs/2012-01/ (Higher Education Funding Council for England, 2012b, p. 146).
23. Assessment Framework and Guidance on Submissions. Online at: http://www.ref.ac.uk/pubs/2011-02/ (Higher Education Funding Council for England, 2011, p. 48).

24. Submissions for the impact section allow for research published from 1993 to 2013. Submissions for the output section only allow for research published from 2008 to 2013.
25. I am grateful to an anonymous referee for this point.
26. Compare a Philosophy department that focuses on metaphysics to one that focuses on applied ethics.
27. Some of the experts who judge impact rankings will be 'research users' from outside academia. They may be more familiar with the sort of impact generated by applied research. Arguably, in some fields, one can only reliably judge the value of impact from 'the inside'. It may take research users years of study in those fields before they can reliably evaluate the value of impact. Thanks to Ben Kotzee for this point.
28. Online at: http://texashighered.com/7-solutions (Texas Public Policy Foundation, 2008).
29. If we were deciding whether to ultimately endorse these policies, we would need to evaluate their conceptions of what is good for the state. But my argument is more modest. I only argue that their conceptions of the epistemic good are incorrect. It is possible that their conceptions of the epistemic good are incorrect, but their conceptions of the good for the state are correct.
30. I am grateful to Ben Kotzee, Andrew Howat, and an anonymous referee for their insightful comments on an earlier draft, and to Stephen Mexal for his advice about education policy.

REFERENCES

Aristotle (1984) *The Complete Works of Aristotle*, J. Barnes, ed. (Princeton, NJ, Princeton University Press).

Baehr, J. (2010) Epistemic Malevolence, in: H. Battaly (ed.) *Virtue and Vice* (Oxford, Wiley-Blackwell).

Battaly, H. (2010) Epistemic Self-indulgence, in: H. Battaly (ed.) *Virtue and Vice* (Oxford, Wiley-Blackwell).

Battaly, H. (forthcoming) Varieties of Epistemic Vice, in: J. Matheson and R. Vitz (eds) *The Ethics of Belief* (Oxford, Oxford University Press).

Brady, M. (2009) Curiosity and the Value of Truth, in: A. Haddock, A. Millar and D. Pritchard (eds) *Epistemic Value* (New York, Oxford University Press).

Collini, S. (2012) *What Are Universities For?* (Harmondsworth, Penguin).

Fricker, M. (2007) *Epistemic Injustice* (Oxford, Oxford University Press).

Fricker, M. (2010) Can There Be Institutional Virtues?, in: T. S. Gendler and J. Hawthorne (eds) *Oxford Studies in Epistemology*, vol. 3 (Oxford, Oxford University Press).

Goldman, A. (2002) The Unity of the Epistemic Virtues, in: A. Goldman, *Pathways to Knowledge* (Oxford, Oxford University Press).

Grimm, S. (2008) Epistemic Goals and Epistemic Values, *Philosophy and Phenomenological Research*, 77.3, pp. 725–777.

Grimm, S. (2009) Epistemic Normativity, in: A. Haddock, A. Millar and D. Pritchard (eds) *Epistemic Value* (New York, Oxford University Press).

Higher Education Funding Council for England (2012a) A Brief Guide for Research Users. Online at: http://www.ref.ac.uk/users/

Higher Education Funding Council for England (2012b) Assessment Framework and Guidance on Submissions: Main Panel D Criteria. Online at: http://www.ref.ac.uk/pubs/2012-01/

Higher Education Funding Council for England (2011) Assessment Framework and Guidance on Submissions. Online at: http://www.ref.ac.uk/pubs/2011-02/

Hookway, C. (2003) *Truth, Rationality, and Pragmatism* (Oxford, Oxford University Press).

James, W. (1922) *Pragmatism* (New York, Longmans, Green and Co).

James, W. (1988) *William James: Writing 1902–1910*, B. Kuklick, ed. (New York, Library of America).

Kvanvig, J. (2003) *The Value of Knowledge and the Pursuit of Understanding* (Cambridge, Cambridge University Press).

Lynch, M. (2004) *True to Life* (Cambridge, MA, MIT Press).

Montmarquet, J. (1993) *Epistemic Virtue and Doxastic Responsibility* (Lanham, MD, Rowman and Littlefield).

Peirce, C. S. (1992) *The Essential Peirce Vol 1: Selected Philosophical Writings 1867–1893*, N. Houser and C. Kloesel, eds (Bloomington, IN, Indiana University Press).

Texas Public Policy Foundation (2008) Seven Breakthrough Solutions. Online at: http://texashighered.com/7-solutions

Young, C. (1988) Aristotle on Temperance, *Philosophical Review*, 97.4, pp. 521–542.

Zagzebski, L. (1996) *Virtues of the Mind* (Cambridge, Cambridge University Press).

8

Three Different Conceptions of Know-How and Their Relevance to Professional and Vocational Education

CHRISTOPHER WINCH

INTRODUCTION

Relatively little attention has recently been paid to the social aspects of practical knowledge or know-how. Indeed, the growing literature on the relationship between *knowing how* and *knowing that* pays little attention to this relationship. Yet understanding it is very important to an adequate understanding of the various kinds of know-how and their interrelationships. The aim of this chapter is to map the main kinds of know-how that need to be taken account of in a vocational or professional education curriculum, both keeping in mind important philosophical distinctions and at the same time showing how paying attention to the social aspect of knowing how helps to illuminate our understanding of the various kinds of know-how, both philosophically and professionally. It is not to claim that any given programme needs to take all the different forms of know-how into account, but is to claim that the distinctions need to be kept in mind when designing curricula. More positively, a major aim is to shift thinking away from an excessive concentration on *skill* to focus on other forms of know-how whose development is vital to any professional or vocational education worthy of the name and to articulate the main relationships between these different kinds of know-how. It is to be hoped that, by keeping these distinct forms of know-how and their relationships firmly in mind, curriculum designers will find that they have a powerful set of instruments for constructing programmes that are responsive to the richness and complexity of the modern workplace.

Know-how (KH), in contrast to *knowing that* (KT) is a relatively under-theorised epistemic concept, although the philosophical literature on the area has been growing rapidly in the last decade (e.g.

Education and the Growth of Knowledge: Perspectives from Social and Virtue Epistemology, First Edition.
Edited by Ben Kotzee. Copyright © 2014 The Authors. Editorial organisation © 2014 Philosophy of Education Society of Great Britain. Published 2014 by John Wiley & Sons Ltd.

Winch, 2010; Bengson and Moffett, 2012; Stanley, 2011). At the same time, the conceptualisation of know-how in Vocational Education and Training (VET) has, in the Anglophone world, undergone a kind of regimentation, often in the service of a larger normative political project of shifting the balance of power from educational institutions to labour markets (Young, 2012). This, as Young (op. cit.) and others have argued, is part of a 'neoliberal' project to extend the influence of markets on behaviour by making the development of know-how more responsive to the demands of the labour market, through emphasising the visible behavioural and performance aspect of know-how at the expense of what might not be so immediately apparent, but which is, nevertheless critical to the understanding of co-operation and autonomous action in the workplace. This project has co-opted a particular conception of know-how organised around task-types,[1] employing the terms 'skill' and 'competence' as ways of expressing this conception. Quite apart from the narrowing of our understanding of vocationally relevant know-how, this normative project opens the danger of quite serious misunderstandings of important distinctions *within* know-how considered as a broad category, of the greatest interest and relevance to professional and vocational education (PVE). However, it is also important to note that there is a strand of influential philosophical thinking about know-how, broadly speaking in the intellectualist tradition, that emphasises the allegedly non-conceptual nature of know-how, and skill in particular (Luntley, 2011).

This chapter has the main aim of mapping out the terrain of vocationally-relevant know-how, not just with the intention of demonstrating the inadequacies of the project described above but to enable educators and curriculum designers in PVE to have a full picture of the different kinds of know-how that one can reasonably incorporate in both initial (IPVE) and continuing (CPVE) programmes, even if they are not fully realised in all of them. Although the link between know-how and propositional knowledge is an important one for VET (Winch, 2009), it will not be explicitly dealt with in this chapter, except, where relevant, in an incidental way. It should also be stressed that the distinctions made are done so for a particular purpose, to indicate the range and scope of different kinds of PVE. They are not meant to be either absolute or watertight distinctions.

Why, then, attempt to make such distinctions? There are linked philosophical and practical reasons. The principal philosophical reason is that of gaining clarity about know-how so that we can understand it better and resolve connected puzzles. One major way in which these puzzles arise is through attempts at *reduction*, either of know-how to knowing that (broadly speaking the intellectualist tradition) or of knowing that to know-how (what is sometimes known as 'strong anti-intellectualism' (Fantl, 2008)). Attempts at reduction usually arise through commitment to a larger metaphysical project, whether it be a form of behaviourism (and hence materialism) or a form of Cartesianism (with, however, a materialist emphasis e.g. Fodor, 2008). Since I do not have a larger metaphysical intent I will simply claim that keeping an open mind on reduction and placing clarification on the agenda as the main priority is the best way to understand know-how philosophically. Doing so involves paying close attention to important distinctions, whether or not they eventually succumb to one sort of reductionist project or another (something about which I am highly sceptical).

The practical reason for taking such distinctions seriously is easily explained. Workers need to know how to carry out a wide variety of interrelated actions in order to be effective. Enterprises and the organisations which prepare people for working life need to be clear about what type of actions they need to prepare people to carry out and what the relationships between them are. In other words, they need a conceptual map in order to plan what they are going to do. Trying, Procrustean fashion, to squeeze this variety into the restricted vessel known as 'skills', as happens so often in the UK, US and Australia, is unlikely to help employers and employees to be clear about how to act effectively in the workplace. In what follows some important (but non-exhaustive) distinctions between different kinds of know-how and their relationships will be explained.

I SKILL

The concept of *skill* has its primary use in the performance of relatively restricted types of tasks typically, but not exclusively, requiring hand-eye co-ordination and/or manual dexterity. Examples would be: planing a piece of wood, drawing a bow, baking a cake, writing a letter. Some skills can also be exercised without overt physical action, such as performing arithmetical calculations 'in one's head'. As readers will be aware however, the term 'skill' is also used quite promiscuously to refer to the carrying out of very broad tasks (e.g. flying a passenger plane from A to B) or activities that can only with difficulty be described as tasks (e.g. parenting). The term 'skill' is often employed for areas of activity which are not explicitly task-related (e.g. communication skills). The argument is that these examples of 'conceptual inflation', while not always resulting in overt nonsense, are in fact examples of covert nonsense which can lead to both conceptual and practical confusion. The term 'skill' should, therefore, in professional contexts, be pruned back to something much closer to its core usage. Even within this core usage, however, 'skill' manifests great complexity and subtlety.

The exercise of skill is an example of intentional activity. An agent has the intention to carry out a task and the exercise of an appropriate skill is the means of doing it. In this sense, the exercise of a skill is the activation of an agent's disposition. Skills are also normatively bound, both constitutively and evaluatively. Only certain kinds of agency will count as the exercise of a specific skill (planing wood cannot be done by using a hammer) and, typically, there are criteria for *how well* the skill is exercised and for the use of a complex evaluative vocabulary, both positive and negative, to convey such appraisals (she danced gracefully; he diced the onions efficiently). While the intentional nature of skill performance is relatively easy to grasp, the normative nature of skills, particularly in terms of evaluation, is complex. It is worth pointing out, however, that the exercise of skill is an example of *agency*. Although manifested in action, it is always more than merely the manifestation of *behaviour* and purely behavioural measures of skill are in danger of missing out this intentional element (Taylor, 1968).

One further, and vitally important point about the normative aspect of skill attribution needs making. It also applies to the other forms of knowing how that we will go on to consider. Central to the exercise of know-how by humans is that an exercise, or potential exercise, of know-how is appraisable, either as a correct or incorrect example of a type of know-how or through the evaluative vocabulary mentioned above. In other words, although exercise of know-how does not necessarily involve the use of language, understanding know-how, both by the agent and by observers, does. Know-how is a *conception-dependent* concept and types of know-how only exist to the extent that they are understood as such (Searle, 1995; McNaughton, 1988), and fall under concepts understood by those participating in the form of life in which the relevant kind of know-how is exercised and hence are part of the language used by those participants. If one takes the view that an *ab initio* private language is not intelligible, then human kind know-how is only intelligible within a social environment mediated by a public language. This is not, of course, to deny that know-how and appraisal of know-how may not be undertaken by solitaries; rather that such activity can be conducted *ab initio* outside a social medium (Winch, 1998; Verheggen, 1995; Malcolm, 1990).[2]

Describing Skills

The exercise of a skill usually involves the exercise of a *technique* or way of achieving the end to which the skill is directed. According to some intellectualists a key feature of know-how is that it consists in the exercise of a technique or way of carrying out the relevant activity (cf. Stanley and Williamson, 2001). It is not an exaggeration to claim that much of the debate about the coherence of the intellectualist position has centred on an interpretation of the sense in which 'knowing that w is a way to F' can be coherently described as 'know how to F'.[3] Confusingly, the technique is also often referred to as a 'skill', leading to the conflation of skill with technique. In order to carry out a task T, one usually needs to employ a way *w* of doing so. It does not follow, however, that knowing that *w* is a way to perform T constitutes a person's skill. First, because someone may be able to describe *w* without being able to perform it. This reflects an ambiguity in English in the sense of 'know how'. 'I know how to plane a plank of wood so that it is even' can mean *either* I can in fact do so, *or* I can describe how it is done (or both). Context usually ensures that English speakers do not confuse the two senses of 'know how' but other languages make the distinction explicit (German: *können/wissen wie*; French: *savoir faire/savoir comment faire*—cf. Rumfitt, 2003). However, the English elision of the two senses means that it is easier in philosophical discussions to conflate the two when no particular context is in mind. Bengson and Moffett (2007) present arguments from an intellectualist perspective to suggest that there is no equivocation between the two senses (for a critique of this view see Winch, 2010, pp. 29–35). They in turn characterise know-how as 'reasonable conceptual mastery' of the relevant tasks (op. cit., p. 33).

Turning back to skill, conceptual conflation encourages the idea that 'skill' as *agent property* and as *technique* are the same. 'Skill' as agent property carries the sense that a skill is something that is an attribute of an agent, which he may exercise in various ways. It is likely to involve mastery of a technique. A 'technique' on the other hand is a way of acting which may be incorporated into the know-how of different people. This conflation has, in turn, two undesirable consequences. First, it makes it easier philosophically to identify the two reductively by assimilating know-how in the practical sense to know-how in the descriptive sense, so that to say that someone knows how to do something is to say no more than that they possess a technique (Stanley and Williamson, 2001; Stanley, 2011), and second because it encourages educators to assimilate skill as agent property to nothing more than the agent's possession of a technique. We should resist this for two reasons. First, it may be possible to practise a technique which is partially constitutive of an agent's know-how and still not be able to perform the tasks which involve the technique, because the agent cannot perform the technique in circumstances relevant to carrying out the task. Someone may, for example, have mastered the technique of laying bricks but cannot do so in relevant circumstances (e.g. a construction site) because he lacks the experience or character to cope with heights, weather and the exigencies of time and cost. This brings us to the second point; skill as agent property involves a person's character, which affects the way that they perform a task; their diligence, persistence, attention to detail for example are all elements of their skill and cannot be reduced to their possession of a technique.

This brings us to the distinction between 'skill' and the adverb 'skilfully'. The relationship is a complex one, easy to misunderstand. First, a skill can be exercised in a non-skilful way. This can mean either of two things. First that the skill is exercised (the technique applied) to a threshold level that satisfies the description of the task-type to be accomplished, without justifying the application of any positive evaluative vocabulary. Second, it can mean that the task is of such a basic order that evaluative vocabulary is simply not applicable. To say that a task has been performed skilfully is to say that the appropriate positive evaluative vocabulary is applicable to the performance. In this sense 'skilfully' is a thin placeholder term substituting for thicker positive evaluative vocabulary: gracefully, accurately, speedily, considerately etc. This use of 'skilfully' also brings out the teleological aspect of talk about skill. It indicates the extent to which the end to which the task-type is directed has been successfully accomplished and partly indicates *how* it has been successfully accomplished.

The Tacit Dimension of Skill

Although skill almost invariably involves the practice of a technique, and techniques can very often be described, the exercise of a technique can never be adequately captured in a description. There are a number of reasons: first, a description will be incomplete—it can do no more than sketch a procedure. Second, *demonstrating* the technique does overcome this problem, but even this, often highly instructive as it is, cannot substitute for the tacit elements involved in, for example, actually feeling the firmness of the tightening screw, the sensation of losing control in a bend or the growing confidence in controlling one's breathing and, more generally, the extended kinaesthetic awareness of handling an implement (Polanyi, 1958). Mastery of a technique thus has an irreducibly tacit element. There is nothing mystical about this. Polanyi's phrase 'we know more than we can tell' (1967, p. 4) makes sense to the extent that it means that our know-how is usually not exhausted by any description of our actions (Hutchinson and Read, 2011). Does this compromise the claim that know-how is language dependent? No, when all one can say when description is exhausted, is that one does it 'like this' accompanied by action, we should remember that 'like this' an ostensive expression, occupies a conceptual space which is partially constituted by talk about the skill, including descriptions of it. To say that, in these circumstances, there is a non-conceptual element to one's know-how is misleading if one means that this element of action is divorced from conceptual understanding (Luntley, op. cit., p. 12). The situation is very similar to the case of ostensive definition described by Wittgenstein (cf. Wittgenstein, 1953, para 29).[4]

Third, techniques are mostly exercised, especially when they are no longer being practised in a preparatory way, in operational conditions such as those on a construction site described above. In this sense, it is no exaggeration to say that although exercising technique T is often a necessary condition of *knowing how to F*, where F is a type of task, it is very often not sufficient since T, mastered in certain favourable conditions, cannot be practised in a wide range of operational conditions, let alone practised with expertise. English usage does not suggest a firm distinction between practising a technique and knowing how to do something but there does seem to be an important conceptual distinction between the two, in the sense that it is possible to be able to practise a technique for the accomplishment of F but not to know how to F in a range of contextually relevant conditions in which the accomplishment of F is called for (cf. Stanley and Williamson, ibid.).

Finally, in relation to the last point, practising a technique, particularly when such practice is skilful and justifies the application of 'intelligence epithets' (Ryle, 1949, chapter 2) also involves the exercise of judgement. Very often, judgement involves not just whether or not to exercise a technique but the 'fine tuning' of the technique to particular circumstances which may take account of the factors involved in operational conditions. Such judgements, although not always strictly speaking episodic in nature (they may be invoked *post hoc* to justify an action) are very often episodic in that they involve, for example the weighing up of alternative courses of action and the decision to opt for one rather than another. In the first two cases where we say that the exercise of technique does not exhaust what we mean by possessing a skill, we are drawing attention to the subtlety involved in mastery of the technique which cannot be captured by mere description of the technique. In the last two cases, we are drawing attention to distinctions between mastering T where T is necessary for knowing how to F and actually knowing how to F. In this latter case, knowing how to F may involve personal qualities of character and judgement which the practice of a technique by itself may not.

Transferability

It is sometimes said that a skill is 'transferable'. This has to mean more than merely that a skill exercised in situation S can also be exercised in situation T of exactly the same kind. An ability that is only exercised once is only doubtfully a skill. At a minimum one would expect repetitions of the practice of a technique in a range of *similar* situations. Exercising a skill (and other forms of know-how) is part of a practice in which more than one person takes part. Although there may be solitary practices that are derivative of social ones, there cannot be an *ab initio* solitary practice in this sense. Taking part in a practice also involves being involved in recurrent activity bound by common purposes. Someone who successfully accomplishes an activity through deception or fluke may be said to be *conforming* to the rules of the practice but not *following* the rules of the practice which are socially constituted (Wittgenstein, op. cit., para 199 ff.). One may not necessarily expect repetitions in an indefinite range of different and especially more demanding conditions. However, it is often the case that the same technique may be required in different *projects*. For example, techniques practised by carpenters in furniture making may also be applicable in the construction industry. However, it is usually the case that such transferability presupposes *adaptability* to the new operational conditions of the different project. The mere possession of a potentially transferable skill cannot imply that the skill (as a personal attribute) is actually transferable. Transferability in this sense should be contrasted with *transversality*; a property, properly speaking, not of skills but of a different type of know-how (see next section).

II ADVERBIAL VERBS

Not all know-how should be conceptualised as *skill*. Skills, as we have seen, consist largely in the carrying out of types of task, often in a range of different conditions. They do not consist merely in the mastery of technique. However there is a range of actions and abilities which cannot be identified with types of task but which are, neverthe-less, also connected with goals and circumscribed by norms. Exam-ples include: obeying, hurrying, attending, co-operating. . . . They are connected with the ways in which certain actions are carried out and some of them are associated with *thinking* in a broad sense of that term (Ryle, 1979). Their criteria of identity are more diffuse than those for skills, and although it is probably an exaggeration to call them family resemblance concepts, they do come in many different instantiations in a range of different contexts, which, at their extremes, may be very different. Thus, as is the case with family resemblance concepts, there is a range of criteria of necessity and sufficiency for identity which shifts as one moves from context to context (Beardsmore, 1992). For example, *planning* in one context, such as architecture, may involve the drawing up of diagrams as a requirement, whereas this need not be the case with cooking. Indeed, in the latter case it may in some circumstances be careful and systematic cooking itself that is *suffi-cient* to characterise it as planned. It is not so clear however, that there is not some common thread that runs through the range of such concepts of second-order abilities. Some of these are of particular importance for our understanding of know-how in general and of PVE in particular. These are associated with longer-term episodes of agency than those that are usually associated with the tasks usually related to skills.

For lack of a better term I will call these *projects*, or activities that demand intentional action over an extended period of time, involving the carrying out of articulated sequences of tasks in the pursuit of a larger goal such as the production of an artefact or service. Key forms of know-how here are*: planning, controlling, co-ordinating, commu-nicating* and *evaluating*. These and their relationships will be dis-cussed in more detail below. It can be seen that these fall into Ryle's category of 'adverbial verbs' by virtue of the fact that they are not associated with any particular type of task or skill and therefore to designate them as 'planning skills' or 'communication skills' is mis-leading, although they may make use of such skills. The reason is not only that they may be manifested in different ways through the per-formance of different kinds of task, but also that a particular form of their manifestation is not sufficient to guarantee that they are actually exercised. To take an example, *communicating* may be carried out in various ways through speech, writing, signalling etc. and different forms of communication may be appropriate to different contexts. However, although it may be necessary to adopt one of these methods of communicating in order to communicate, doing so does not guar-antee that one does, in fact, communicate. This is not merely because one may not succeed in getting oneself understood, but also because one may fail to say anything coherent (that *could* be understood see the example in Hertzberg, 2012). Crucially, it is the *manner* in which one acts which determines whether or not an act of communication takes place. Exercising appropriate 'communication skills' will not be enough.

It is the fact that one exercises one's skills in writing, for example, not just to articulate grammatical and meaningful sentences, but so that one has something to say which is understood by someone else in a particular context (Rhees, 1998, chapter 10). One way of putting this is that the act of communicating, which may well consist of *skilled* performances of articulation or writing, may not be sufficiently thoughtful or coherent to constitute an act of communication (something that could be understood in appropriate circumstances). In such circumstances we might say that someone was not communicating, but 'going through the motions' of doing so—that is, successfully performing tasks that were partially criterial for an action of this type, but failing to do so in such a way that the second-order act (of communicating, for example) *was* actually performed.

Thus, not only is the manifestation of one of these abilities *polymorphous* (it can take different forms), but it cannot be identified with any sufficient set of such forms, but needs to be manifested in a manner which actually realises the intended purpose, for example a piece of writing that really does communicate something meaningful or coherent, at least to some extent.[5] This does not mean that there needs to be a mental accompaniment or precursor, it can mean that the ability is exercised with sufficient care and attention to characterise it as communication, rather than merely going through the motions of communicating. At first sight this looks like the distinction made above between mastery of a technique and knowing how to do something that involves using the technique. These former kinds of ability do indeed involve the notion of a threshold level of performance below which, for example a piece of writing is not even a grammatical or meaningful sequence, but the latter involve something more, namely the realisation of the purpose of communicating what it is intended. The ability to communicate is evidently not the mastery of one set of skills, as there are different ways of communicating. Neither though is it merely the mastery of different sets of skills. An illiterate may be very effective at oral communication, but he cannot communicate if he does not have something meaningful to say, in a manner which is capable of being recognised as such by an audience in an appropriate context.

But his ability to communicate effectively also depends on being able to say something meaningful in a wide range of situations, very often to different audiences. With a polymorphous activity, the successful accomplishment of the objective is much more related to the context in which the activity is carried out than is the exercise of a skill and its success is even more dependent on the ability of the agent to respond to the exigencies of context. The same type of activity (e.g. planning, co-ordinating) can be manifested in the exercise of different sets of skills, depending on context. A skill, on the other hand, really does need to be the accomplishment of the same type of task in different circumstances, albeit attuned to contextual exigencies. As we saw, it is doubtful whether the exercise of a technique in a limited range of circumstances would be sufficient to characterise someone as skilled in the relevant task-type. The bare use of technique to a threshold level does not count as know-how, even though one could, at a stretch, describe it as a skill in the sense of nothing more than the manifestation of technique. Here it very similar to enactive know-how in the sense of giving an account of what is involved in the know-how rather than the know-how itself (Rumfitt, op. cit.). In the case of a polymorphous activity, there is no reason to suppose that it is, in every case, the accomplishment of the same type of task that is in question, but the accomplishment of *different* types of tasks in a wide variety of different contexts. It is evident that some at least of these abilities not only presuppose the existence of a social context for their learning and exercise, but that it also makes no sense to think of them as solitary activities: communicating and co-ordinating are obvious examples, but many forms of planning and evaluation have an essential social dimension. Furthermore, the accomplishment of such tasks must be effective beyond the threshold performance of the presupposed skills. Just as the evaluative vocabulary of 'intelligence epithets' is often ascribed adverbially (*A* delivered the speech clearly and concisely), so exercise of an 'adverbial verb' is built into the performance of tasks in the service of a larger purpose than the accomplishment of the task to which the skill is directed, and it is built into it in such a way that it has to be of a certain quality in order to count as that kind of ability. This means that it must be carried out with a degree of care and attention that transcend the performance of the tasks which are means to the end. There can be acts which look like planning, communicating and so on, which *appear* to be manifestations of a polymorphous ability, but which are not actually acts of planning or communicating because they do not succeed in accomplishing more than the underlying tasks on which the ability, in that particular context, depends.

An activity like *planning* which is manifestly associated, in different situations, with *different* types of task like drawing, discussing, soliloquising, writing notes and so on, is an example. And even though in many situations planning almost requires such acts in order to *be* planning, the performance of such acts, without the care and attention that goes into the accomplishment of the purpose, will fail to be planning and will only succeed in being the outward manifestation of that ability through the performance of such tasks as drawing, soliloquising etc.—these could be called 'planning skills' exercised to no more than a threshold level. The case of planning is further complicated by its 'forward reaching' quality, which means that planning can only be judged to be such either if it continues to be manifested in the set of activities that constitute *realisation of the plan* or, more rarely, if one can reasonably infer that the agent would realise the plan if he had been allowed to. And here the inference often depends on what we know of the agent's *prior* ability to realise a plan in other circumstances. Sometimes, as in the example of some kinds of cooking (see above) it also make sense to say that the planning is immanent in the realisation of a project (see also Weil, 1955b, p. 89) or through explorations with the material, or sometimes as accompaniments of an activity in a social context through, for example, a conversation about the topic.

Another respect in which polymorphous action differs from skill is its sensitivity to context. A skill is associated with a task-type and the task may or may not be accomplished. Context will very often affect whether or not the skill can be practised. As we saw, it is possible to be able to practise a skill in a particular context without knowing how to accomplish the tasks for which practice of the skill is a necessary condition in a range of more demanding situations. With a polymorphous activity, the accomplishment of the objective is even more related to the context in which the activity is carried out and its success is largely dependent on the ability of the agent to respond to the exigencies of context by exercising different skills in different contexts in order to accomplish the objective. Polymorphous abilities are *second-order abilities* which are manifested in first-order activities such as the performance of tasks, possibly articulated sequences of tasks, and are partly manifested in the manner in which these articulated sequences of first-order tasks are performed. The context in which they are exercised is important, not just for their identification (which may be manifested in different task-types in different contexts), but also in respect of the evaluations that are possible for them. It thus seems to be a consequence that the individuation of these second-order abilities is more complex than the case with skills. Skills can be individuated by the task-type to which they apply and contextual variation can sometimes blur the boundaries of one task-type and another. In the case of second-order abilities, however, variation is much wider and thus so is individuation.

Like first-order abilities, polymorphous abilities are apt for the use of evaluative vocabulary to describe the success or lack of it with which they are carried out. Given that such activities as *planning* or *evaluating* may look very different according to the different contexts in which they are done (contrast planning the building of a house with planning a lesson—not to mention the multifarious ways in which either of these types of activities can be carried out), we can expect the evaluative vocabulary that is deployed in the assessment of second-order abilities of this kind to vary considerably across these contexts as well. This point actually leads to a puzzle about them. Although such abilities are often called *transversal* or *extra-functional* (Hanf, 2011, p. 57), indicating that they occur across a range of different spheres of human activity, it does not follow that they are *transferable* abilities even in the limited sense that we saw that skills are. Because of their context dependency, their criteria of identity shift considerably and it follows that manifestation of the ability in context *A*, which is sufficiently accounted for by characteristics *a*, *b* and *c* will not necessarily be the same as its manifestation in context *B*, where characteristics *c*, *d* and *e* may be sufficient. This contrasts with the relatively stable criteria of identity of a skill across different contexts. The skill, largely but not completely identified with mastery of a technique for the performance of a task-type in relevant conditions, can be identified through the type of task, in whatever context it occurs. We cannot, therefore, make any assumptions that the ability of someone to plan, co-ordinate or assess manifested in one sphere of activity will be manifested in another, let alone in the same way. Nevertheless, there is a sense in which we *do* expect this kind of transfer and it is, to some extent, reasonable to do so. The sense in which this is the case will be returned in the final section of this chapter.

Second-order Abilities and Thinking

There is a current of philosophical reflection that makes a strong association between second-order abilities and *thinking* (e.g. Ryle, 1979). When Wittgenstein (1967) calls thinking a *ramified concept* ('A concept that comprises many manifestations of life. The *phenomena* of thinking are widely scattered': Wittgenstein, 1967, para 110) he has at least partly in mind the ways in which context and type of activity affect its manifestation. But in what sense does it make sense to say that second-order abilities are closely related to thinking? To understand this, it is helpful to go back to the earlier discussion of the relationship between the practice of a skill and the use of evaluative terms to appraise it. When know-how manifested through skill is praised, the *manner* in which the action is carried out is being assessed and very often this will include for example, consideration of the degree of *attention* and *care* with which it is done, as well as consideration of whether or not action was preceded by judgement or reasoning.

While this is true of first-order ability, it is even more true of some second-order abilities, whose more nebulous nature means that their very *identification* requires that they display some of the attributes of thinking. While it is possible to perform the types of first-order activity associated with, say controlling or co-ordinating without actually controlling or co-ordinating, it is not possible to actually control or co-ordinate without manifesting certain qualities in the articulated sequence of first-order activities that, in the appropriate context, constitute controlling or co-ordination. These are the kinds of activities which, if they are to be distinguished from their facsimiles, have to be done in a certain manner, that is, with care, attention and judgement. These attributes of manner are not optional extras, but intrinsic features of the second-order activity and we associate them with thoughtfulness in action and thinking, even if the thinking in question is not necessarily episodic or semi-episodic ratiocinative soliloquising conducted with care and attention. Thus, although thinking is quite properly associated with many first-order abilities, it is *immanent* in any second-order activity of the kind associated with the bringing into effect of an intended sequence of actions that results in the creation of an artefact or a service, even though it may well look different in different contexts.

III   PROJECT MANAGEMENT

We have discussed abilities exercised in activities related largely to the accomplishment of relative restricted types of tasks such as *skills*. It is not so nearly true, however, of the kinds of abilities designated by adverbial verbs. For this discussion I will concentrate on those that are central to vocational and professional activity, namely: planning, co-ordinating, controlling, communicating and evaluating. They may, to some extent, be employed in the exercise of skill and related forms of know-how associated with the accomplishment of tasks, but are arguably more at home on a broader canvass where an agent's intentional rationality is employed in the forming and putting into effect of a project that extends over time and involves the articulation of a series of interconnected activities oriented towards the production of a complex good or service.

This family of second-order activities is clearly a close one, and the boundaries between them are not always obvious when they are expected to be exercised jointly, as is the case in many professional and vocational activities. However the distinctions that they express matter. Furthermore, their specification relative to different occupations is important and in some cases their exercise is more dependent on social considerations than is the case for others. It is worth pointing out, however, that German VET regulations specify the acquisition of social competences as part of a form of occupational capacity, emphasising the importance of social interaction in the successful pursuit of a recognised occupation. The close links between them are recognised in, for example, German VET specifications (for Germany see KMK, 2011, particularly pp. 14–17).

While there is no obvious conceptual cut-off point between a task and a project we can specify the attributes of: *complexity, length, difficulty* and *manifest intentionality* in drawing the contrast between the two. *Manifest intentionality* is a key attribute.[6] It signifies the fact that the forming and execution of a plan, is a key feature of projects, while not of tasks, where execution alone is the imperative. In the case of a skill, a task is set and one's intentional rationality can then be directed towards its accomplishment. In the case of task-types that have been repeatedly accomplished by an agent or which are very simple, the intentional rationality (in the sense of forward planning) involved may be minimal, although situational judgement may be called for. A project, on the other hand, is typically a form of agency whose contextual features require some originality in devising a strategy and procedures for its accomplishment. Thus the contrast would arise, for example between the following: building a house rather than a wall; a plumbing system rather than a stretch of piping; writing a book rather than a short stretch of prose; successful healing of a patient rather than the dressing of a wound; a year of farming rather than the planting of turnips.

The process of devising and putting into effect of a project I will call *project management*. Much paid work does not involve project management. Work that involves the decomposition of tasks into such tiny and specialised sub-segments that they can virtually be done by an automaton, clearly does not involve project management, or even much in the way of the exercise of skill. However, the *division of labour*, or the practice that has existed since time immemorial, of allocating different spheres of activity to different individuals or groups, is perfectly compatible with the pursuit of project management. The division of labour is recognised, for example, in the division of different types of economic activity into *sectors* and the division of types of work into *occupations*.[7] Within a given division of labour it is possible to devise occupations whose main aim is the creation of goods and services characteristic of the segment of human endeavour which the occupation is designed for or has evolved to address. Such creation may, and frequently does have the characteristics of project management.

It involves what commentators like Marx and Kerschensteiner have claimed is *the* characteristic feature of human action: the forming and putting into effect of a plan. This is not to be reduced to separate activities of *planning* and *execution*, although there are no doubt various more or less definite sequences of activity involved in project management. Project management is not the mere ordering of a set of tasks, but the articulation of an extended form of agency which involves thought in the broadest sense. To be more specific, although planning and execution are key features of project management, it is erroneous to think that this is all that there is to it. Planning, to take the most obvious example, may involve prior activity such as constructing a blueprint, but it need not. As already noted, it may to a greater or lesser extent be immanent in the carrying out of the project. It may also involve complex forms of social interaction that occur both prior to and during the carrying out of the project.[8]

However, there is much more to it than that. *Controlling* the execution of a project for example, involves monitoring and attending to processes as well as the accomplishment of specific physical and mental tasks. It is controlling, rather than merely performing that marks out activity performed within the context of a recognisable project rather than as part of a fragmented labour process managed by someone else.[9] As such it involves thought as part of its very nature. *Communicating* and *co-ordinating* are likewise very often features of both planning and execution and are often a component of controlling. Communicating is obviously an integral part of the social aspect of project management and is key to the success of most types. It takes place through different media, with other individuals with different knowledge and status and can often be very demanding, not only requiring clarity, but also tact and understanding. Successful communication is also very often the means by which successful co-ordination takes place, that is, the joining together of different components in a project so that the whole is successfully carried out.

Just as second-order know-how necessarily involves thought and attention, so also does project management, not only by subsuming the intellectual activities involved in second-order know-how, but also through the articulation of a complex and extended form of agency. As noted earlier, this does not entail that intellectual and non-intellectual activities are always articulated in sequences of the former (typically embodied in planning of some kind) followed by the latter, but they may occur in a more integrated way such that the intellectual work required for the enactment of the project is immanent in many of the activities directly needed to bring it about. Project management does not, therefore, require a strict division between intellectual and manual labour, although it is necessarily itself an intellectual form of agency.

Self-management is a necessary part of project management. In forming and carrying through a project an agent manages him- or herself as an agent in its enactment. In doing so, and in encountering obstacles and problems along the way, he learns about his own capacities and their limits and, in doing so can learn how to push those limits back. In an important sense therefore, agents engaged in project management learn about themselves and, in doing so, acquire attributes which, although not strictly transferable, allow them to act confidently in situations which are, to varying degrees, cognate with those that they have already encountered. Specifically, the confidence to approach a project in the expectation of a successful resolution, gained through the experience of success in exercising skills, planning, overcoming difficulties and solving problems, often in concert with other people, develops attributes of character that are a personal resource other contexts. There is ample evidence that forms of apprenticeship that involve extensive project management lead to occupational and even sectoral mobility.[10] It should not be forgotten, however, that such qualities can also be developed *within* one's chosen occupation, allowing one to rise within it to positions of greater autonomy and responsibility, as with the German *Meister* qualification.

To summarise, the ability to manage a project, necessarily built on second-order abilities involving forms of independent action, is crucial to the development of personal characteristics that have an important role to play, not just at work but in other areas of life where self-knowledge, persistence, confidence and cooperativeness are valuable attributes. This points to the way in which project management, developed in work contexts, where coping with the exigencies of non-simulated environments is paramount, has profound educational benefits for individuals *as persons* as well as for their capacities as workers.

What is the relationship between *skill, tranversal ability* and *project management ability*? I suggest that it is a kind of nesting relationship. There will be no project management ability without some transversal ability, even though different projects may require different mixes of transversal ability. Similarly, one cannot exercise an ability like the ability to plan or to co-ordinate without exercising some skills, even though these may vary widely from activity to activity or even from person to person. Finally, it is doubtful whether one could be skilled at anything without possession of an appropriate technique, although as we have seen, possession of a technique is very often not sufficient for ascription of a skill. There thus appears to be a hierarchical relationship between skill (and its technique component), transversal ability and project management ability. This is not just an abstract conceptual point, but has significant practical implications, particularly for the design of professional curricula. If, for example one cannot manage a project without possession of the appropriate transversal abilities and skills, then a curriculum that ignores this relationship and fails to provide appropriate forms of ascent from one kind of know-how to the next is likely to end in disaster (see Winch, 2013 for more on this).

IV   CODA: TOWARDS OCCUPATIONAL CAPACITY

As noted in Section III, the ability to manage a project successfully is, in many countries, not just a precondition of becoming a practitioner of that occupation but potentially of others as well. However, whatever occupation one settles on, *occupational capacity* is important and presupposes the abilities discussed in the previous sections. This is particularly the case in those societies which have well-developed and formally defined conceptions of an occupation such as the German *Beruf*, which entail a wide ranging, interlocking sphere of activity as well as an established place in the social order for individuals who acquire occupational capacity (*berufliche Handlungsfähigkeit*) and practise it.[11]

What does a fully-formed occupational capacity look like? Self-evidently it encompasses the varieties of professional know-how already described, in particular the ability to manage a project in the sense described in the previous section, but there are other important attributes. These include systematic knowledge, the ability to keep abreast of changes in the occupation and the environment in which it is practised and an appreciation of the standards of excellence that apply to the goods and services produced as well as to the way in which these standards are understood in the wider society (see MacIntyre, 1981; for a sympathetic critique, see Hager, 2011).

This is not the place to present a full account of occupational capacity but I have, within this chapter, described the kinds of agency which are essential to its successful development.

NOTES

1. When one ascribes skill to an individual it relates to more than one (token) task, but to a range of tokens and potential tokens which have much in common. How clear the boundaries are between one type of task and another is sometimes unclear, hence problems with 'transfer'.

2. 'Animals know how to do many things and they do not possess language.' True, but this is no objection to the claims made above. Some attributions of know-how to animals are figurative and some are legitimate extensions of our concept of know-how to the animal world, including recognition of primitive normative and evaluative behaviour (see Baker and Hacker, 1984, pp. 254–255).

3. Stanley and Williamson's preferred construal of know-how constructions is: roughly that to say that *A knows how to F* is to say that *A knows that w is contextually appropriate way to F in a practical mode of presentation, where 'w is a contextually appropriate way to F' is a Russellian proposition* (op. cit., pp. 426–427).

4. I owe this observation to Alan Cribb.

5. An apparent counterexample would be *trying* to do something and not succeeding in doing it. *Trying* has the transversal properties described above and yet one can try and fail. However, one can only be said to be trying if one does actually make a serious effort to do something, whether or not one fails. One can 'go through the motions' of trying without actually doing so. Thus even in such a case, there is a 'success criterion' for correct attribution.

6. See Marx's statement: 'We pre-suppose labour in a form that stamps it as exclusively human. A spider conducts operations that resemble those of a weaver, and a bee puts to shame many an architect in the construction of her cells. But what distinguishes the worst architect from the best of bees is this, that the architect raises his structure in imagination before he erects it in reality' (Marx, 1970a [1887]). There are problems connected with the apparently asocial nature of this definition, which plays down the social aspect of creative and imaginative endeavour.

7. It is an oversimplification to describe occupations as subdivisions of sectors, as many of them cut across different sectors, see ILO (2012) classifications.

8. For a striking example related to construction, which stands in contrast to Marx's example, see Weil, 1955a, pp. 133–4.

9. See for example, Smith, 1981 [1776], pp. 785–786, for an account of the likely effects of extreme forms of the fragmentation of the labour process.

10. Wolf, 2011, e.g. pp. 33–4.

11. Greinert, 2007; Hanf, 2011.

REFERENCES

Beardsmore, R. W. (1992) The Theory of Family Resemblances, *Philosophical Investigations*, 15.2, pp. 111–130.

Bengson, J. and Moffett, M. A. (2007) Know-how and Concept Possession, *Philosophical Studies*, 136, pp. 31–57.

Bengson, J. and Moffett, M. A. (2012) (eds) *Knowing How. Essays on Knowledge, Mind, and Action* (Oxford, Oxford University Press).

Baker, G. P. and Hacker, P. M. S. (1984) *Language, Sense and Nonsense* (Oxford, Blackwell).

Fantl, J. (2008) Knowing-How and Knowing-That, *Philosophy Compass*, 3.3, pp. 451–470.

Fodor, J. (2008) *LOT2* (Oxford, Oxford University Press).

Greinert, W-D. (2007) The German Philosophy of Vocational Education, in: L. Clarke and C. Winch (eds) *Vocational Education: International Approaches, Developments and Systems* (London, Routledge), pp. 49–61.

Hager, P. (2011) Refurbishing MacIntyre's Account of Practice, *Journal of Philosophy of Education*, 45.3, pp. 545–561.

Hanf, G. (2011) *The Changing Relevance of the Beruf*, in: M. Brockmann, L. Clarke, G. Hanf, P. Méhaut, A. Westerhuis and C. Winch (eds) *Knowledge, Skills and Competence in the European Labour Market* (Abingdon, Routledge), pp. 50–67.

Hertzberg, L. (2012) Rhees on the Unity of Language, *Philosophical Investigations*, 35.3–4, pp. 224–237.

Hutchinson, P. and Read, R. (2011) De-mystifying Tacit Knowing and Clues: a Comment on Henry *et al.*, *Journal of Evaluation in Clinical Practice*, 17.5, pp. 944–947.

International Labour Organisation (ILO) (2012) Online at: http://unstats.un.org/unsd/class/family/family1.asp (accessed 17 October 2012).

KMK (Kultusminister Konferenz) (2011) *Handreichung für die Erarbeitung von Rahmen-lehrplänen der Kultusminister Konferenz für den berufsbezogenen Unterricht in der Berufsschule und ihre Abstimmung mit Ausbildungsordnungen des Bundes für anerkannte Ausbildungsberufe*. Online at: http://www.kmk.org/fileadmin/veroeffentlichungen _beschluesse/2011/2011_09_23-GEP-Handreichung.pdf (accessed 17 October 2012).

Luntley, M. (2011) What Do Nurses Know?, *Nursing Philosophy*, 12, pp. 22–33.

MacIntyre, A. (1981) *After Virtue* (Notre Dame, IN, University of Notre Dame Press).

Malcolm, N. (1990) Wittgenstein on Language and Rules, *Philosophy*, 64, pp. 5–28.

Marx, K. (1970a) [1887] *Capital*, Volume 1 (London, Lawrence and Wishart).

McNaughton, D. (1988) *Moral Vision* (Oxford, Blackwell).

Polanyi, M. (1958) *Personal Knowledge* (London, Routledge).

Polanyi, M. (1967) *The Tacit Dimension* (New York, Anchor).

Rhees, R. (1998) *Wittgenstein and the Possibility of Discourse* (Cambridge, Cambridge University Press).

Rumfitt, I. (2003) Savoir Faire, *Journal of Philosophy of Education*, 100.3, pp. 158–166.

Ryle, G. (1949) *The Concept of Mind* (London, Hutchinson).

Ryle, G. (1979) *On Thinking* (London, Hutchinson).

Searle, J. (1995) *The Construction of Social Reality* (Harmondsworth, Penguin).

Smith, A. (1981) [1776] *Adam Smith: The Wealth of Nations* Book V (Indianapolis, IN, Liberty Press).

Stanley, J. (2011) *Know How* (Oxford, Oxford University Press).

Stanley, J. and Williamson, T. (2001) Knowing How, *Journal of Philosophy*, XCVIII.8, pp. 411–444.

Taylor, C. (1968) *The Explanation of Behaviour* (London, Routledge).

Verheggen, C. (1995) Wittgenstein and 'Solitary' Languages, *Philosophical Investigations*, 18.4, pp. 329–347.

Weil, S. (1955a) *Oppression et Liberté* (Paris, Gallimard).

Weil, S. (1955b) *The Need for Roots (L'enracinement)*, A. Wills, trans. (Boston, MA, Beacon Press).

Winch, C. (1998) *The Philosophy of Human Learning* (London, Routledge)

Winch, C. (2009) Ryle on Knowing How and the Possibility of Vocational Education, *Journal of Applied Philosophy*, 26.1, pp. 88–101.

Winch, C. (2010) *Dimensions of Expertise* (London, Continuum).

Winch, C. (2013) Curriculum Design and Epistemic Ascent, *Journal of Philosophy of Education*, 47.1, in press.

Wittgenstein, L. (1953) *Philosophical Investigations*, G. E. M. Anscombe, trans. (Oxford, Blackwell).

Wittgenstein, L. (1967) *Zettel* (Oxford, Blackwell).

Wolf, A. (2011) *The Wolf Report* (London, HMSO).

Young, M. F. D. (2012) Education, Globalisation and the 'Voice of Knowledge', in: L. Lauder, M. Young, H. Daniels, M. Balarin and J. Lowe (eds) *Educating for the Knowledge Economy: Critical Perspectives* (London, Routledge), pp. 139–151.

9
The Epistemic Value of Diversity

EMILY ROBERTSON

The epistemic value of generating knowledge from the social location of marginalised groups has been affirmed by a variety of scholars from standpoint theorists to multiculturalists and advocates of alternative epistemologies (Banks, 1993, 1998; Collins, 2004; Harding, 1991, 1993; Mills, 1998). Defenders of the epistemic value of diversity hold that what passes for 'knowledge' in many fields is not in fact universally valid but rather represents the interests and perspectives of the typical knowledge producers, usually white males. From this point of view, marginalised groups have different experiences, perspectives, and social locations that hold promise for generating a better understanding of social systems, especially systems of social oppression. Advocates of diversity are split on whether inclusion results in a revised, universally valid understanding that is more objective than the traditional one or in multiple 'situated knowledges', i.e. in a proliferation of perspectives generated by different forms of marginalisation, no one of which can claim to be privileged (Anderson, 2012).

While the *injustice* of excluding members of marginalised groups from knowledge production and dissemination has been widely accepted, the epistemic relevance and role of marginality and greater inclusiveness in creating more justified knowledge claims are contested (Bar On, 1993; Janack, 1997; Ruitenberg and Phillips, 2011; Siegel, 1995). Some epistemologists understand the advocates of diversity as simply calling attention to sources of bias, a vice already acknowledged in traditional epistemology.[1] Further, the idea of 'alternative knowledges' based in different social locations appears to endorse a version of knowledge-relativism that by the lights of many epistemologists leads to incoherence (Boghossian, 2006). Yet supporters of diversity more commonly resist the 'relativist' label, emphasising instead the 'socially situated' nature of knowledge production, including the variety of ways inquiry is affected by the socially-located interests and perspectives of the knowledge producers. Thus

Education and the Growth of Knowledge: Perspectives from Social and Virtue Epistemology, First Edition. Edited by Ben Kotzee. Copyright © 2014 The Authors. Editorial organisation © 2014 Philosophy of Education Society of Great Britain. Published 2014 by John Wiley & Sons Ltd.

we should ask not only whether a claim is true but also whose interests it serves and who benefits from the acceptance of the claim (Haraway, 1988; McLaren, 2007). Finally, critics of the relevance of diversity to epistemology argue that advocates are confusing sociology of knowledge with epistemology. Surveying the uses of the term 'epistemology' in the educational literature on multiculturalism, Phillips (2011) finds that 'epistemology' is used to describe how views about knowledge and the preferred modes of inquiry arise within particular social groups and vary among them. But these are he holds, historical and sociological questions, not the truly epistemic question of whether the beliefs generated are 'well-enough justified to count as knowledge rather than belief' (p. 19). In short, looking at the social causes of why people hold the beliefs that they do is a different issue from the normative epistemological project of determining the conditions under which their beliefs are true.

I will explore the question of the value of diversity to epistemology from the perspective of applied social epistemology (Goldman, 2010).[2] Since advocates of the relevance of diversity are clearly pointing to the role of social factors in knowledge production, social epistemology is a promising lens for examining their claims. Social epistemology studies what Goldman calls 'social pathways to knowledge' (science, law, education, media, government, etc.) in terms of their generating, or not, true beliefs for agents (Goldman, 2002, p. ix; Goldman, 1999). Issues in applied social epistemology 'commonly involve matters of *institutional design*, where the problem is to configure or reconfigure social institutions so as to promote truth acquisition or error avoidance' (Goldman, 2010). Work of this nature, Goldman (2010) holds, is typically interdisciplinary and not a matter of 'pure, a priori philosophy'. Since applied social epistemology critically analyses knowledge production and dissemination systems and develops possibilities for improvements, social epistemologists' focus is on our actual epistemic situation rather than on ideal knowers and necessary truths. I hold that from this perspective, diversity is an epistemic virtue, as well as a moral one. My argument, however, does not support alternative epistemologies, cognitive relativism, or the replacement of truth as an epistemic goal by, for example, beliefs that have progressive consequences. It is, then, an argument with modest conclusions.

'Diversity', of course, can mean many things. I have in mind the inclusion of the voices, experiences, perspectives, questions, interests, and social location of those groups who have been traditionally marginalised in the institutions of knowledge production and dissemination. Those who hold that diversity is of epistemic value hold that the social location of knowledge producers is relevant to an evaluation of the claims the systems produce, particularly in social science, including educational sciences, the context I am considering. Supporters of the epistemic value of diversity note that one's social location may affect one's access to knowledge, the questions that are deemed important to investigate, the weight given to various criteria of justification such as which testimonial sources are trustworthy, and the broader background beliefs against which new information is judged, among other consequences. Critics of the epistemic value of diversity note that, while these factors help to explain the origins of the inquiry a researcher conducts, and hence the origins of the claims he or she makes, they do not bear on whether or not the researcher's claims are justified. From this perspective, it appears that the proponents of the epistemic value of diversity are committing the genetic fallacy.

When one takes the individualist stance of traditional epistemology, this critique has merit. But let us consider the epistemic merits of diversity from the stance of applied social epistemology, focusing especially on the issue of testimony. Individuals cannot assess the truth of many claims for themselves but rather must depend on the testimony of more expert or qualified others. In such cases, the task of the knower is to determine whether the source of the claim is trustworthy. Trustworthiness consists of at least two factors: (1) the recipient of the testimony must have reason to believe that the source is honest and sincere in making the claims; and (2) the recipient must have reason to believe that the source is competent with respect to the knowledge claimed (Coady, 1992).[3] If one discovers, for example, that a study of a new drug was funded by the company that developed the drug then that is relevant to the degree of trust one might reasonably place in the reported results of the study. This information shows that the researchers or their sponsors had a motive for suppressing negative information about the drug, i.e. that they had reasons not to fully disclose the results. Studies comparing results of research conducted by drug companies, or by academic researchers funded by drug companies, with independent studies show that drug company related studies are more likely to report favourable results (Rehman, 2012). If such relationships are commonplace in drug studies, then a social epistemologist might recommend policies intended to increase the likelihood of the public's receiving better information about the drugs they take and to enhance the public's ability to place reasonable trust in the testimonial sources of their information. For example, the likelihood that such scientific studies will produce favourable outcomes for agents is enhanced when journals make it mandatory that funding sources be disclosed by authors. Indeed this is now common practice and research shows that funding sources are figured into physicians' judgements of the credibility of drug studies (Rehman, 2012). Thus in social epistemology, the genetic 'fallacy' is not necessarily a fallacy. Again, this mode of applied epistemic analysis deals in probabilities and not necessary truths. It is certainly possible that some drug companies and the researchers they support are entirely above-board in reporting results. But the empirical data show a significant tendency toward reporting more favourable results given direct funding by drug companies and hence provide reasons supporting public scepticism and to recommend policy changes.

Is there a plausible argument that something similar holds for the social position of researchers in a scholarly community? One might think not. In the case of the drug companies we can assume a monetary motive for intentionally suppressing negative results. I am not arguing (and most advocates of diversity do not argue) that if the research community is composed of members of the dominant group that leads to intentional distortion of the research outcomes. But philosophers of social science often grant that the social location of the researchers and their corresponding experiences may be relevant to the questions they choose, the way they frame the problems to be studied, and the theories they employ. In the context of discovery such biases may be expressed without affecting the truth of the outcome, which is determined in the context of justification, the traditional story goes, and that is the truly epistemic matter. Furthermore, all researchers have a social location. If having a social location were inevitably a source of bias, there would be no hope for trustworthy findings.

But if the researchers are all or nearly all members of dominant groups, here are some possible outcomes even under the circumstances where all of the researchers are of good will and all of their findings are true (I'm granting for the sake of this part of the argument that the context of justification works as it should in weeding out false claims):

(a) Members of marginalised groups may discover that the problems that concern them about the phenomenon in question are not represented in the research. As a result, they may suffer from what Miranda Fricker (2007) calls 'hermeneutical injustice', a form of epistemic injustice that leaves its victims without a conceptual framework for articulating their experiences either to themselves or to others.[4] Hermeneutic injustice occurs because the marginalised groups in question have not been party to the development of the available frameworks for articulating experience. One of Fricker's examples concerns trying to communicate the experience of sexual harassment prior to the development of the term. Racial profiling in the United States offers a second example. It was a common experience among Blacks and Latinos before the term was coined, but

Whites were sceptical until the term and the data that supported it became widely available. To take another example, recently people with intellectual disabilities have rejected the term 'retarded' as a slur although the field of 'mental retardation' had used it for years. These examples show that inclusion of the experiences and perspectives of marginalised groups in knowledge production can change the conceptual landscape in epistemically fruitful ways.

(b) The knowledge generated largely by dominant groups may be biased in the sense of giving an incomplete picture of the domain of study, one biased toward the interests and experiences of the dominant group. For example, Kathleen Nolan's (2009) study of discipline policies in a Bronx high school that featured 'zero tolerance' for offenders went beyond an analysis of the statistical data on school infractions to include yearlong participant observations in the school. While the statistical data indicated that crime and violence were down in the school after the new policy was initiated, Nolan's study showed how the policy created a school to prison pipeline for young black men that led to new forms of educational and economic exclusion. Nolan says that 'the official mantra, "crime is down", is, at best, only a small slice of the reality of urban schooling' (p. 46). This 'small slice' that fails to include the consequences for the offenders provided an inadequate basis for evaluating the policy. Of course, the outcomes of research are always incomplete since we can never address every aspect of the phenomena of study. However, incompleteness itself does not necessarily count as bias or negatively affect the policy recommendations that may be based on the study. But when the incompleteness is skewed as in the example above, the social pathways of knowledge production have consequences that are not only unjust but also thwart the development of effective public policies by providing an inadequate basis of knowledge for action.[5]

Is it possible that the outcomes of knowledge production controlled by dominant groups may not only be incomplete in important ways but also wrong, where the reasons for the mistaken outcomes are reasonably related to the lack of diversity in the research community? (Obviously all research findings are fallible, hence could be wrong.) Levisohn and Phillips (2011) examine multicultural educator James Banks' description of his elementary school textbooks that described slaves as 'happy and loyal'. Recalling this experience, Banks wrote:

> When I entered graduate school . . . I studied with professors who understood my nagging questions about the institutionalized representations of African Americans in American culture and facilitated my quest for answers .. . . My epistemological

quest to find out why the slaves were represented as happy became a lifelong journey that continues . . . I have lived with these questions all of my professional life. I will describe my most recent thinking about them. *I now believe that the bio-graphical journeys of researchers greatly influence their values, their research questions, and the knowledge they construct* (Banks, 1998, p. 5; emphasis in original, as cited in Levisohn and Phillips, 2011, p. 56).

Analysing this passage, Levisohn and Phillips describe Banks's point as 'an empirical one, not a philosophically epistemological one' (p. 56). Banks is interested, they say, in how such a false depiction of slavery could have been 'accepted and promulgated', not in 'debating its merits, examining the evidence, considering the justifications', which would have been a normative epistemological enterprise. But are Banks' interests purely historical or sociological? I think it's plausible to suppose that what Banks is interested in is how the discipline of history and the textbook industry that disseminated their findings could have gotten it so wrong, as Levisohn and Phillips acknowledge, but that he's likely also trying to analyse and improve those social pathways to knowledge. I assume his position is that if the experiences and perspectives of the enslaved African-Americans had been part of the data, such a result would have been less likely. If African-Americans had been members of the research community and among the textbook producers, inclusion of the African-American experience also would have been more likely.

Can such a claim be sustained? Once again it's important to note the probabilistic nature of applied social epistemology. Being a member of a dominant group does not necessarily mean that one will be unable to recognise the evils of the institution of slavery. Nor is the perspec-tive of members of marginalised groups necessarily more veridical or less partial than that of members of dominant groups. It could be the case that the views of the marginalised as well as the dominant are distorted by relationships of domination and oppression (Freire, 2000). But as Sandra Harding (1991, 1993) has argued, it's not nec-essarily the *perspective* of the marginalised, i.e. their way of seeing the world, which constitutes an epistemic improvement over that of the dominant group. Rather, the perspectives of the marginalised are data for examining the social system from their social location. It's surely plausible that a better understanding of the system can be obtained when the experiences and perspectives of the marginalised are included. For example, slave narratives from 2300 former slaves produced by interviews conducted in the late 1930s through the Works

Progress Administration have helped to correct the record of 'the happy slave' that motivated James Banks (Rawick, 1972–79). Their inclusion as data has resulted in an improved understanding of the institution of slavery.

That the inclusion of the perspectives and experiences of marginalised groups improves social pathways to knowledge so as to make true belief more likely shows diversity's relevance to knowledge construction. However, it might be said that this point can be readily accommodated within traditional conceptions of epistemology. Knowledge requires at least true belief on this account. Justification is included as well if testimony under appropriate conditions is a proper source of justification. Nothing I've said supports the position that different groups possess different 'knowledges' except in the sense that they may have different experiences that lead them to know or believe things that escape others' attention and that the reports of their experiences may function as data that allows researchers from whatever social location to generate better accounts of the social structure. Thus there is no commitment to relativism in this argument. Social position may confer a presumptive epistemic privilege but it can be overridden just as eyewitness accounts that are given epistemic privilege in courtrooms can be overridden. Within applied social epistemology, the epistemic contribution of social location in knowledge construction can be accommodated without incurring a commitment to relativism or to the replacement of truth accessible to all as the desired epistemic goal. Nevertheless, I think it would be a mistake to suppose that the challenge of diversity to epistemology leaves everything exactly as it is. It has become commonplace to comment on the individualism implicit in traditional epistemology (Robertson, 2009). I've argued above that fully understanding the value of diversity for epistemology requires taking the perspective of applied social epistemology where empirical findings are relevant in the interest of the normative goal of increasing true beliefs, and decreasing false beliefs generated and dispensed by our knowledge systems. Epistemology in this mode is not the traditional *a priori* enterprise.

The shifts in epistemic perspective indicated above have potential consequences for education. '*Sapere aude*! Have courage to use your *own* understanding!' was Kant's (1996)[1798] candidate for the motto of the European Enlightenment. He added: 'If I have a book to have understanding in place of me, a spiritual adviser to have a conscience for me, a doctor to judge my diet for me, and so on, I need not make any efforts at all. I need not think, so long as I can pay; others will soon enough take the tiresome job over for me' (pp. 51–52). Kant's conception of intellectual maturity lives on in some current conceptions of autonomy and critical thinking as educational goals. The commitment to thinking for oneself is common despite wide spread acknowledgement that the epistemic individualism of the Enlightenment is not viable. The majority of what we know we undoubtedly have learned from others' testimony. Even our efforts at being critical depend on critical traditions that are not usually of our own making. Nor is this solely an issue for lay people in relationship to experts or authoritative sources, as Kant seems to imply. Knowledge making within scientific communities depends on one scientist trusting the word of other scientists whose data and findings he or she may not be in a position to evaluate (Hardwig, 2006). Indeed it would be impossible and counterproductive to expect to inspect the reasons for all our beliefs. Are our normative educational goals out of step with our current understanding of the nature of knowledge and knowledge creation? How can the injunction to use one's own reason be squared with the facts of epistemic dependence?

In his 1937 lecture on teaching controversial subjects, Edward Thorndike argued that schools should distinguish between questions students should try to figure out for themselves and those where they should defer to experts. He proposed the following general rule: 'When we lack the necessary knowledge and some impartial expert has it, the right answer in any controversy is, "Ask the expert".' 'The important lessons', he said, 'often are to learn to distrust one's own judgments and the propaganda of parties who take a profit by influencing one's judgments, to trust the real experts, and to find who they are' (Thorndike, 1937, pp. 18–19). He added that he did not know of one school in the country whose curriculum addressed this problem.

Helping students figure out whom to trust for their information is a complex problem. There are many reasons for lacking trust, some justified and some not. I believe that global warming is primarily caused by human actions, specifically by the burning of fossil fuels that generate greenhouse gasses. I haven't done the studies to support this claim or even evaluated the evidence (it's beyond my competence to do so) but I know that the overwhelming majority of climate scientists support this view. I accord them epistemic authority in this area and so accept the belief. The Los Alamitos United School District in California, however, has required teachers who teach about global warming to demonstrate 'political balance' by including the views of those who deny global warming or its human causes (Pagaza, 2011). That requirement teaches students that climate change is scientifically controversial when in fact it is not. Ironically, under these conditions, the educational system itself is not to be trusted as a social pathway to knowledge.

Few educational issues are more urgent than teaching students what sources of information to trust and why. Our democratic future depends on a citizenry capable of making informed judgements in this area. Further, students need to be taught why they should support social pathways to knowledge that make us more likely to arrive at true beliefs. Diversity of representation is one major factor in justified trust that applies to many of our cognitive institutions. Understanding structural injustice and how it can affect education, the media, and knowledge production in scholarly communities is not only a matter of education for social justice but is also epistemologically central.

On the one hand, students need to learn how knowledge is produced within scholarly communities and why it is worthy of provisional trust. For example, why should the results of a well-designed scientific experiment receive credibility? How do historians use primary sources in constructing their accounts of the past? Historian Kevin M. Kruse (2012) has argued that decline of public trust in institutions and professionals since 1970 has abetted manipulation of citizens by politicians who have determined that they can safely disregard the facts. Understanding why the results of scholarly inquiry can be worthy of trust means that students need to know more than is commonly the case about how knowledge is created. Trickle-down versions of sophisticated views of the social construction of knowledge can lead to the belief that it's all just made up to accord with someone's political agenda. Or deeply rooted political and religious views can lead to an unwillingness to accept research findings that appear to conflict with them. This is likely the case with some of the deniers of global warming or its human causes in the United States. And a politically balkanised media exacerbates public confusion about the status of knowledge. The educational system should not promote a wholesale scepticism about knowledge since widespread citizen lack of trust in knowledge systems has a potentially high cost, both to individuals and to the public at large. On the other hand, students as future citizens and individual knowers do need to learn how not to be gullible and to be critical consumers of views distributed by established practices and institutions. Which sources are to be trusted and why? What are the factors that degrade the credibility of the scholarly communities that merit reform, sometimes through public policy? Who has been included and who excluded in the production and dissemination of knowledge and with what outcomes?

Elizabeth Anderson (2011) has argued that laypersons with a high school education and access to the Internet can judge the credentials and honesty of putative 'experts' by answering questions such as the following: Is the information coming from laypersons or from those with the appropriate educational credentials? Are they active scholars who are regarded by other scholars as major contributors to the field? Do they have conflicts of interests? Have they been charged with academic dishonesty? Students could be taught to conduct such investigations. Nevertheless, Anderson holds that social circumstances, such as the politically balkanised media and residential ideological segregation that makes citizens unlikely to talk with any but the likeminded, explain why citizens do not in fact conduct such inquiries with much frequency.

While educational institutions cannot themselves change the social practices Anderson describes, schools do in fact represent a space where citizens of differing perspectives interact with each other even when their communities are relatively ideologically homogeneous (Hess, 2009, p. 80). Beyond the basic agenda of checking the trust-worthiness of the sources of information, educational institutions have a responsibility for developing both an appreciation of social pathways to knowledge, as described above, and an understanding of ways in which social pathways to knowledge can be corrupted and the need for citizens to support reform measures. Understanding the epistemic reasons for inclusive communities is an important part of this project.

One way of accomplishing this task is by helping students explore paradigmatic examples in various fields of study. For example, Omnia El Shakry (2010) describes her approach to teaching about the Middle East in the twentieth century on an American Historical Association forum about teaching controversial issues. In discussing contemporary Islamic movements, she focuses on historical figures who represent a range of views. One such thinker is Sayyid Qutb who has been presented in the American media as a main Islamic radical and terrorist. Drawing on Qutb's entire body of work, El-Shakry introduces students to his writings on Islam, social justice, and capitalism, as well as his more radical works. Her students come to see Qutb as a complex scholar committed to confronting questions of human freedom and servitude. Her students receive a picture, she says, that contravene the accounts they may receive from NPR or the *New York Times,* which 'present Qutb as a poster boy for Islamic terrorism'. She holds that her educational task is to do 'more than merely summarise contemporary debates' by complicating 'such *public* debates, which so often truncate historical evidence for the sake of political arguments'.

El-Shakry is a university professor. But public school teachers also can help students examine received views to appreciate the importance of multiple perspectives. For example, in a two-year qualitative, practitioner research study in a Chicago public school, Eric Gutstein (2007) helped his largely Latino/Latina seventh-grade math students examine the public information disseminated about a proposed gentrification project in their community. When the developers and city officials who supported the project stated that 20% of the new housing would be 'affordable', the students used their mathematics to discover that the housing would not be affordable for members of their community, given their mean incomes. Their study led to wider discussion within their community about whether 'development would bury the barrio'. Gutstein approached his teaching from the perspective of critical pedagogy and his goals were to develop his students' understanding of social injustices and their agency in addressing them. But although it was not his primary focus, Gutstein was also teaching his students that an account of the development created by its advocates and disseminated through the newspapers did not represent the interests of the residents of their community and that a better understanding could be created by including their perspectives.

El-Shakry concludes her discussion by endorsing educators' responsibility to 'foster disagreement and challenge their [students'] thinking in ways that led [sic] them to question received ideas, accepted narratives, and easy generalizations'. Few educators would disagree. But the complicated task of educators includes not only teaching students to think for themselves but also to be good consumers of public knowledge as well as vigilant citizens who support policies that maintain credible social pathways to knowledge that are more likely to generate true beliefs for us all. Diversity, I hope to have shown, is a key element of this enterprise.

ACKNOWLEDGEMENT

I thank Ben Kotzee for his helpful comments on earlier drafts of this chapter.

NOTES

1. Within feminist philosophy of science, Sandra Harding (1991) calls this position 'feminist empiricism' (pp. 111-112). She cites Marcia Millman and Rosabeth Moss Kanter (1975) as her only examples of people holding this viewpoint. In a more recent account, Heidi Grasswick (2006) counts Helen Longino (1990) and Lynn Hankinson Nelson (1990) as feminist empiricists, although she grants that they would not accept many aspects of Harding's definition. See also Elizabeth Anderson's (2012) helpful account of contemporary feminist empiricism.
2. Alvin Goldman (2010) notes that social epistemology includes both theoretical and applied issues, but holds that the applied issues are 'more distinctive' to it.
3. Elizabeth Anderson (2011) has suggested a third requirement that she calls 'epistemic responsibility': testifiers should be 'responsive to evidence, reasoning, and arguments others raise against their beliefs' (p. 146).

4. In Fricker's (2007) formulation, epistemic injustice is a form of injustice that harms a person in his or her capacity as a knower. Hermeneutic injustice is one of two forms of epistemic injustice that Fricker analyzes. The other form is testimonial injustice. In this type of epistemic injustice, an individual is regarded as a less trustworthy informant than he or she should be because of systematic social prejudice against a group of which he or she is a member.

5. See Elizabeth Anderson, 2004 and 2006, for extended analyses of examples of the negative consequences of the lack of inclusion of diverse experiences and interests in research for the making of public policy.

REFERENCES

Anderson, E. (2004) Uses of Value Judgments in Science: A General Argument, with Lessons for a Case Study of Feminist Research on Divorce, *Hypatia*, 19.1, pp. 1–24.

Anderson, E. (2006) The Epistemology of Democracy, *Episteme*, 3, pp. 9–23.

Anderson, E. (2011) Democracy, Public Policy, and Lay Assessments of Scientific Testimony, *Episteme* 8.2, pp. 144–164.

Anderson, E. (2012) Feminist Epistemology and Philosophy of Science, in: E. N. Zalta (ed.) *The Stanford Encyclopedia of Philosophy*. Online at http://plato.stanford.edu/archives/fall2012/entries/feminism-epistemology (accessed 12 December 2012).

Banks, J. (1993) The Canon Debate, Knowledge Construction, and Multicultural Education, *Educational Researcher*, 22.5, pp. 4–14.

Banks, J. (1998) The Lives and Values of Researchers: Implications for Educating Citizens in a Multicultural Society, *Educational Researcher*, 27.7, pp. 4–17.

Bar On, B-A. (1993) Marginality and Epistemic Privilege, in: L. Alcoff and E. Potter (eds) *Feminist Epistemologies* (New York, Routledge).

Boghossian, P. A. (2006) *Fear of Knowledge: Against Relativism and Constructivism* (Oxford, Clarendon Press).

Coady, C. A. J. (1992) *Testimony: A Philosophical Study* (Oxford, Clarendon Press).

Collins, P. H. (2004) Learning From the Outsider Within: The Sociological Significance of Black Feminist Thought, in: S. Harding (ed.) *The Feminist Standpoint Theory Reader* (New York, Routledge).

El-Shakry, O. (2010) Lessons from the Modern Middle East, from the *Controversy in the Classroom* forum column in the May 2010 issue of *Perspectives on History* Online at http://www.historians.org/perspectives/issues/2010/1005/1005for11.cfm (accessed 12 May 2010).

Freire, P. (2000) *Pedaogogy of the Oppressed*, 30th Anniversary edn. (New York, Continuum).

Fricker, M. (2007) *Epistemic Injustice: Power and the Ethics of Knowing* (Oxford, Oxford University Press).

Goldman, A. I. (1999) *Knowledge in a Social World* (Oxford, Clarendon Press).

Goldman, A. I. (2002) *Pathways to Knowledge* (Oxford, Oxford University Press).

Goldman, A. I. (2010) Social Epistemology, in: E. N. Zalta (ed.) *Stanford Encyclopedia of Philosophy*. Online at http://plato.stanford.edu/archives/sum2010/entries/epistemology-social/ (accessed 12 February 2012).

Grasswick, H. (2006) Feminist Social Epistemology, in: E. N. Zalta (ed.) *The Stanford Encyclopedia of Philosophy*. Online at http://plato.stanford.edu/archives/fall2012/entries/feminist-social-epistemology/ (accessed 12 December 2012).

Gutstein, E. (2007) 'And That's Just How It Starts': Teaching Mathematics and Developing Student Agency, *Teachers College Record*, 109.2, pp. 420–448.

178 *E. Robertson*

Harding, S. (1991) *Whose Science? Whose Knowledge? Thinking from Women's Lives* (Ithaca, NY, Cornell University Press).

Harding, S. (1993) Rethinking Standpoint Epistemology: What is 'Strong Objectivity'?, in: L. Alcoff and E. Potter (eds) *Feminist Epistemologies* (New York, Routledge).

Hardwig, J. (2006) Epistemic Dependence, in: E. Selinger and R. P. Crease (eds) *The Philosophy of Expertise* (New York, Columbia University Press).

Haraway, D. (1988) Situated Knowledge: The Science Question in Feminism and the Privilege of Partial Perspective, *Feminist Studies*, 14.3, pp. 575–599.

Hess, D. E. (2009) *Controversy in the Classroom: The Democratic Power of Discussion* (New York, Routledge).

Janack, M. (1997) Standpoint Epistemology Without the 'Standpoint'? An Examination of Epistemic Privilege and Epistemic Authority, *Hypatia*, 12, pp. 125–139.

Kant, I. (1996) [1798] An Answer to the Question: What is Enlightenment? in: L. Cahoone (ed.) *From Modernism to Postmodernism, An Anthology* (Malden, MA, Blackwell).

Kruse, K. M. (2012) The Real Loser: Truth, *The New York Times*, 6 November, p. A29.

Levisohn, J. A. and Phillips, D. C. (2011) Charting the Reefs: A Map of Multicultural Epistemology, in: C. W. Ruitenberg and D. C. Phillips (eds) *Education, Culture and Epistemological Diversity: Mapping a Disputed Terrain* (Dordrecht, Springer).

Longino, H. E. (1990) *Science as Social Knowledge: Values and Objectivity in Scientific Inquiry* (Princeton, NJ, Princeton University Press).

McLaren, P. (2007) *Life in Schools: An Introduction to Critical Pedagogy in the Foundations of Education*, 5th edn. (Boston, MA, Pearson Allyn & Bacon).

Millman, M. and Kanter, R. M. (1975) Editor's Introduction, in: *Another Voice: Feminist Perspectives on Social Life and Social Science* (New York, Anchor Books).

Mills, C. W. (1998) Alternative Epistemologies, in his: *Blackness Visible: Essays on Philosophy and Race* (Ithaca, NY, Cornell University Press).

Nelson, L. H. (1990) *Who Knows: From Quine to a Feminist Empiricism* (Philadelphia, PA, Temple University Press).

Nolan, K. (2009) Critical Social Theory and the Study of Urban School Discipline: The Culture of Control in a Bronx High School, in: J. Anyon (ed.) *Theory and Educational Research: Toward Critical Social Explanation* (London, Routledge).

Pagaza, N. (2011) School Board orders Global Warming Classes to Include Conservative Views' LosAlamitos-SealBeachPatch, [11 May]. Online at http://losalamitos.patch.com/articles/global-warming (accessed 10 December 2012).

Phillips, D. C. (2011) A Critical Review of Representative Sources on Multicultural Epistemology, in: C. W. Ruitenberg and D. C. Phillips (eds) *Education, Culture and Epistemological Diversity: Mapping a Disputed Terrain* (Dordrecht, Springer).

Rawick, G. (ed.) (1972–79) *The American Slave: A Composite Autobiography* (Westport, CN, Greenwood Press).

Rehman, J. (2012) Can the Source of Funding for Medical Research Affect the Results? *Scientific American Guest Blog* [23 September]. Online at http://blogs.scientificamerican.com/guest-blog/2012/09/23/can-the-source-of-funding-for-medical-research-affect-the-results/ (accessed 10 December 2012).

Robertson, E. (2009) The Epistemic Aims of Education, in: H. Siegel (ed.) *Oxford Handbook of Philosophy of Education* (Oxford, Oxford University Press).

Ruitenberg, C. W. and Phillips, D. C. (eds) (2011) *Education, Culture and Epistemological Diversity: Mapping a Disputed Terrain* (Dordrecht, Springer).

Siegel, H. (1995) What Price Inclusion? in: A. Neiman (ed.) *Philosophy of Education 1995* (Urbana, IL, Philosophy of Education Society).

Thorndike, E. L. (1937) *The Teaching of Controversial Subjects* (Cambridge, MA, Harvard University Press).

Index

abstract thinking, 80–82
academic standards, 114–15
Adler, Jonathan, 46
adverbial verbs, 152–8
agency, 148, 149–50, 155
  cognitive, 10, 92–100, 101, 102–103
  occupational capacity, 163
  project management, 159, 161
Alston, W P, 77
analytic epistemology, 1, 37
Anderson, Elizabeth, 174–5, 176, 177
Anscombe, G E M (Elizabeth), 9–10,
  45, 48, 55–75
anti-intellectualists, 12
anti-reductionists, 9, 33, 37–8, 41
applied social epistemology, 167, 168,
  171, 172
argument, 38–9, 40, 42, 43, 50
Aristotle, 2, 7, 11, 98
  development of capacities, 79, 80,
  89
  intellectual virtues, 118, 120
  moral vice, 125–7
  moral virtues, 128, 131–2
attentiveness, 106, 108, 112, 113
authority, 5, 41, 48–51, 63–5
  Anscombe's teachers, 48, 56, 62–5,
  69–70, 72

Banks, James, 170–171, 172
beliefs, 3–8, 14–34, 55–72
  diversity, 167, 168, 172, 174
  epistemic insensibility, 128–9,
  131–5, 139, 140–141
  false, 42, 43
  interpreter, 60–62
  justification,4–5, 7, 42, 77
  learning from others, 36, 39, 41–50,
  53
  megalomaniac, 62–5
  teachers of philosophy, 65–7
  virtue epistemology, 92, 93, 94, 95
Bialik, C N, 60

bias, 166, 169, 170
Brandom, Robert, 10, 76–7, 79, 81–9

Carroll, Sean, 137
Cartesian Epistemic Autonomy
  (CEA), 15–17, 32
  early education, 21–4
  intellectual autonomy, 25–41
  very young children, 17–21
choice, 125
cognitive achievements, 10–11,
  96–100, 101, 102, 103
cognitive activity, 108
cognitive agency, 10, 92–100, 101,
  102–3
cognitive attainment, 92, 93, 94, 95,
  96–100
cognitive success, 92, 94–100, 101
collective intentionality, 78, 88
Collini, Stefan, 138–9, 141
communicating, 153–5, 158, 160
complete epistemic independence, 16,
  27
conditional principle, 39, 42, 53
constructivism, 77, 84
context and skill, 148–9, 151, 153–8
continuing professional and vocational
  education (CPVE), 146
continuum of cognitive
  attainment, 96–100
controlling, 153, 158, 160
conversational activity, 58
cooking, 153, 156
co-ordinating, 153, 155, 158, 160,
  162
Craig, Edward, 6–7
creationists, 49, 61
creativity, 113, 118
credulity, 38, 41, 58
critical thinking, 4–5, 23, 111, 116,
  120–121, 173
curiosity, 8, 11, 106–108, 111, 113,
  115, 118

Education and the Growth of Knowledge: Perspectives from Social and Virtue Epistemology, First Edition.
Edited by Ben Kotzee. Copyright © 2014 The Authors. Editorial organisation © 2014 Philosophy of
Education Society of Great Britain. Published 2014 by John Wiley & Sons Ltd.